HEALING BEYOND MEDICINE

GW00601834

HEALING

BEYOND

MEDICINE

Alternative Paths to Wellness

DR. HANS HOLZER, Ph.D.

LONGMEADOW PRESS

Cover design by Kelvin P. Oden
Interior design by Richard Oriolo

Library of Congress Cataloging-in-Publication Data

Holzer, Hans, 1920–
    Healing beyond medicine : alternative paths to
wellness / Hans
Holzer.
      p.   cm.
    Includes index.
    ISBN: 0-681-00459-2
    1. Mental healing.   2. Healing.   3. Alternative medicine.
I. Title.
RZ400.8'52—dc20   94-19204
                                          CIP

Printed in United States of America

First Edition

0 9 8 7 6 5 4 3 2 1

CONTENTS

HEALING BEYOND MEDICINE

INTRODUCTION

W hen I first became professionally interested in what we now have come to call "alternative medicine," the subject was considered "way out" by even the most friendly and unbiased readers of my books. A majority of professional doctors were outright hostile. Those who agreed with my views regarding the necessity of a scientifically enlightened search for new ways to make people well, especially where conventional "school medicine" had failed, often did not want their views attached to their names out of fear of being shunned by their patients or professional societies.

But that was in 1967. By 1973, my first book dealing with unorthodox and psychic healing, *Beyond Medicine*, had been a success. When I revised it in 1987 and added new, up-to-date material, the book became very popular again, although not with the official institutions of the medical profession or their journals, or with those who review books dealing with health and healing.

Now it is 1993 and the earliest material, *once again brought up to date*, along with additional new and vitally important material, will be placed before the public. But there is a great deal that is different today.

Desperately aware that no real cure exists for such illnesses as cancer, AIDS, multiple sclerosis, and other illnesses, many physicians are beginning to listen, perhaps for the first time, to alternative paths to healing—so long as they are followed with due caution and a scientific orientation. Traditional medical doctors are not likely to change much in their outlook, but they may suggest something different when it is clear they have failed their patients. And that something different is what this new book is all about.

*   *   *

A Chicago woman in her middle forties, suffering from terminal cancer, was cured by healer Henry Rucker within one week. No recurrence of any malignancies was observed medically four years later.

Paulette E., age twenty-two, suffered from severe cancer of the cervix, as diagnosed by laboratory tests. She was completely cured within three months by absent treatment from healers Phyllis and Sidney K.

James Douglas DePass was cured of a serious stomach ailment by healer Betty Dye of Georgia, in a single treatment.

Britain's Harry Edwards cured Gladys Cudd of consumption while she was a teenager, about to die. Today, many years later, she is a practicing healer herself.

U.S. Army Sgt. Charles F. Piper was cured of a long and severe sinus condition in one dramatic healing encounter with Betty Dye of Georgia.

Arthur Orlop of Germany prescribed a natural remedy for insurance inspector Helmut Jaeckel: it cured a fungal infection which had resisted all medical attempts to cure it.

In 1967 Isa Northage of England removed malignancies from the jaw of Mrs. Sylvia Hudstone through psychic surgery in the presence of a professional nurse.

The cases briefly mentioned here are told in all detail, with full documentation, of course, further on in this book. There are many thousands of such instances where unusual healing has taken place. How is this possible? Why don't we know more about such things? It *is* possible, and those who wish to listen can hear a great deal about such things; psychic healing and unorthodox medical healing are not secrets. But the greatest disease of them all is ignorance. Ignorance yields to enlightenment. Enlightenment is possible when all the facts are known: here then are the facts.

"As long as you're healthy" is a favorite saying of our times and the idea that good health represents a most valuable asset seems to run through all cultures and economic strata. "Be healthy" is a jovial Jewish expression: "*Salud, dinero, y amor*"—"Health, money and love"—is a Spanish toast, putting health first; the French toast "*votre santé*"; the Germans "*Auf dein Wohl.*" In English we do the same, saying, "To your health."

We spend billions on the maintenance of good health, consider the expansion and building of hospitals a major factor in our budgets, have a special department of health in our government, and open our ordinary conversation with a perfunctory question as to the state of one's health. We consider the profession of medical doctor an honorable one and encourage our children to seek it.

Yet, with all this preoccupation with the state of health, and the increased reliance upon the services of medical specialists, we are less and less sure of our well-being. The more sophisticated our method of treating illness has become, the less successful it seems to be in a greater variety of cases. We have become used to the idea that the physician no longer makes house calls except in dire emergencies or when the patient is wealthy enough to insist upon it. We are quite used to having our druggist give us a drug for whatever ails us, making sure that it is the newest and latest discovery on the market.

Moreover, by departmentalizing our lives and putting total reliance on the specialists in health, we have finally abandoned the ancient Greek ideas of total health or the totality of illness. To the

Greeks, if one part of the body or mind was ailing, there was something wrong with the entire person. To the modern specialist, the ailing part or area is of immediate interest. He concerns himself less and less with the significance such an illness may have for the rest of the person. When the subject of the trinity of personality—body, mind, and spirit—comes up, the majority of medical practitioners look dumbfounded. Of course, not every modern physician insists that man does not have a soul, but there are few who will not just treat the body and leave the soul to the minister.

What is certainly becoming clear to the thinkers among us is that all is not well with a purely mechanistic concept of life. Developments in technology and the increasing ability of man to perform seeming miracles in life and laboratory have been paralleled by a decline in the cult of the individual. Yet it is that very individuality— the uniqueness of the human personality—that lies at the core of perfect health and perfect well-being. In an age when men are increasingly turning into numbers, a minority wants to call attention to another aspect of human development: the danger of ill health resulting from too much conformity and neglect of individual needs.

Along with these concerns, competent observers have pointed out for many years that there is another order of things, apart from those recognized by conventional medicine. People *are* being treated *successfully* with methods outside the realm of orthodox medical science—a fact that is a thorn in the flesh of those medical practitioners to whom their own art is beyond all questioning and, conversely, a ray of hope to those for whom conventional medicine has done nothing, or very little.

That "unorthodox" area of healing is the subject of this book, and it must be approached with caution. Whenever we leave the seemingly safe path of conventional science or scientific investigation to look into areas not yet fully charted, there is always the danger of reading too much into one's findings, self-delusion, and plain error of judgment. And since we are dealing here with man's well-being, we cannot afford a very large margin of error. Every precaution must therefore be taken, every attempt must be made to verify and evaluate the information obtained to exclude negative factors.

But with all this in mind, there remains an overwhelming residue of factual information that seems to point in the direction of areas of healing where medicine has not yet dared to tread. This book will concern itself with the theories and facts of unorthodox healing to the extent that these practices and facts can be and have been verified by competent witnesses and authorities.

A great deal indeed lies beyond medicine, and this knowledge should be dispersed to as large a segment of the population as is willing to learn of it. *Healing Beyond Medicine*, in popular terms, conveys this necessary information so that everyone can understand it and apply it to himself.

From where I stand, along with an increasing number of others like myself, M.D.'s, Ph.D.'s, and technical people—the answer lies not in better pills, better radiation, and better surgery. The answer lies in the better understanding of the nature of man, and the holistic appraisal of what causes disease—rather than dealing exclusively with the symptoms and the results of disease. Man is born to be harmony—body, mind, and spirit. Any science that denies this triune balance as necessary to deal with man as a whole, fails in the very essence of life: restoring that harmony that ought to be always there within us.

Unorthodox medical treatments and psychic healing are meant to enlarge the perameters of healing, encompassing both conventional methods of treating illness and apparently unusual ones: the object is not be right or to take credit, but *to heal*.

As the years race by, much of what we thought to be inviolable scientific truth has had to be altered, reexamined and sometimes replaced with different views, for science is not knowledge, but the quest for knowledge, and it is forever a moving force, changing with the times.

My own personal conviction is, whenever possible, to strengthen the triune person—body, mind, spirit—to heal itself; when that fails for whatever reason, let someone with a larger amount of vital energies infuse that energy into the sagging aura or energy field of the patient, and thus stimulate healing and recovery.

I am not, however, suggesting that these unorthodox, alternative ways to heal the sick should replace any or all conventional medical treatments. Much that is done in modern medicine is life saving and proper. Just as much is life taking and wrong. Nor is each and every remedy from the rain forest or the alternative medical practioners right or a panacea for all that ails mankind. Some of it may even be dangerous if taken in the wrong doses or without proper care and knowledge of its nature and effects. But the overwhelming majority of these methods lead to well-being, saving lives, giving hope, and defying critics who fear anything new and not part of the curriculum taught in medical school.

Even the U.S. government has found the belated courage to resist the long-entrenched pressure groups of the American Medical Association and their pharmaceutical brethren, by establishing an office looking into the claims and benefits of alternative medicine. This Office of Alternative Medicine is headed by Dr. Joseph J. Jacobs. No better person could have been chosen to head it than this doctor of Native American descent, coming from a background where ancient healing wisdom has always existed, and blending it with his training as a modern doctor.

Large numbers of people die unnecessarily, or suffer unrelieved, because too many physicians in America, and elsewhere, still go "by the book." Only, in 1993, there are many pages missing from this "book"—pages containing, in many cases, the difference between life and death.

Professional arrogance, financial considerations, and plain ignorance among those on whom we rely to keep us healthy and prolong our lives, are not going to halt the progress toward a more open concept in healing. A medical profession which uses the best of both worlds—conventional and alternative medicine—often only recently has discovered ways of dealing with illnesses. This is no time for narrow-minded professionalism or the defense of "school medicine"—if the rain forest herbal medicine works, so be it, and let us find out why it does! Let those with medical credentials not label anything outside their ken and past training as charlatanism, quackery, or plain useless. Let them open up their minds toward the healing that comes from the earth, from people living closer to nature than our academics usually do, and incorporate those new findings into their programs.

Using the best that is in modern medicine, and the best that alternative medical science offers, especially from nature herself, will, and must, create a healthier world.

Prof. Hans Holzer, Ph.D.
October 1993

Part I

ALTERNATIVE

PHYSICAL

HEALING

The Nature of Man: What Exactly Is Healing?

Basically, my point of view is that man should be functioning properly on the three levels of body, mind, and spirit. Of course, with this view we already have a bit of a problem. The majority of medical doctors will deal primarily, or even exclusively, with the body, some with the mind (though that area is still pretty controversial), and leave the spirit to the safety of their theological colleagues—where anything goes and proof is not necessarily required.

There are increasing numbers of properly trained doctors, and others in the health field, who have taken the holistic approach. Man is a triune entity and can only be dealt with *as such*. Sometimes when science cannot properly describe or explain the nature of "something," but has sufficient evidence, through observation, or perhaps even through experimentation, of what that "something" does, we can learn what the nature of that "something" is by analyzing the results. Drawing conclusions based on parallel cases, on similarities, and on differences, we will sooner or later get back to where we started from in this quest: the nature of that "something."

Thus, somewhere between the extremes of belief and faith, and hardheaded re-creation in laboratories as proof of existence, lies the "natural" answer to our existence. We were meant to be as perfect as the "materials" used in making us allow, and when something goes wrong with us, we have every right to ask: how come?

It is no accident that the terms health and healing are related; for healing is the act of restoring or improving our condition when it is required.

Medical doctors are trained to look for illness; it is the enemy that must be attacked by any and all means, so that the patient may be whole again. But somewhere along the time track of our modern world, the shift from truly restoring health to suppressing pain and discomfort has resulted in a school of medical practice that is more concerned with making patients *feel good* than actually making them *well*. This is regrettable, as so many serious illnesses still defy understanding, let alone cures.

It is therefore only good sense to broaden one's outlook and look to nature for remedies and truth. Hiding behind the artificial shield of "scientific evidence," much that has been discovered is kept from those who need it most: people who have not been cured by conventional medicine. In this book we will open the door a bit more to that knowledge and its application.

We are talking here of healing *the person,* not just containing a disease or alleviating pain. Only when we accept the reality of our triune nature can we hope to win the battle against illness. Remember, there is no such thing as *ill health.* Health is always *wellness;* its absence or diminution comes not necessarily from the body alone, but also can have mental or even spiritual origins.

*　　*　　*

Take the case of John D. He is ill with an incurable disease. He has been to doctor after doctor, specialist after specialist. He has consulted the best in the medical field and received no hope that his illness can be cured. What is he to do? Resign himself to living with this disease, or dying of it, just because the medical fraternity cannot help him? Most men do just that. Or they ignore their disease and fall victim to it. A few, however, go on; they look for help outside medicine, *beyond medicine.*

John D. has a friend who had been ill and who had gone to a healer and been cured. He asks his friend where he can find this healer. He travels fifty miles to meet the man who has helped his friend. John D. is a skeptic. He wonders how a man without medical training can do what all those superbly trained, highly skilled experts could not do for him. But he has no choice; he is desperate. He wants to be well. He puts himself into the hands of the healer. The healer passes his hands above John D.'s body, barely touching him, or he shakes hands with him and then quickly grabs his shoulders and holds him for a minute or two. Perhaps the healer massages his neck or the afflicted part of the body gently and for a short time. Rarely does the healer speak as he works, except perhaps to reassure his patient that all will be well. The healer does not promise; he tries his best. John D. may have to come back another time or perhaps three or four times. The fee is not high—much less, in fact, than the average physician charges. There is a gentle handshake and John and the healer part.

The following day John D. feels better. Suggestion? Perhaps. Two or three days pass, and there is a remarkable difference in his state of health. If this is suggestion, John D. is all for it. After two or three weeks he consults his regular physician. A checkup reveals that the disease is receding. One more visit to the healer, again the laying on of hands, the gentle touch, the farewell. A month later medical authorities pronounce John D. fully cured. They have no explanation. They call it "spontaneous remission."

With some diseases spontaneous remission is possible. With John D.'s particular disease it is not. Nevertheless, the physician refuses to look elsewhere for the reason for the improvement. John D. tries to explain that he had gone to see an unorthodox healer, but halfway through his explanation he sees disapproval on the face of his physician and he stops. What is the point? But John D. *is* cured, and he stays cured. The years pass, and there is no return of the dreaded disease that would—should?—have finished him off.

The case of John D. is not an actual case from my files. It is a composite of many cases, but is typical of many occurrences that are happening daily, all over the world.

What exactly is healing? The restoration of complete health and the undoing of damage, temporary or permanently, to one of the three components—body, mind, and spirit. To heal, as the term implies, is to bring back to health, to make someone *hale* again.

The underlying principle behind healing is the assumption that man is *supposed* to be in good health at all times, that any deviation from the perfectly functioning organism is contrary to nature's intent. This is the basic law of all healing: illness is *not* a natural component of human life. Illness is contrary to nature and, if you wish to equate nature with God, to God's image represented by man. To the healer, illness is a state of imbalance caused by a variety of reasons, and if the full organism is to regain its *normal* state—perfect functioning—that state of imbalance, whether it be physical, emotional, or mental, must be corrected.

This, in general, is the approach of the nonmedical healer. To him man is one—body, mind, and soul. Traditionally, in the West, man's belief has included the concept that nature or God sends man illness to test him or perhaps punish him. In this framework it is difficult to convince man that he *should* be well and that any deviation from the state of perfect health is not due to some hostile force outside of his control but, to the contrary, is very much a matter that he himself can deal with.

The healer's approach seems a little strange to Western man, who has been brainwashed by the technological approach to healing and the very limited acceptance by orthodox medicine of anything that cannot be produced, dissected, or reconstructed in laboratory experiments. In the East, a better understanding of the nature of man has always prevailed. As V. and J. Lawson-Wood state in their fundamental work, *Five Elements of Acupuncture and Chinese Massage*: "Life process, or more appropriately existence process, is not simply a series of static conditions, but complexes of processes occurring as rhythmic creations of tensions and relaxations of these tensions." Chinese medicine men have always been aware of a subtle flow of energy through the human body, and their methods of healing are based upon this assumption. "Every cosmic system in process has its microscopic counterpart in man."

The understanding that man is a whole, unified organism, and that his body cannot be separated from mind or spirit, comes easily to "primitive man." Quite naturally he accepted his being on earth as an act of deity, and in identifying deity with nature he developed a natural religion in which all power flowed from above, from the deity or the various expressions of that deity into man, at the whim and will of the superior powers, but subject to certain actions and attitudes on man's part. Thus the priest was the healer of primitive society.

Of course, every major world religion contains elements of healing in its priesthood. But there is a fundamental difference between the Western (Christian) attitude to healing and that of other peoples. From the beginning of Christianity, healing was held to take place at the discretion of the deity and for those who had pleased the deity by adhering to "official" Christianity.

As time passed, it is true, Western man acquired a more sophisticated, and scientific, understanding of the human body and its workings. Doctors become professionals in their own right, no longer priests or, as they often were in the Middle Ages in Europe, barbers.

With the coming of modern times, the religious aspect of healing lost out to the scientific. The pendulum, indeed, swung the other way. Instead of extracting that which seemed valid in ancient traditions and even in folk medicine, the medical fraternity tended to pooh-pooh anything they could not reproduce or test in the laboratory. Clinical testing and so-called laboratory conditions became the symbols of medical accomplishment, together with an all-encompassing desire to synthesize as many healing ingredients in nature as possible. Applying technology to the problem of healing man, the medical profession increasingly disregarded the human element, eliminating the uniqueness of each case and its considerations and driving toward a mechanistic, fail-safe view of medicine in which individual failure is of less and less significance.

Today large slices of human experience are simply ignored because they no longer fit in with the edifice of medical philosophy accepted as the norm.

Such an attitude inevitably brings with it the illusion, or rather self-delusion, that one's profession has attained the highest possible state, and that very little that is not predictable lies beyond. That, in fact, is the opinion of the overwhelming majority of medical doctors today: we have reached great heights of medical knowledge, and while we may not know everything, we are driving toward further knowledge along predictable lines. Healing methods not conforming to this medical edifice are ignored for as long as possible. When they can no longer be ignored, "scientific" explanations are arrived at and adhered to.

In such a situation, anyone practicing healing outside the medically approved system is clearly held to be an enemy of the system and must therefore be suppressed. Thus we have the paradox that in a world in which orthodox medical science does not have all the answers and in which multitudes still suffer, unorthodox healers who are successful in their profession are frequently persecuted by medical authorities and, when that is not possible, derided, their results dismissed as fraud, accidents, or "natural remissions."

Curiously, but predictably, many of these orthodox medical men, who are so quick to condemn anything unorthodox or contrary to the rules and regulations they themselves have promulgated, are totally unqualified to determine what is best for their patients.

"In due course I entered medical school and received there, like every other medical student in the world, an inadequate education," writes Dr. Danny Abse in *Medicine on Trial*. New discoveries are made every day, yet only a minority among medical doctors acknowledges these changes and tries to adjust to the new findings.

For example, orthodox medicine teaches that infectious diseases, such as a common cold, must have some physical origin, probably a virus. Thus, antibiotics are given even though most doctors know perfectly well that the common cold will not respond to such treatments.

Arthritis, a crippling disease afflicting millions of people, has as yet not yielded to the science of the physician. No cure is in sight. Yet, the American Medical Association, in a small pamphlet on this disease, states, "Secret remedies and mystical deception have no place in the care of arthritis." Without examining the unorthodox possibilities for any potential clue to a containment of the disease, the orthodox fraternity rejects them—without offering anything in their stead.

I have already pointed out that illness is the absence of good health, an abnormal state in need of correction. To accept illness as part of one's state of being represents a twisted view of the universe. Of course, generally, diseases will respond to medical treatment. But what happens if a condition does not respond despite every effort? If good health is the norm for the body, and medical treatment can effect no improvement, then the reason for the illness must be looked for in other areas, such as karmic preconditions, failure to understand self or to live in harmony with self, or psychic incursions. Consequently psychic or other forms of unorthodox healing may well hold the answer to such conditions.

To understand the processes involved in unorthodox forms of healing, it is necessary to understand what exactly man is in terms of parapsychological research. It appears that man is composed of two essential elements: an outer, denser layer of matter called the physical body; and an inner, finer substance called the etheric body. It is the inner substance that contains the personality itself. At the time of death the outer layer is dissolved; the inner layer continues to function in a dimension properly attuned to it. This "non-physical half of our universe," as I call it, is that "world of the mind" mentioned by Professor Joseph B. Rhine, formerly of Duke University, and it is undoubtedly the same realm that religion likes to call Heaven and Hell.

If we assume the existence of a concentric dimension in which mental energy is the sole reality, the phenomena of parapsychology are no longer miraculous or even astounding. Yet we must abandon, in our thinking, the barriers of time and space that we are brought up on if we are to arrive at an adequate understanding of the nature of these phenomena. A psychic person does not perform "miracles" or circumvent the laws of science; a psychic simply leaves the denser atmosphere of the physical world temporarily, for various periods of our time, and partakes of the inner dimension in which the phenomena take place. While doing this, the psychic learns of events in the so-called past of which he normally would have no knowledge; he learns of thought imagery within another person of which he could not have conscious knowledge; he may even learn of situations in the so-called future that have not yet become objective reality.

It is difficult for some to envision a universe in which future events are already in existence, at least in the planning stage, because this concept presupposes a universal law beyond our common law of cause and effect and, moreover, hints strongly at the existence of a superior governing body that administers this law for the benefit of the universe of which we on earth are part. By accepting such a view, we are inevitably approaching a religious orientation, although one far removed from the conventional, establishment religion. Such a rational and universally applicable system contrasts directly with orthodox religion's merit system whereby the good are rewarded and the bad punished.

If the universal law were administered by a superior body independent of denominational obligations, the need for establishment churches would be nonexistent and man could obtain his link with the deity directly and without the need to practice certain rituals or undertake obligations of any kind. Yet the purely scientific evidence *does* point in the direction of precisely such a system's being in existence beyond the context of rational, scientific knowledge.

The dual nature of man and the existence of the universal law beyond the law of cause and effect are of great importance if one is to understand how healing works. The duality implies that the healer deals not merely with the physical body but more importantly with the etheric body "underneath" it. The existence of a universal law necessitates the acceptance of arrangements permitting healers to draw upon extraordinary powers, involving seeming chance connections and likes between people, to make healings possible. It is my firm conviction that there is no such thing as a coincidence or an accidental happening but that all events in our lives are somehow governed by universal law, moving us about in such a manner that we encounter others of significance to us at certain times in our lives. These encounters occur naturally—they are chance meetings—on the surface, but when looked at in the light of esoteric philosophy, they are seen to be important and significant milestones in our lives. I maintain that these arrangements are due not to chance but to a well-planned system in which every individual is a subject governed by his own actions, by possibly the actions done in an earlier lifetime, and by the working of the universal law.

Much is made by the medical fraternity of inherited diseases or tendencies. This emphasis is based upon the belief that physical characteristics are of major importance in a person's makeup. Weaknesses or tendencies inherited by a person from his father or mother or even his grandparents are sometimes held responsible for the occurrence of a disease in the patient. That, too, is a mechanistic and materialistic view of the universe. True, we do inherit our physical body from our immediate parents. But our personalities stem from another source. If reincarnation is a fact—and I have demonstrated along with others, such as Dr. Ian Stevenson, that the evidence points indeed in that direction—we must also accept the concept that the individual is free from the karmic debt of his father or mother. Only his own karmic debt can be considered when evaluating the absence or presence of disease in a person's present life.

Much confusion exists in the mind of the public concerning healing: what it represents, and what comes under the heading of healing and what does not. Many think that all healing is a matter of belief and suggestion. Nothing could be further from the truth. Unorthodox healing, that is to say, healing taking place contrary to current medical thinking, includes a number of approaches. (These will be discussed later in much more depth.)

First of all there is *psychic healing*. In this form of mediumship, the healer draws psychic energy from his own self, principally from the solar plexus areas (stomach and top of head), and through his hands places this energy around the body of the patient, in particular in the areas in which he has seen or felt the presence of illness. Diagnosis always precedes healing. Psychic healers are able to look at a person and see discolorations in the person's aura or magnetic field. They will then tune in on that area. The psychic healer rarely touches the skin of the patient. His healing takes place at the periphery of the personality where the aura ends and where it is therefore more sensitive, just as nerve endings are more sensitive than the middle parts of nerve tissue.

Psychic healing takes place whether or not the patient believes in it, in fact whether or not the healer himself believes in it. It is a purely mechanistic ability to draw certain energies from the personality and apply them where they are needed. The ability to be a psychic healer has nothing to do with the healer's religious attitude. Some psychic healers are spiritualists and prefer to ascribe their abilities to the intervention of spirit entities, but the fact seems to be that the results are the same whether or not the healer is a spiritualist or merely a person possessing extraordinary healing powers.

Physical healers are those who touch the body of the patient and apply a combination of psychic energy and directional massage, similar to the magnetic strokes of Dr. F. A. Mesmer, the father of modern hypnosis. The physical healer may or may not manipulate the body of his subject, and his healing is due primarily to the *laying on of hands*, through which the process of healing takes place. When a priest or, in rare cases, a layman places his hands on a patient, in order to heal him, physical healing is involved even though there may be spiritual overtones to the process.

In *hypnotherapy*, and even more in *psychotherapy*, suggestion is used to promote healing within the patient himself. These forms of healing assume that the patient has unresolved conflicts, which can be brought to the surface and disposed of. Having done this, the healer then places constructive suggestions into the unconscious mind of the patient. When the patient awakens from the hypnotic state, these suggestions implanted in his unconscious begin to work. He may not be aware of them, but they work nevertheless.

Hypnotherapy differs from psychotherapy in that it is a simpler form of healing utilizing only hypnotic suggestion, whereas psychotherapy relies in addition on the psychic energy forces within the patient and the awakening of these slumbering forces to help with the healing processes.

Further along the road to physical forms of healing lies *dietetic therapy*, in which certain combinations of foods are prescribed by the healer for specific illnesses. These illnesses are not necessarily all physical in nature, they may also be spiritual or mental. Nevertheless, the intake of certain foods or the absence of certain foods are thought to be of paramount importance in restoring the balance of health in the patient. The greatest of all dietetic healers was of course the late "sleeping prophet": Edgar Cayce of Virginia Beach, whose prescriptions frequently puzzled the medical fraternity but were, in retrospect, found to be effective.

Similarly, herbal healing, which consists of the use and intake of specific natural herbs in order to combat illness, both physical and mental, is a form of unorthodox healing in the sense that the prescriptions rely on existing plants and natural ingredients rather than on artificially combined or synthetically created elements, the introduction of which into the human body is not necessarily to the body's advantage. Dietetic and herbal healing require an intimate knowledge of nature far beyond that which most professional physicians have today. Consequently, there are very few healers who work in this branch of therapy, and one finds most good herbal healers among the followers of the "old religion," the Wicca or White Witchcraft of western Europe, since the knowledge of nature's herbs represents a major tenet of their religion.

A particularly American phenomenon, *faith healing*, derives its benefits entirely from an assumed link with the deity in which the healer is merely a channel of expression through which divine thought flows directly to the patient. Faith healing works best with mass audiences, apparently because the energy created by the large number of believers present is utilized by the healer to bring about his amazing success. Faith healings are not necessarily the result of religious belief, fanaticism, or a kind of hysteria. All of these elements are present, but it would appear that the faith healer, in invoking divine guidance, manages to unleash within himself certain forces that radiate outward from his body and interact with the auras of the afflicted. Thus, ultimately, the success of the faith healer lies in the freeing of psychic energy within his own personality and the successful communication of that energy to those who need to partake of it in order to be healed, though I doubt that any faith healer will agree with this description of his powers. Most faith healers are devoutly religious, especially those of the fundamentalist persuasion. Any thought that man possesses within *himself* the powers to heal others would be in contravention of his traditional views of God and universe.

Other forms of religious healing are related to faith healing in that they too partake of the divine expression as the source of the healing. What happens at places like Lourdes or other less famous shrines is not simply explained by religious sentiment on the part of the believers and the power of autosuggestion. How religious healings work will be discussed in chapter eight.

Medical Men
and Unorthodox
Healing

Even though the august American Society for Psychical Research has maintained a medical section for many years, and even though individual doctors have expressed an interest in psychical research and ESP, the society and these individual doctors did this apart from the medical profession, carefully avoiding any clash with the American Medical Association. To the majority of physicians, the idea that a healer without a degree in medicine could accomplish part or all of what he, the medical doctor, is trained to do is not only unthinkable but downright in conflict with his own best interests as a professional man.

There are exceptions, of course. Enlightened physicians have learned, if nothing else, that their knowledge is limited. Such physicians welcome information and new facts from any source, whether or not that source has been given the official stamp of approval through the bestowal of a medical degree.

Doctors who admit the existence of unorthodox healing are

usually quick to explain that we do not know why and how such cures come about. Even though they readily admit the existence of healing outside of orthodox medicine, they are far from recognizing the purveyors of such healing practices as their equals or even as professionals. The only difference between the skeptical doctor and the enlightened one, in this respect, is in the nomenclature: the orthodox physician calls anyone not an orthodox physician a quack; the enlightened doctor, who admits of the possibility that healing works, refers to healers as lay healers or untrained healers. It does not occur to him that the training that the unorthodox healer has had or the knowledge that he has obtained one way or another also constitutes a body of learning, although different from his own conventional education.

On the other hand, there are a few courageous medical doctors who not only acknowledge the existence of unorthodox healing, including psychic healing, as a reality, but who go so far as to include it in their own work if they are fortunate enough to have psychic healing powers in their makeup to the extent that they can be called upon in their medical work. Naturally such M.D.'s would be subject to prosecution by their own fraternity as well as by various government agencies if they were to admit to this activity openly and freely. We have not yet reached the point in our society where a person can dispense medical assistance outside officially approved channels.

It stands to reason that there would be a certain percentage of psychically gifted people among professional doctors as well as among other segments of the population. Some of these gifted individuals may use their extrasensory powers without realizing that they possess them: the physician whose diagnosis is nearly always correct, the doctor who puts his hands on the patient without giving him any medicine and finds that his patient responds immediately. Such matters are frequently dismissed as "excellent bedside manners," "psychological effects," or, at the very best, intuition.

Even the term intuition is suspect in the eyes of the orthodox physician; for it implies the coming into play of feelings, something the old-fashioned practitioner of the medical arts despises. Emotional reactions and textbook medicine are deadly enemies. But unless more and more medical doctors with impeccable records as physicians come forward and freely admit that they have used or are using their psychic healing powers to help their patients, and study these effects, and publish them so that the skeptical element among their colleagues might benefit from this knowledge, psychic healing and other forms of unorthodox medicine are likely to remain scorned by the very men who could apply these methods better than anyone.

Not all medical doctors refuse to be identified with some form of research in this area, however. Several years ago I was invited to participate in a forum discussion on psychotherapy. The meeting was under the sponsorship of the Parapsychology Foundation and the late Eileen Garrett. To my surprise, one of the participants was an old acquaintance whom I had not seen in many years, Dr. Walter Engel, the noted psychoanalyst and pupil of Carl Jung. Dr. Engel explained that he had lately become very much interested in psychical research and was no longer hostile to the idea that man might possess extraordinary powers, which a trained researcher could tap and use with favorable results.

Another psychoanalyst of great stature, Dr. Robert Laidlaw, for years worked with the late Eileen Garrett and, after her death, continued his interest in parapsychology, including psychic healing. In fact, it was he and a group of others who lately investigated the English healer George Chapman. While this does not necessarily constitute blanket approval of all healers or all healing practices, it does constitute a step forward in that these eminent medical men are seriously investigating the powers of individual healers. They are not doing so for their own amusement or to gratify their curiosity. They are doing this in order to learn more about the art of healing.

At the University of California, Los Angeles, Dr. Thelma Moss had been investigating psychic healing with a group of associates. Their investigation included laboratory experiments in which a healer is brought together with actual patients. The results are carefully observed and recorded. Dr. Wilhelm Beyer, a general practitioner of Überlingen, Germany, has been interested in healing approaches to possession and obsession for many years.

Another European doctor, the psychiatrist L. Kling of Strasbourg, France, has for some time specialized in the treatment of the so-called possessed with the well-known parapsychologist Professor G. Frei. Dr. Kling had looked into the possibility that some of the schizophrenic cases he had been dealing with might be cases of possession and therefore accessible to treatment by other methods than the conventional ones. In 1967 he sent me one of his patients, J. P. Kieffer, who had been judged a schizophrenic. "Psychiatrically speaking the diagnosis is clear, but that isn't enough by any means," Dr. Kling wrote. He explained that the subject was rational most of the time and understood fully what implications were involved. I met the man in Paris and questioned him thoroughly. My findings indicated that the individual was indeed mediumistic and subject to influences from discarnates.

The late Dr. Edward Bach, of London, England, was probably the greatest pioneer of herbal medicine. Originally trained as a conventional physician and bacteriologist, Dr. Bach soon broke away from his early teachings and set out to discover the healing powers of plants. "His ideal of a simple way to heal all disease persisted, and as he grew older it became a conviction and the activating force behind his whole life's work," writes Dr. Bach's biographer, Nora Weeks, in *The Medical Discoveries of Edward Bach, Physician.* "For throughout the years he practiced as pathologist, bacteriologist, and homeopath, his one aim was to find pure remedies, a simple form of treatment to replace the complicated scientific means which gave no certainty of cure." As a homeopathic physician, Dr. Bach followed the dictum to treat the patient and not the disease—that is to say, to treat the characteristics and the personality of the patient as well as the illness itself. Dealing with a part of the body apart from the whole, as is the custom in conventional medicine, is contrary to the beliefs held by homeopathic physicians. Bach's books, notably *The Twelve Healers and Other Remedies* and *Heal Thyself,* which is called an explanation of the real cause and cure of disease, are still available, and a newsletter dealing with Bach's amazing herbal treatments can be obtained from the Dr. Edward Bach Healing Centre, Mount Vernon, Sotwell, Wallingford, Berkshire, England.

In another chapter I will deal with the mysterious but very real

Dr. N. of California, a physician and psychiatrist attached to a major hospital, whose amazing prophesies I published for the first time in 1967.

Dr. J. Z. is a young physician attached to Long Island, New York, hospital. "Since my third year in medical school," the doctor explained, cautiously, "I have often *felt* diagnoses before they were confirmed by clinical and laboratory testing. I am not saying that these were intuitive feelings, but rather a sort of 'sixth sense' about what the patient had. I am sure that these feelings had a lot to do with my medical knowledge combined with common sense, but these feelings went beyond this realm. I have often diagnosed and been correct despite what the medical signs had indicated. These diagnoses could not be simply explained. They were in the realm of a feeling that came to me. I am not saying that I am some sort of physician mystic, diagnosing by an inner voice. I have not uncommonly been wrong. These feelings, however, have been borne out a good percentage of times more than I feel would be coincidental. I am not advocating practicing medicine or diagnosing on the basis of these feelings. I am simply saying that these feelings have occurred, exist, and will probably continue to happen."

Dr. H. W. is the principal psychiatrist at a major correctional institution in the eastern United States. He also has a private practice in psychiatry and is a respected physician. Dr. W. and I together have attempted various experiments with healing.

Even though he seeks no patients, having more than enough to do as it is, I have on occasion sent him cases from among those who appeal to me for help. In some cases Dr. W. has paid personal visits; in others he has arranged for absent healing, that is to say, telepathic sending forth of energies channeled to the particular needs of the patient. Dr. W. has never guaranteed any results when unorthodox means were employed, nor does he feel that a healer should ever do so.

Dr. W., a member of his county's medical association, has been associated with several large state hospitals and a private psychiatric hospital prior to being associated with the state hospital for criminals he is now connected with. He has practiced medicine for about thirty years, primarily as a psychiatrist, although he was in general practice for the first ten years of his medical career, and his comments, made during an interview, on medicine, psychic healing, and related subjects, are very significant.

"Do you know of any cases where psychic healing has entered the picture successfully?" I asked him in the interview.

"Yes."

"Have you yourself ever witnessed any cases of psychic healing?"

"I've not only witnessed them, I've *done* them," he said.

"What were the diseases involved? Were those mental or physical diseases?"

"To my knowledge I have only been able to help mental diseases."

"For instance?"

"I have a very busy psychiatric practice," Dr. W. went on. "I found that I was mentally healing some of my patients without touching them or going near them. This realization came very gradually. I found that I was putting *too much of myself* into my patients."

"Do you mean to say that you've had actual success healing patients without the ordinary methods of interview and analysis?"

"I felt that there was a psychic thing happening, that I actually helped the patient with the nonverbal part of my mind. *I felt that I was actually pushing energy at them to heal them.*"

"Did you see this energy pass?" I asked.

"No."

"Did you feel anything going from you to the patient?"

"Yes. It felt like I was pushing an invisible beam of energy toward them."

"Did you put any specific thoughts onto that beam or was it just a general power?"

"Just a general force," he said. "I'm sure that this force exists."

"Did some of your patients ever comment upon being healed in this manner?"

"No."

"Did you ever ask them about it?"

"No."

"Have you ever considered yourself psychic?"

"Yes."

"Have you had ESP experiences?"

"Yes. I can predict the death of a patient within an hour, I did this repeatedly in a hospital; I said that a particular patient was going to die within a particular hour of a particular night."

"What made you foretell these things?"

"It just came into my mind spontaneously along with the particular patient."

"Did you ever diagnose patients by unusual means?"

"No more unusual than any other *good* internist or psychiatrist. They all do it, but may not be aware of it."

"Have you ever seen the human aura?"

"No."

"Do you accept its existence?"

"Yes."

"What do you think it is?"

"The biomagnetic field of the human being."

"When you send out a force, does it connect with the physical body of the patient or with this bioelectrical field?"

"The biomagnetic field. There are *two* of them in every human being, and they are detectable by instruments; this has been known since 1936. They are the alpha and beta fields."

"Can you tell me some incidents in your medical career where seemingly miraculous healing or spontaneous healing has taken place due to your agency?"

"I've done more with my hands placed close to their head than I have been able to do across a room."

"Have you actually cured a case where orthodox methods have failed?"

"I had one girl just recently who was very hysterical in a sudden attack provoked by fear. I straightened her out in two minutes flat."

"How did you do that?"

"With my hands."

"How did you use your hands?"

"In her particular case I used one hand a couple of inches in front of the head and the other behind."

"Do you stay still or do you move the hands about?"

"I don't move them."

"How long do you stay in that position?"

"A minute or two. That's about all it takes."

"Does the patient feel anything while that goes on?"

"Heat."

"Is this healing permanent? In this specific case you're referring to, did she then have no further recurrence of the problem?"

"Not as far as I know. They would have called me."

"In your stay at the state hospital where, I believe, you were a resident psychiatrist for a number of years, have you ever tried healing on some of the inmates?"

"Mentally, yes. On one occasion five of us took a man over a shock. He had been told in error that he could go home; we had to take him into a room and tell him that he couldn't."

"Who were the others?"

"Correction officer, supervisor, and two professional employees."

"How did he react?"

"He did not go into the violence we had expected, nor did he become depressed or suicidal as we had feared."

"Was this perhaps due to logical thinking and talking rather than any form of healing?"

"No."

"Do you think healing took place?"

"Yes."

"In which way?"

"Simply by the mental force of the five individuals involved."

Dr. W. makes no extraordinary claims as far as his healing powers are concerned, but the fact that he combines orthodox knowledge of psychiatry with a natural gift for healing is in itself remarkable. One must keep in mind, of course, that psychiatry itself deals with mental forces and that therefore the relationship between psychiatry and psychic healing would naturally be a close one if properly understood and applied. But healing has been used success-fully in the more physical branches of medicine as well.

One of the most extraordinary medical personalities of our time is Dr. Douglas Baker, a native of London who spent his growing years in Natal, South Africa. Dr. Baker was slated to take a leading place in commerce and to become the managing director of a large printing concern. Despite his assured position in commerce, he had taken an interest in the study of zoology and of aboriginal languages and communication. At the University of Natal he became interested in the mysteries of the Zulus, and in studying their strange means of communication, he became aware of telepathy for the first time. He graduated with a bachelor of arts degree in 1949, but his interest in the world of the occult persisted, eventually forcing him to enter a retreat to think things out for himself. As a result of this mystical and spiritual experience he decided to change his life and began the study of medicine so that he could devote himself to helping mankind.

At the age of thirty-five he entered medical school in England. He qualified in medicine in 1964. He edited the medical society journal, *North Wing,* and while doing research into the history of medicine became interested in magnetism as a possible therapeutic agent. With the late George Delawarr, who had developed a radionic instrument that would prove to be useful in what Dr. Baker came to call biomagnetism, he delved into various mysteries of human personality, including the photographing of thought forms as well as the study of magnetism in relation to human personality and the body. As a result of their researches in 1967 Dr. Baker and George Delawarr published *Biomagnetism—Preliminary Studies of the Effect of Magnetic Fields on Living Tissues and Organs in the Human Body*, a highly technical book describing the techniques the two men had developed and their applications and possible results from these applications. The same team followed up the first book with *Double Blind Clinical Trials to Assess the Effect of Electromagnetism on Serum Cholesterol, Prothrombin Time and Blood Pressure,* and a large teaching hospital in London, St. Mary's, investigated some of their findings, undertaking clinical trials using the equipment developed by them. Subsequently a paper was published confirming that magnetism appears to affect the blood pressure, the level of blood cholesterol, and the clotting time of blood. In essence the magnetic therapy units used by Dr. Douglas Baker consist of a console containing a tape recorder with tapes specially programmed for various diseases. These tapes in turn activate the creation of a low-level electromagnetic field, which is transferred to various points of the human body through solenoids placed directly on selected spots of the body where, in the opinion of Dr. Baker, the magnetic energy should be applied for best results. (Purely experimentally Dr. Baker has also developed a larger unit fitting around the head and another fitting around an arm or wrist.)

A low-level magnetic field is set up and maintained for anywhere between five and thirty minutes. The treatments are no miracle cures, and frequent application is necessary to obtain results. Dr. Baker's treatment presently works best with the lowering of blood cholesterol and blood pressure, important factors in coronary diseases and in the treatment of postcoronary cases. He has also been able to obtain significant lowering of blood sedimentation rates in arthritic complaints. Less spectacular but no less important are beneficial results obtained with this treatment in cases of eczema, shingles, and general hypertension.

Patients feel absolutely nothing, nor are there any side effects from the treatment. Patients can take the treatment at Dr. Baker's country clinic or in London. Dr. Baker has developed ambulatory units, as well, and in certain cases the patient may use a home unit.

I first met Dr. Douglas Baker at his country house at Little Elephant, Kentish Lane, Essenden, Herfordshire, England, in the summer of 1970. He showed my wife and me around the premises, including the laboratory and the cubicles upstairs used for the treatment of his patients, and we discussed his methods. Later he arranged to send me one of his units, which I've had in my possession ever since.

The presence of Dr. Baker's unit in my office has brought some fringe benefits to the cause of biomagnetism that were not originally expected of it. When Shawn Robbins, a young psychic I have trained and worked with for some time, asked that I attempt to help her with her somewhat restricted eyesight and headaches, I suggested that she try the biomagnetic healing method.

The machine in my office is there purely for experimental purposes, and no treatments are administered to outsiders. However, in the use of Dr. Baker's machine on Shawn Robbins and other psychics I have worked with, such as John Gaudry, a remarkable development was observed: their psychic perception increased by as much as 100 percent. Not only did the magnetic field set up by the machine clear whatever complaints the mediums came to me with, such as headaches or eye strain, but their psychic abilities were remarkably stronger immediately after the treatments.

One can only conclude that the magnetic field in some way joined with the natural magnetic field within the personality of the mediums to create a stronger psychic force. We do not as yet know a great deal about the manner in which psychic ability is focused and applied, so there remains much to be researched in this area. However, Dr. Baker's biomagnetic apparatus has definitely been tied to significant changes in the performance rate of several psychics tested by me over long periods of time.

Dr. Douglas Baker's research is clearly significant, as is indicated by the reaction to his 1970 U.S. speaking tour, arranged by Dr. Robert Laidlaw, the well-known psychiatrist and head of the department of psychiatry at Roosevelt Hospital, New York.

During his many lectures Dr. Baker made no extravagant claims. With his British sense of understatement he merely presented what he had found to be factual.

"It is natural that there are problems to be overcome in presenting a new discovery which is outside current medical orthodoxy," Dr. Baker says. "The caution with which the medical profession treats any new departures is absolutely proper. At the same time caution must not lead to apathy or make impossible the impartial scrutiny of a potentially beneficial discovery. Caution has been a prime concern of Magnetic Research, Ltd., lest anything should leak out which might stimulate unfounded hopes on the part of sufferers from certain serious diseases. The company has not indulged in so-called fringe medicine; nor does it claim to cure—though in fact its case books contain many incidents of difficult conditions alleviated through applications of magnetism. What it does claim is to have discovered a technique of applying magnetic fields with the assistance of medical knowledge in such a way that changes are recorded in subsequent laboratory tests. Thus the company has accumulated clinical evidence that by the methods it has developed new therapeutic approaches may be possible to certain diseases which until now have proved intractable to orthodox medicine."

Between five and ten thousand people have consulted Dr. Baker and been treated by his methods. *Psychic News* quotes the wife of a medical doctor who had suffered for years with a disease called purpura. The doctor's wife is quoted as stating, "My husband gave me up and was delighted that I had found an unorthodox treatment which helped my complaint." Another patient, a teenage boy suffering from extremely low blood cholesterol causing frequent blackouts, is quoted as stating that the doctor's weak pulsating magnetic field treatment had raised his blood cholesterol to a normal level. When the treatment was stopped the young man's blood cholesterol reverted to its abnormally low level again.

According to the same source, a middle-aged man with high blood pressure and an arthritic knee testified to general improvement after a session with Dr. Baker's magnetic instrument.

Before the treatment he could hardly walk and had had to change his job to avoid exercise. After the treatment he returned to his original overseer's work, his blood pressure greatly reduced.

One would think that a man with the proper medical credentials who turns out to be a pioneer in progressive medicine, trying to expand the horizons of knowledge by as yet unorthodox but apparently valid methods, would be welcomed by the medical fraternity and officialdom as well. Yet in California, during a talk on "Magnetism, Its History and Current Applications" in which Dr. Baker outlined some of the discovered effects of magnetism and radionics, mentioned in his 1967 book, *Biomagnetism,* claimed that magnetism had affected the blood pressure of his subjects—specifically mentioning Reverend the Honorable Andrew Elphinstone—and described how some twenty out of thirty rheumatoid arthritics had responded favorably to magnetic treatment, two plainclothes detectives from the Los Angeles Police Department taped his talk and then arrested him. It was alleged that these were false claims and that, in fact, any suggestion that magnetism or radionics are healing and treating methods is false. Dr. Baker's radionics and magnetic instruments were confiscated.

Fortunately Dr. Baker was able to obtain the help of a prominent authority specializing in medical jurisprudence, Mark Joseff, Ph.D., who secured Dr. Baker's immediate release and, subsequently, a reduction of the charges.

When news of the incredible charges against Dr. Douglas Baker, a member of the College of Surgeons, was released, researchers all around the world rallied to his cause, and in September 1971, all charges against Dr. Baker were totally dismissed—leaving only a sizable debt incurred in the defense of Dr. Baker, not to mention the unnecessary cost to the taxpayer. Why would the Los Angeles District Attorney choose to attack a man of Dr. Baker's standing? Could it be that some of his colleagues in the AMA felt threatened by the possibilities of new methods, methods that seem to be promising in the treatment of disease, and methods with which they themselves were not familiar since their own education lay back some years?

The late Dr. Herman P. Saussele was born in Germany. He came to the United States at age fourteen and worked at first in the family bakery business in St. Louis. But all through his life he was interested in the esoteric and wanted to dedicate himself to the art of healing. Finally, at age fifty-eight, he entered the Missouri Chiropractic College and completed its four-year course, graduating as a practicing doctor of chiropractic in St. Louis. Before his death at eighty-five, *Healthways* magazine, the magazine of the American Chiropractic Association, reported, "Dr. Saussele is an unusual individual, a bouncing man in his mid-seventies who boasts, 'I haven't been sick since 1929 and that is quite a statement to make in 1968.' "

I met Dr. Saussele in St. Louis a few years ago. In a modest suite at 3189 South Grand Boulevard, Dr. Saussele dispensed a combination of nutritional counsel, general psychological advice on the art of proper living, chiropractic when and where needed or requested, and a fascinating field of unorthodox medicine called *iridology*.

Dr. Saussele followed the teachings of a pioneer in the field of iridology, another chiropractor by the name of Dr. Bernard Jensen, whose book, *The Science and Practice of Iridology*, published in 1952 at Hidden Valley Health Ranch, Escondido, California, is a kind of bible for the few practitioners of this very special form of healing. "By way of definition," Dr. Jensen writes, "iridology is a science whereby the doctor or operator can tell from the markings or signs in the iris of the eye the reflex condition of the various organs of the body. In other words, it is the science of determining acute, sub-acute, chronic, and destructive stages in the affected organs of the body through their corresponding areas in the iris. Drug deposits, inherent weaknesses, and living habits of the patient are also revealed in the iris of the eye."

According to this method tissue changes resulting from proper or improper treatment also show up in the iris of the patient. Thus it is possible to determine whether a prescription or treatment actually works through periodical checkup and iris diagnosis. Dr. Jensen points out the comparatively low percentage of accurate diagnoses obtained by conventional medical methods and offers the iris diagnoses as an addition to the storehouse of medical knowledge, *not* to replace any existing methods. And as Dr. Jensen points out, changes do show up in the color and texture of the human iris. As new tissue replaces old tissue it can be evaluated by the medical doctor. "It is impossible to tell from the eyes what germ life exists in the body, but when tissues have degenerated to the stage where germ life exists in various parts of the body, it will be reflected in the iris," says Dr. Jensen.

It was this system that Dr. Herman Saussele practiced with all of his patients, prescribing either homeopathic remedies, dietetic supplements, or chiropractic adjustments, as the case might be.

Does it work? Eugene C. Henkel, Jr., father of five children and a railroad ticket office clerk, visited Dr. Saussele in October 1953. At the time Henkel was, at age forty-nine, hunchbacked; he had a stiff neck; he could not raise his arms over his head; and he was unable to drive to work. He had been told by an orthodox M.D. to get a wheelchair. Dr. Saussele's iris diagnosis revealed that the patient had in the past suffered various respiratory disturbances, a matter that was immediately verified. Dr. Saussele prescribed a treatment consisting of special foods, vitamins, food supplements, and exercise. Today Henkel drives about fifty thousand miles a year in connection with his own business. He is still somewhat stiff and somewhat stoop shouldered, but no longer crippled or in pain.

Mrs. Agnes Ludbeck visited Dr. Saussele on April 24, 1961, when she was fifty-five years old. She had been under medical treatment for high blood pressure, which Dr. Saussele found to be 206 over 110. Ludbeck had been to an eye specialist for trouble in her eyes. The specialist had treated her for two years but had assured her that there was nothing wrong with her except atmospheric pressure. She herself wondered if there was some systemic condition, but he reassured her and advised her to keep putting drops into her eyes and not to worry about it. On examination Dr. Saussele found this patient to suffer from diabetes and a blood sugar count of 254 milligrams (the normal limit is 120 mgs.). The woman came to see Dr. Saussele once a week and received supplements for liver and pancreas treatment.

A year later she quit her job and retired to Troy, Missouri. At that time her blood pressure was down to 158 over 84, and her blood sugar to 158 mgs. But being away from Dr. Saussele's care did something to her system. Two years later she was hospitalized in Troy, unable to walk. Her disease was diagnosed as diabetic neuritis. Friends brought her back to St. Louis and Dr. Saussele. Three days after he started treatment, she began to limp around by herself; three weeks later she was fine.

Richard Janson came to Dr. Saussele's attention on November 5, 1963, at age eighteen. He then weighted 72 pounds and was very much debilitated. The boy had been in and out of medical hospitals without success. Dr. Saussele started to work on the boy at Christmas 1963. Because of the young man's condition, the doctor had to go to his house to treat him, but Dr. Saussele's healing worked so well that the young man was able to go back to school by May 1964, and to graduate. Unfortunately, he had a relapse and Saussele had to start all over again.

The doctor discovered then that certain psychosomatic factors had also come into play. He began to reeducate the young man's thinking, preaching a positive mental attitude and referring him to a classic book on the subject, Claude M. Bristol's *The Magic of Believing*. By fall of the same year the young man was able to get a job.

Dr. Saussele saw him every week until October, 1965. When Dr. Saussele next saw the young man, at Christmas, 1967, when the boy was home on leave from the U.S. Navy, he weighed 142 pounds.

After I had learned of Dr. Saussele's work, I had arranged to visit his office to submit to his iris diagnosis. Of course, he knew nothing of my medical history. He put me in his chair and examined my eyes carefully. Employing a large magnifying glass, he scrutinized my eyes minutely, jotting down his findings as he went along. Each sector of the iris represents a different part of the human system, iridologists claim, and according to the coloring and shape of a particular part of the iris, Dr. Saussele drew certain conclusions.

"You have a thyroid condition," he said. "I can see it right here in your eye." I nodded. I had been under treatment for a sluggish thyroid gland for years and was at this time taking half a grain of thyroid extract twice a day.

The doctor shone a light into my eyes, in order to get a reflex reaction. "This is a gastric reflex, and here we have a gall bladder reflex and a liver reflex. In other words you have a nervous digestive system." I nodded an emphatic yes. "And a nervous stomach." Again I nodded. Dr. Saussele's iridological findings were absolutely true.

Healing is the major component of the teaching of the late "sleeping prophet" Edgar Cayce, about whom many books have been written and whose great work is being carried on by his sons at the Association for Research and Enlightenment (ARE) in Virginia Beach, Virginia. Cayce, an untutored photographer, went into trance states during which he was able to diagnose the illness of people about whom he knew nothing. The language and contents of these diagnoses were such that only a trained medical doctor could have undertaken them. Nevertheless, Edgar Cayce had no such training nor was there any fraud or delusion involved. Many of the prescriptions given to the thousands of people who sought Cayce's help turned out to be unknown to the orthodox medical fraternity. Nevertheless, these remedies all worked and much was learned by those willing to learn from the study of the Cayce records.

Today, Cayce's diagnoses in specific cases are carefully filed away for those who wish to consult them when similar diseases require it. Those joining ARE obtain the so-called Black Book, a list of the most common diseases and a record of what Edgar Cayce prescribed in individual cases as remedies. Connected with the Association for Research and Enlightenment in Virginia Beach, Virginia, is a pharmacy specializing in Edgar Cayce prescriptions: the Heritage Store, P.O. Box 77, Virginia Beach, Virginia 23458. Items for sale are prepared under strict supervision of the ARE authorities and tie in with specific recommendations or prescriptions made by the late seer. From personal experience I can state that such prescriptions have, not infrequently, proved amazingly effective where conventional medicines have failed me.

Because this is a controversial program, ARE has always maintained close liaison with medical doctors friendly toward their cause— for example, in a symposium called the Triune Concept of Healing, held in New York, Edith Wallace, M.D., and Robert G. Brewer, M.D., discussed the Cayce concept of healing as it applied to conventional medicine—because ARE believes that in a combination of Cayce's prescriptions with the methods and prestige of establishment medicine lies the greatest hope for mass acceptance of the Cayce teachings.

As a first step in that direction, ARE maintains a special clinic at Phoenix, Arizona, where medical doctors treat patients with reference to the Edgar Cayce material. The clinic is housed in a pleasant suburb of Phoenix, with the mountains as backdrop. It consists of a complex of one-story buildings and a small garden. By no means comparable to a hospital or a large research establishment, the clinic is nevertheless run along orthodox lines in the sense that patients are seen by appointment, medical records are kept, and the entire operation is undertaken with the full approval and blessing of Arizona medical authorities.

Established in early 1970, the clinic had from the beginning been the special project of Dr. William McGarey and the ARE Board of Trustees. Dr. McGarey lives in Phoenix, the climate is favorable for the treatment of a number of diseases, and the atmosphere is unhurried and free from the sort of pressures prevalent in large metropolitan centers.

On a visit to the Phoenix center, I discussed the program with the manager, McCaleb.

"How did the ARE hope to benefit the world by establishing this clinic?" I asked him.

"More than 50 percent of the Cayce readings are physical readings. Studying those readings, we try to verify them and learn from them."

"How does this work as far as patients are concerned?"

"First of all, we have to take all the readings on a specific disease and study them. It takes about an hour per reading to synthesize this material and come up with what we think the source of the readings is trying to work from, what attitude or basic laws are involved. Then we come up with a general prescription or a therapy approach for the disease and apply it to a group of patients and see how it works; we modify as we go along."

"In other words, the patients coming here are being treated by methods prescribed by Cayce previously for similar cases?"

"Correct. Modified in some cases by the doctor's own knowledge."

"What range of disease is being treated here? Is there any limitation?" I asked.

"There are 233 diagnoses that have been discovered in the readings of what we would call separate diseases. We've only started to work on a few of these; it will take a bigger staff to get to all of them."

"Are there any diseases that have not been touched at all?"

"Yes. While we have a young intern studying the readings on cancer, we have not yet tried to deal with it."

"What are the principal diseases you deal with?"

"Epilepsy, myasthenia gravis, spearodermia, arthritis."

"You say there should be a larger staff. Do you have any assistants?"

"We have fifteen full-time people and five part-time people working here. Our limitation is strictly financial. The main source of our funding comes from seeing general practice patients. The doctors work here at a decreased personal salary and the difference goes into building up the staff; we're adding new doctors as fast as we can generate the funds to put them on the payroll."

"How many M.D.'s do you have on the staff?"

"Four."

"Are they specialists or general practitioners?"

"Dr. McGarey is a specialist in Cayce's approaches, and of course in neurological diseases, particularly multiple sclerosis. We have a specialist in obstetrics and gynecology; Dr. Gladys McGarey, a general practitioner; and Dr. Arthur Wright, who is a general practitioner who came to us from New Hampshire, and who also understands the general thrust of the Cayce readings. He's here learning to apply that to his medical practice."

"How does the American Medical Association feel about your enterprise? Do you have any problems with them?"

"No. Our doctors are members in good standing; for example, the McGareys have a long association with the county medical society here. This was another reason for being in Phoenix. Had we picked up the McGareys and moved them to Virginia Beach, there might have been some trouble with the medical association there. Here everybody knows the McGareys as good, reputable doctors, and no one is concerned with the fact that they are doing something a little unorthodox."

"Do you cooperate with hospitals in the area?"

"Our doctors are on the staff of several hospitals, and they put patients into them when the occasion arises."

"Are you publishing anything applying to this particular clinic?"

"Dr. McGarey has just had an article published in the county magazine on healing around the world. We're just starting our second year of the *Medical Research Bulletin*, which goes, free of charge, to all our cooperating doctors and is available for subscription to lay people."

"Who are the cooperating doctors?"

"The cooperating doctors are those who have indicated a desire to receive information from the ARE. They fall into two categories: those who simply want to receive the information, and those who are also willing to take ARE patients who wish to have a Cayce style treatment rather than a standard medical approach."

"Where are these doctors located?"

"All over the country."

"Can you name one or two?"

"Dr. Fred Lancer in Chattanooga; Dr. Robert Forbess, a dermatologist in San Diego. There are approximately two hundred M.D.'s and D.O.'s, participating. Also, around six hundred chiropractors."

"How many of them are pure M.D.'s?"

"Around a hundred pure M.D.'s."

"How many patients a week are seen here at the clinic?"

"Each doctor is working a full schedule, between twenty-five and thirty-five hours of actual patient time each week. A standard unit is fifteen minutes. Consultations take half an hour; complete physicals take an hour and a half. Our complete physical is as complete as any you can get in a general practice office."

"Is there a lab connected with this clinic?"

"We have a small lab for routine work. There is a lab here in town that we send most of our work out to, Arizona Health Labs."

"How are the patients charged?"

"The fees are, in general, the standard fee for medical treatment in the city of Phoenix."

"There are no extra charges for being treated with ARE methods?"

"No, we try to hold our fees down. We are charging a hundred dollars for a complete workup and that is considered fairly low."

"Suppose somebody wants to come here and has no funds?"

"We are currently collecting what we call the 'Indigent Patient Funds.' As time goes on, we will be able to take on indigent patients who have a serious need and who fit into research programs. I might add that when we go into our arthritis project—when there will be fifty patients treated here and fifty 'controls' treated at another clinic—our fifty patients will not be charged."

"Do you work with Blue Cross and any other organization along those lines?"

"Our insurance policy is standard. We have a full-time insurance girl who fills out the forms for our patients regardless of what insurance company they deal with."

"Have you ever supplemented the Cayce readings with related material from other sources?"

"There is a great interest on the part of our doctors for all types of healing. However, the Cayce material has so much breadth and depth that it is going to be many years before we can get too far beyond a level of simple interest."

"Do your doctors go outside the clinic to treat patients?"

"We do make house calls on our regular patients who need it."

I thanked the manager for his time and went over to Dr. William McGarey's office. The doctor turned out to be a pleasant, soft-spoken gentleman who worded his replies to my questions carefully and, perhaps understandably—after all, it isn't every day that you can question an M.D. and a member of the AMA on his work in psychic healing.

"Dr. McGarey, how many years have you been interested in the Cayce readings?" I began.

"I've been in the ARE since 1957."

"When did the idea strike you to use the material from the readings in your practice?"

"Almost at once, because I looked at these ideas and thought, if Cayce can search a person's unconscious mind, then there must be some basis for understanding it. When you first read the Cayce material, it is confusing to the medical mind because he talks in strange terms. He talks about 'coagulation' when he means 'cell construction.' In the practice of medicine we don't even *think* of cell construction."

"Do you think that the source which gave Cayce his information was medically trained?"

"I think the source was Cayce's unconscious mind reaching out and contacting the unconscious mind of other people. Cayce had the past life experience of having been a healer himself, back in Persia, thousands of years ago."

"Do you feel that there is an understanding of medical technology, medical terminology in the readings?"

"To a certain degree."

"Is it beyond what he as a conscious person would have known?"

"Yes." Dr. McGarey was emphatic.

"Do you find that any of this material could be derived from the minds of discarnate physicians?"

"Some of it, but not all of it."

"You refer to strange expressions. Are they strange in the use of words, or strange because of the ideas expressed by them?"

"Strange in the use of words. The ideas expressed are physiological ideas. The difference, I think, between the way he talks about the body and the way doctors and other people think about it is the difference between function and structure. Cayce talks as if a function is a real entity. In other words, a function is a living, active process and maybe function actually creates structure. The way he looks at it, an individual is a *spiritual* being *first* and manifests, through mind, as a *material* being. If this is true, then the spirit creates and the physical body is the result. If this is so, the spiritual being is the function, or the power, or the life force, and the physical structure, all parts of it, are there in order to let that life force manifest. Therefore, this structure is a result of function or of life. The function becomes the life process. The structure is just a means whereby it can express itself.

"In medicine we think in terms of *structure*. We think this man has liver disease, or lung disease, or his heart is abnormal, or he has brain disease, or he has an appendix that is inflamed. The way Cayce talks about it, one of the forces within the body has become unbalanced with the other forces, a system is out of coordination with another system, or the liver is not coordinating in its function with the kidneys because they're both eliminatory organs and the function of elimination has to come about or the individual dies. It is a different approach, from the standpoint of function, and the way we *currently* think about it, the structure is the thing we go by."

"How do *you* feel about it? Who is right?"

Dr. McGarey did not pause for a second.

"Oh, I think Cayce is right," he said.

"Would you define then the approach to healing using this, shall we say, progressive medicine?"

"I don't think it is a progressive stance toward medicine, since it hails back to the way Cayce did it ten thousand years ago in Persia. It is as ancient as man. I've come to call it *physiological rehabilitation.* Physiology is the study of the functioning of the parts of the body, the parts that keep the body alive."

"Are you using Cayce's recommendations as to medicine and treatments?"

"I'm using the principles he talked about, not the specific medications. I think he was talking in principles. He would have someone get a series of colonics and have another person take castor oil, or Epsom salt baths, then he'd have another person take a massage for the same purpose—to stimulate the eliminations of the body."

"But you will adopt the method according to the needs of the individual patient, is that right?"

"That's right."

"What about some of the substances Cayce does prescribe that are at variance with the accepted methods of treatment for these diseases?"

"It depends on what you're comparing it to. For instance, in arthritis we use atomadine, which is a type of iodine preparation. Iodine is used in medicine all the time, as in drops of SSKI (saturated solution potassium iodine). But the atomadine Cayce suggests is an iodine trichloride solution. He says that iodine stimulates all the glands of the body to function more normally. It acts as a cleansing agent and an aid to the function of the cells. Atomadine used over a period of time builds up, and that is the way I use it, in ascending dosages from one drop a day up to five drops, which is still a minimal amount. Then he says use an Epsom salts bath to eliminate *through the skin,* which is an eliminatory organ. Eliminate some of the toxins.

Some people in medicine, especially the physical therapists, use all sorts of physical therapy methods to combat arthritis. But the difference is this: I believe that arthritis is just a result of the body malfunctioning. If I can get the body functioning properly, arthritis will *not* be present. Aspirin used to contain the disease is not a cure."

"Do you feel the same way about cancer?"

"I have not researched cancer, and so I'm not sure what Cayce said about cancer. He did say there were nine different kinds. With leukemia, he said that tincture of iodine taken and mixed with blood drawn from the patient and then injected back in would cure maybe fifty percent of the cases of non-acidic leukemia."

"Has this ever been done?"

"No. Because he said first of all you have to test it in animals in order to determine the dosage and determine the side effects and so it has never been done. There is a good reason—no money."

"What diseases do you specialize in here?"

"We work with arthritis and respiratory diseases, the usual thing that you see in a general practitioner's office."

"You don't concern yourself with physical diseases, accidents, and things of that sort?"

"Not so much, although the healing of the body after an accident is much improved if you pay attention to the *functions* of the body."

"Have you done any work with mental patients?"

"Some. We have psychiatrists cooperating with the Edgar Cayce Research Foundation Program, and some are using Cayce's suggestions on schizophrenia."

"Which area do you feel strongest in?"

"I would be equally divided between respiratory diseases and arthritis, spearodermia, and pelvic diseases of women, which, I think, respond very well to Cayce's suggestions."

"Do you ever get involved with vitamins or other forms of dietary treatments?"

"Not vitamin treatments, diet treatments as such. We're working with a human being who is a manifestation of spirit. We're trying to bring that person to a wholeness. If we give a lot of vitamins to cure arthritis, then we may be avoiding a real confrontation of the human being."

"You are trying to heal the *whole* organism even though only *part* of it is affected."

"I think it is *all* affected. Cayce said that the body, the mind, and the spirit are one. If they are one, then a kink in one is a kink in another."

"Do you have any work with hypnosis?"

"No."

"Do you do any work involving the aura?"

"No. I'm interested, but I don't see the aura."

"Are you aware of the implication of auric treatments?"

"Yes."

"Is there any plan to develop that?"

"Yes, but it is in the future. I think that we need gradually to orient doctors in this whole field of parapsychology as such, the activity of the spiritual nature of man as it affects medical practice. I think doctors will *have* to become acquainted with it or they'll pass into oblivion."

"Do you perform surgery here?" I said, changing the subject again.

"Minor surgery. If someone cuts their hand, I sew it up. Or taking off little cysts or something of that nature."

"Isn't that in contradiction of Cayce's ideas on wholeness?"

"No, he said that if you have castor oil consciousness, use castor oil, and, to paraphrase that, if you have surgery consciousness, use surgery. Some people are in a state of awareness where surgery is the thing that they need at this time, this place."

"Are there any surgeons operating under the Cayce directive?"

"Yes. There's one in Bethesda, Maryland, Dr. Robert Brewer. He's going to be on our symposium next year. This is the fifth time. We are also having Dr. Ernie Petche, who is a psychiatrist from California, and William Tiller, who was head of the Department of Material Sciences at Stanford University, a physicist."

"In your treatment do you ever have reference to prior incarnations as being, in some way, connected with diseases?"

"Sure, because people who come to me understand about reincarnation and it makes treatment a whole lot simpler. I think that whether reincarnation happens or not, it is much more reasonable to think in terms of it than not and so you can explain and understand things and thus act in accordance with reason a lot better if you know that something may be *karmic* in its origin."

"Do you yourself accept the karmic origin of much disease?"

"Yes."

"Is there some way of evaluating the karmic element in disease and thus of reversing the process?"

"I think so. I think that the karmic element almost always comes from manifestation of glandular malfunction."

"In understanding the cause do you feel that the disease can be checked?"

"Sometimes. It depends, I think, on what the person has chosen even before he is born. If he were born without limbs, this is a *karmic* affliction. We don't know enough yet to help a person grow new limbs, although the potential is there. Potential is in each cell of the human body, and this has been demonstrated by physicians who do research. But that kind of karmic affliction may be something he has chosen to live with through a whole incarnation."

"Have you had any personal problems with the American Medical Association because of your views and your work?"

"I had one case, when I was giving a lecture and the people in that city got overenthusiastic and sent announcements to all the doctors. The president of their society wrote a letter to the secretary of our society and said, 'What about this guy talking about the unconscious mind? Is he some kind of a nut?' and our secretary wrote back and said, 'No. He's got ideas of his own and he's a respected member of the medical community.'"

I was deeply impressed with Dr. McGarey's sincerity and level-headed approach to the problem at hand: how to reconcile orthodox medical training with the Edgar Cayce teachings. Quite obviously the two are on a collision course. If the doctor is right in supporting the Cayce view of man, and I am convinced that he is, then much of what he was taught in medical school can no longer be true. For instance, the traditional view of the body as a superior animal, developed through the long and arduous process of evolution from lower animal forms, and essentially subject to the laws of the physical universe only, is diametrically opposed to the teachings of Cayce and most other esoteric teachers, that the physical is merely an expression of the spiritual and that the spiritual has created the physical manifestation, not vice versa.

Surely, an entirely new form of medicine lies just beyond the horizon. Fortunately the Association for Research and Enlightenment in Virginia Beach and in the many branches throughout the United States is doing everything within its power to shed additional light upon these amazing teachings of a man without medical training, without superior knowledge and, for that matter, without any ambitions to be anything but a humble vehicle.

The clinic at Phoenix is merely one attempt to acquaint the general public with the Cayce material and to use it in a practical way to heal the sick. On still another level, physical therapy, Harold J. Reilly, of New Jersey, has been active in the field of body conditioning and rehabilitating through exercise and a planned program of physical activity. What makes the Reilly method different from any other form of physiotherapy is of course his relationship with the late Edgar Cayce. "One of the most interesting and intriguing experiences I have had is that of helping to condition hundreds of men and women referred to me by the famous miracle man of Virginia Beach, the well-known psychic, Edgar Cayce. For about two years before I had even met the man and continuing seventeen years after until his death, he advised people to come to me for conditioning. As this advice was given in a trance state I felt curiously honored to have been selected from out of the ether to give a special type of therapy I was already using for general conditioning. I was further flattered when this strangely gifted man came in for my personal manipulations," writes Harold Reilly in one of his books, *Easy Does it*. Reilly preaches physical conditioning as a philosophy of life. To him, the health and function of muscles, glands, organs, mind, and *spirit* all depend on the movements of the body. Many public figures, Hollywood stars, and athletes have used Reilly's services over the years. Many came to Reilly to improve their figures, to lose excess weight, or to have their health restored when under stress, but many others came because Reilly was the man to see if one was interested in the Edgar Cayce philosophy of life. Somehow Harold Reilly, who holds a doctorate in chiropractics, is the physical exponent of the Cayce teachings. After a patient has been ministered to by someone practicing on the basis of the Cayce readings, he is frequently sent to the Reilly clinic for a combination of rest and toning up. Up to June, 1960, Reilly handled about 1,000 cases referred to him by the Edgar Cayce foundation. He arranged for treatments in his drugless therapy field for patients requiring osteopathy, chiropractic massage, hydrotherapy, homeotherapy, and other forms of treatment requiring no drugs whatsoever.

As Dr. Reilly reported in the *Searchlight*, a publication of ARE, the patients sent to him fell into four categories: those having to do with the increase of circulation, those having to do with the increase in the elimination, those having to do with relaxation, and those having to do with the proper approach to eating. Harold Reilly was able to show them the way to better health, but to maintain good health, patients were required to continue a balanced program of specific exercises at all times.

So great was and is Edgar Cayce's impact on the American scene that it was perhaps inevitable that people, sooner or later, would claim to be carrying on the work of the late seer of Virginia Beach. Well-meaning psychics and not so well-meaning opportunists have come forward to claim contact with Edgar Cayce. "Get help now from Dr. Ernesto A. Montgomery, the West Indies prophet. Not since the great Edgar Cayce has so amazing a prophet and healer appeared," is the somewhat all encompassing statement put forward by a well-known Los Angeles psychic reader.

Two housewives in Cincinnati, Ohio, who have worked together for years in what they believe to be a contact with the late Edgar Cayce, I have investigated carefully myself. One of the two women, the medium, received "Cayce's messages" in trance; the other took them down for posterity. As with all such messages, I take great care to differentiate between the patently false or erroneous and the possibly genuine. In the case of the two ladies in Cincinnati, the alleged Cayce speaking to me through the entranced medium was unable to answer a number of key questions put to him. The information had been supplied to me by Hugh Lyn Cayce, son of the late Edgar, and included names and situations that could have been answered only by the authentic Edgar Cayce.

Similarly, a dentist in the Midwest laid claim to being a mouthpiece for the late Edgar Cayce. Despite her apparent sincerity and conviction that she was indeed the chosen one, none of the material obtained through her can be verified sufficiently to support her claim.

It would appear that Edgar Cayce will choose his mouthpiece very carefully so as not to create conflict or doubt in the minds of researchers as to the genuineness of the communications. Thus far no one has come forward with sufficient evidence to support a claim of being the mouthpiece of the late Edgar Cayce. This may yet happen in the future, and when it occurs, it will benefit mankind beyond belief; for if the incarnate Edgar Cayce was able to prescribe medications for thousands of people, relying only on the knowledge given him in trance by discarnates, how much greater must the knowledge of the discarnate now be, after he himself has crossed the threshold into the world of spirit and become acquainted with its laws and truths.

At this writing, the Cayce Foundation's ARE Clinic in Phoenix, Arizona, is a firmly established alternative center, with Drs. Gladys and William McGarey still at the helm. Those wishing to avail themselves of their counsel or services should contact the Association for Research and Enlightenment (ARE) at P.O. Box 595, Virginia Beach, Virginia 23451. There is also a holistic pharmacy connected with the Association where Cayce-inspired medicines may be obtained at reasonable prices.

Probably one of the most brilliant and innovative medical pioneers is John C. Pierrakos, M.D., researcher and practicing psychiatrist in New York City, who maintains offices at 115 E. 23rd Street.

Dr. Pierrakos, in his treatise, *The Energy Field in Man and Nature*, establishes through experimentation the existence of energy fields in man, plants, and even crystals—thus seriously endangering the cherished notion that the world is divided into organic and inorganic matter. The treatise was published by his Institute of Bioenergetic Analysis, at 71 Park Avenue in New York City. Because of man's energy field (or aura) consisting of three separate layers, healing of the various layers, presents a rational, if unorthodox explanation in respect to the question of how psychic healing works.

"The field phenomena are related to the energy metabolism of the body," writes Dr. Pierrakos, "its production of heat, emotional excitement, rate and quality of breathing, activity, and rest. They are also affected by atmospheric conditions, relative humidity, polarity of charges in the air, and many other unknown factors."

It is clear that the inclusion of this knowledge in the treatment of the ill, even by conventional means, is likely to alter the conservative outlook of the average physician. But for the vast majority of medical practitioners to accept Dr. Pierrakos's findings would mean relearning and rethinking much, an effort human nature seems to resist with most people. But those in need of, or seriously interested in, this approach to human nature and healing, might want to consult the doctor himself.

Another eminent psychiatrist, Dr. Ralph Dickson Yaney, has found the inclusion of reincarnation material in the treatment of his psychoanalytical cases of great value. He uses reputable psychics to obtain past life material about clients and astrological charts, to gain a better insight into his patients' personalities. Whether the reincarnation material is factual or not, it appears that its use in the psychoanalytic process can be quite positive. Dr. Yaney is extremely careful in his selection of sensitives (psychics), and quite knowledgeable in astrology: he uses professional astrological character analysis based on birth, not any kind of fortune-telling. One may debate the methods he uses, but more and more psychiatrists are employing such alternative techniques (as did Carl Jung in his applications of astrology). In fact, in my conversations with several of Dr. Yaney's patients, they all indicated that they were indeed helped by the insights gained from these alternative sources.

For those interested in additional information about alternative medical treatments, *The Healthview Newsletter* is a periodical publication supported by a number of natural-healing oriented physicians, dentists and chiropractors. It is published at 612 Rio Road West, Box 6670, Charlottesville, Virginia 22906.

* * *

Oddly enough, it is conventionally trained psychiatrists and psychoanalysts who are often opposed to the inclusion of non-physical elements in diagnosis and treatments. Freudian and Jungian interpretation is as strong as ever, even though the evidence for extrasensory perception and its various ramifications on the state of the physical body are generally accepted these days.

But, of course, a substantial portion of dream analysis can no longer be interpreted by the "old" standards: clairvoyant dreams cannot be explained on physical grounds, and out-of-body experiences are not "hallucinations," but actual "astral travel" by the inner body. In my current work, *The Psychic Side of Dreams,* I have demonstrated through case histories that many dreams are actually not dreams at all, but states during which genuine psychic material is obtained. Whether it is obtained by the person's own extrasensory abilities, or by some external agency, like a spirit or spirit guide, is a moot question—what matters is the accuracy of the material.

The "unorthodox" of today is the commonplace of tomorrow, of course, and there are a growing number of physicians who are willing to talk about alternative methods and remedies. Those who cling to outmoded beliefs that only a prescription drug manufactured by a pharmacist will do, seem to forget that the very same chemical ingredients contained in the doctor's prescription may well be in the natural medicine (e.g., the herb, the vitamin, the healing plant found in nature). Except in its natural state it may be far more powerful and perhaps different in its effect from synthetic materials.

Every day brings startling "new discoveries" in medicine. Some of these "new discoveries," however, may have been around among alternative-medicine users for centuries. But our greatly improved medical technology is also responsible for discoveries that could not have been made twenty years ago.

A genuine healing physician should be interested in results, whether they come to the patient in the orthodox way, or by an alternative route. Many physicians have forgotten that primary purpose in the rush for bigger and more expensive treatments, medical machinery, and drugs.

THREE

The Dawn of the Age of Alternative Medicine

With AIDS having become an unfortunate household word, and more people dying of cancer regardless of the amount of chemotherapy and radiation they receive (and probably also *because of it*), the wall against alternative ways to save lives has begun to crumble. There comes a time when the orthodoxy cannot remain all-powerful any longer, and slowly—and grudgingly—they must allow attention to be given to healing by methods other than their own.

Not that this is exactly new: psychic healing, chiropractic, and homeopathy go back to the middle nineteenth century. What is new is the attitude of the medical establishment. Born from rarely admitted despair at being unable to conquer some of the worst diseases, the medical establishment is hoping to learn something new from these pioneers in alternative medicine so that they can incorporate those findings into their own practices. I have no quarrel with that, so long as they do not distort or misuse the new ways.

As this happens, the line between practicing physicians and medical researchers grows indistinct and even those outside the strictly medical world, such as technicians and explorers, are allowed to make discoveries and publish their findings.

For instance, Sandra Blakeslee, a medical writer, reports in the *New York Times* of September 7, 1993, that the human nose may hold "an additional organ" for a "real Sixth Sense." What she is talking about is a discovery by Dr. David Berliner, who runs a private lab, to the effect that "humans, like most animals, may exude a copious clowd of odorless chemicals called *pheromones*, that send meaningful signals to other humans. If research now under way pans out, it signifies the discovery of a cryptic sensory system that exists without conscious awareness, yet may influence fundamental human behavior involving sexual reproduction and the ability to discriminate between individuals." What this means, in plain language, is confirmation of the existence of what most of us refer to as "chemistry" between people—an attraction (or lack of it) between two people.

Do enormous magnets affect the human body? That is the question *New York Times* science writer Walter Sullivan asked in February 1983, when reporting the work of Drs. Thomas Tenforde and Michael Raybourn at the Lawrence Berkeley Laboratory of the University of California. The experiments, while entirely safe, have suggested that "human beings are subtly influenced by magnetism. . . . the overall study has also explored the effects of strong magnetic fields on heart performance and has shown that they induce a marked change in electrocardiograms." So-called "unorthodox" healers, rarely medical people, have used magnets to affect the body for many years. As with many people lacking formal training but possessed of intuitive knowledge, they know it works, but do not know how, or why.

Recently, the discovery of morphogenic protein, a protein that can regenerate bones, has shown a new way of healing damaged human bones. As Roy Furchgott reports in the *New York Times* of April 4, 1993, these proteins not only promote bone healing and growth, but may soon be used in dental work such as root canals, and in the repair of duodenal ulcers. Mending fractures with bone protein (its laboratory name is O.P.1.) works by attracting healthy cells from nearby bone and binding them to receptors on the surface of those cells. It then creates a cartilage-forming cell called a chondrocyte, and the gap in the bone slowly fills with cartilage. Gradually, this cartilage hardens into new bone tissue. In time, this new bone takes on the shape and structure of the original bone. This new technique is largely the discovery and work of a research company called Creative Biomolecules, based in Hopkinton, Massachusetts, and of a professor of orthopedic surgery at the University of California, Dr. Marshall Urist.

But while people suffer and die needlessly simply because the average physician will not even discuss alternative ways to help them, there are those among the health fraternity—M.D.'s, Ph.D.'s, and medical researchers without that lofty degree—who offer new ways, documenting them so that both patient and uncommitted doctor can judge for themselves. I am not just talking of the 1990s. Using the psi factor in medicine, that is, the psychical element present, for instance, was the subject of a book called *Psionic Medicine* by J. H. Reyner, George Laurence, and Carl Upton. Its subtitle read *The Study and Treatment of the Causative Factors in Illness.* This book was published in 1975.

The authors state that their book is directed "primarily to those members of the orthodox medical profession who are beginning to mistrust the present preoccupation with the amelioration of clinical symptoms, and who are prepared to believe that these are only the manifestation of deeper underlying causes, to the discovery of which their skills could be more profitably employed."

Reyner also states that only medically qualified people trained in psionic techniques should practice this approach, particularly with diagnosis. This work also points out that "while there has been great progress in understanding the structure of the physical body, this has led to problems, one of which is an undue reliance on the material aspects of medicine and a mistaken belief that a full understanding of the physical mechanism will ultimately provide a cure for all the ailments of the flesh."

Gradually, truth does march on. In December 1991, Natalie Anger, the *New York Times* medical writer, reported on a new attitude toward such states as fever, based on ideas published by Dr. George C. Williams in *The Quarterly Review of Biology*. Biologists refer to the "natural" approach to allowing the body to heal itself as Darwinian. Symptoms such as fever should not be suppressed at all costs, but should be allowed to do its job, which is to fight infection. In this view, standard medical procedures to fight disease sometimes interfere with the body's own natural defenses. There are many people who refuse to take antibiotics or get immunization shots for colds, relying instead on their body's own natural defense systems. This does not mean *all treatment* for serious infection must be suspended. It does mean that far too often suppressive agents are prescribed routinely, even when their absence would promote healing better and faster, supported perhaps by certain natural remedies that do not interfere with the body's own immune and defense systems, but complement them.

We are talking here of the conventional medical system. Doctors trained basically as they have been for years; kept up-to-date not so much by the knowledge of new ideas as by the discovery of new drugs and manmade remedies, thoughtfully and frequently supplied by the pharmaceutical industry that manufactures them. Yet, even in the pharmaceutical industry things are beginning to stir. An "unusual heart therapy," as the *New York Times* calls it, recently won the support and financial approval of a large insurance company. The program, an alternate treatment to surgery and pharmaceutical approaches, combines diet, meditation, exercise, and support groups for the heart patient to reverse the course of heart disease. This "reversal program" was developed by Dr. Dean Ornish, director of the Preventive Medicine Research Institute of Sausalito, California.

Today there is an ever-growing increase in taking alternative medicine seriously. As early as 1980, approximately one hundred establishments throughout the United States provided holistic and "wellness" counseling. As Victor Cohn wrote in the *Washington Post* on December 7, 1980, "a new life-style medicine which teaches us that what we do and eat, smoke, drink, have more to do with our health than all the things doctors can do." And today, there is a magazine called *Health & More Healing*, founded by Julian Whitaker, M.D. In a special edition called "Wellness Today," Dr. Whitaker writes about alternative medical ways to deal with sickness, once again blaming most doctors and drug companies for keeping this information from the public for self-serving reasons. The magazine is published at 7811 Montrose Road, Potomac, Maryland 20854.

Not long ago, renowned journalist Bill Moyers fascinated his public broadcasting audiences with a series dealing with the subject of his new book, *Healing and the Mind*. Whenever anything new in the way of a healing agent or therapy is suggested, some physicians may indeed welcome it and even try it out. But many more will demand what they call "scientific proof" that this new method really works. As if medical science were a monolith, built of stone, not capable of any great changes. The truth is, the word "science" comes from the Latin "scire," which means quest for knowledge, searching knowledge. Not knowing it all.

In 1976, Paul Abell, a Los Angeles acupressurist, had to camouflage his work as "massage" in order to avoid being persecuted by the mainstream medical crowd. Acupuncture and acupressure (pretty much the same idea, but without the needles) is 4,000 years old and based on healing, affecting, and working with the body's "meridians" and "pressure points." Abell's particular therapy is called Jin Shin Ju Jyutsu, which emerged from Taoist philosophy as a healing art to engage both body and mind. "It is a nonmedical, nonmedicinal way to relieve your tensions and replenish your mental and physical energies," Abell states. I know firsthand, because Paul treated me, and I felt different—not by suggestion, but as a matter of practical, observable fact.

The melancholy truth is, we are now rediscovering ancient wisdom, not necessarily discovering new ways to heal. In the futile and erroneous assumption that modern technology and chemistry can better Mother Nature and our inborn systems of self-healing and adjustment, much that is valuable has been left behind and needs now to be reintroduced into our lives. Add to this the arrogant attitude of the technologically superior "West" toward the "superstitious" East, and an entire edifice of healing knowledge is pushed aside. Truly, it is modern man's own folly that causes so much of his suffering.

The opening-up process among an ever-increasing number of medical doctors does not, however, go unchallenged by those who fear for *their* ways. For example, Dr. Robert Atkins of New York City, and author of a very successful diet book, treats seriously ill cancer patients who cannot be helped by conventional chemotherapy or radiation, with a method widely used in Europe, called ozone therapy. In ozone therapy, ozone is introduced into the bloodstream to destroy toxic matter and bacteria. When a patient of Atkins' was admitted to Jacobi Hospital, in New York, after she had complained of weakness, she told the hospital doctor of her treatments by Dr. Atkins. Without so much as speaking with Atkins or evaluating the unusual treatment in any proper way, the admitting physician, Dr. Paul Gennis, took it upon himself to file a complaint against Dr. Atkins, which resulted in Atkins having his licence summarily revoked. Dr. Gennis is quoted by *New York Newsday* as stating, "I cannot imagine what benefit ozone could have. It sounds like quackery to me."

The outcry among other professionals, Dr. Atkins' patients, and the general public familiar with his work was extensive, and the whole matter is now in the courts. Of course, every new discovery has always had to deal with those who fought against it out of ignorance.

But finally, the dawn has come. With a new and progressive government in Washington, the hardliners are no longer altogether triumphant. In late fall 1992, a new government agency, the *Office of Alternative Medicine*, was established, headed by Dr. Joseph J. Jacobs, which will also give grants to deserving researchers in the field. What is particularly promising for future results from this agency is the fact that Jacobs is an American Indian. In fact, he spent two years of his childhood living on a Mohawk reservation in New York State, and last year served as the president of the Association of American Indian physicians. Although educated in all the "right" ways as a doctor (at Columbia University) his Native American heritage makes him the ideal person to head up this office, this "new door" that is finally opening to let the light come into our lives. While his office will deal in a serious and measured manner with such topics as acupuncture, chiropractic, biofeedback, hypnosis, and even guided imagery, it will also look into the medical usage of herbs, vitamins, homeopathy, and even ozone therapy, and any other *well-documented* forms of healing.

In a later chapter I will deal specifically with herbs and the shrinking rain forests where so much can be found that can make us well.

There is abundant literature available dealing with various paths in alternative medicine. Some of this literature tends to be more like a sales pitch (albeit for a good cause), and not every "natural" remedy offered works, or works as well as claimed. Natural and alternative medicine are pathways to maintaining and restoring full health of body, mind, and spirit, but they are no more perfect than man himself.

Those who wish to read about this "movement"—which nowadays is essentially a way of life for many—will find books, magazines, lectures, and seminars everywhere.

Here are a handful of what I consider useful sources. The books by Dr. Herbert M. Shelton on health reform, natural hygiene, and diet. He also has a magazine called *The Healthway Advisor*, published at the headquarters of the American Natural Hygiene Society Inc. at 1920 Irving Park Road, Chicago, Illinois 60613. The Omega Institute for Holistic Studies at PO 396, New Lebanon, New York 12125, and their newsletters. The National College of Naturopathic Medicine, which trains naturopathic doctors and awards a degree that is recognized by practitioners in the field of alternative medicine as valid, is located at 510 SW Third Avenue, Portland, Oregon 97204. Lastly, The University of Natural Healing Inc., founded by Sandra G. Miller, specializes in information dealing with incurable diseases, and tries to help where all other means have failed. They publish a newsletter called *Last Chance*, and are located at PO 8113, 355 West Rio Road, Suite 201, Charlottesville, Virginia 22906.

*   *   *

Now in 1993, acupuncture and acupressure are as common in America (and elsewhere) as chiropractic and hypnosis. Whether some doctors approve of these or not, many people are using alternative methods when standard treatment has not helped them. It is a different approach, and if it works, fine. With rampant and incurable diseases taking an increasing toll in human lives, and causing economic hardships through spiraling costs of medical treatments, which often turn out to be unsuccessful, one would think that *any* avenue leading to relief would be universally welcome. Not so. The FDA, the federal agency regulating drugs, is suddenly getting nervous about the effects of the many vitamins and nutritional supplements on the market. It wants to "regulate" them, which would deprive millions of people of their only way to better health. Naturally, those directly affected are fighting such a notion. But the powerful medical and pharmaceutical lobbies in Washington continue to put pressure on the government to restrict what they quite rightly perceive to be competition. Namely, natural medicines, and therapies that do not bring in any big fees, and "drugs" derived from trees and plants that cost a lot less than the synthetic "remedies" (really poisons alien to the body) that make pharmaceutical companies rich.

But even some of the drug companies know a good thing when they see one, and they are now seriously studying the many medicinal plants and trees in the tropical forests of Central and South America, so that they, too, can offer them to the public—at higher prices, to be sure.

So where is the answer that would reconcile what was, what is, and what may be, in health care? Much of traditional medicine is valid and works. A lot does not and is not harmful. A lot is, however. Natural medicines derived from living plants and trees have exactly the same situation: a lot of them really help, proven by properly monitored surveys (even though the explanation as to why they work is often not known). Some do not work and are harmless. And a few should be taken with care because of potential dangers in the wrong dosages, and there are some false or exaggerated claims put forth by the sellers—just as there are false or exaggerated claims of "regular" medical products. Taking the best and most effective of both systems in the answer. Blending what nature gives us with some of the techniques of modern medicine as partner can indeed give us better health.

Sometimes, however, the two systems are clearly not compatible. Giving cancer patients chemotherapy or radiation will not ultimately cure them, but will surely destroy the person's own immune system from fighting the disease. On the other hand, carefully designed nutritional therapies can and have defeated cancer in many cases, but not with patients who already have had chemotherapy or radiation. Perhaps the problem lies with doctors not having ever been trained in anything but "school medicine." Some of them still wear blinders to anything outside of what they know. Others simply fail to grasp the significance of the interplay between natural, curative medicines and the body-mind-spirit systems that are, after all, also totally natural and do not contain anything synthetic.

On a trip to Los Angeles I once sat next to a gentleman who observed my taking vitamins with my vegetarian lunch. The talk turned to vitamin C, and I explained to him that my vitamin C tablets were derived from plants, not synthetic ascorbic acid, which is the manufactured form of vitamin C on the market. "What's the difference?" he asked. "The difference," I replied, "is that naturally grown vitamin C derived from the Acerola plant, also contains an absorption factor, bioflavin, which, when combined with the vitamin C allows it to do its job in the body fully and properly. Synthetic vitamin C has none of it." The gentleman shook his head. I had failed to convince him. But then he handed me his card; he was president of a large pharmaceutical company.

Lest I be accused of singing only the praises of the "New Age" world of rain forest and plant remedies, let me also point out that much profiteering is going on in that industry, as well. Making a decent profit is every merchant's right and purpose, and those who engage in the manufacture or the providing of natural and alternative remedies are indeed earning their livelihood in a good cause. But there is really no excuse for the spiraling costs of the most popular vitamins, minerals, and natural remedies—any more than such practices in other areas are acceptable or even necessary. Why should a little bottle of tincture of Saw Palmetto, costing $6 all year long, jump to $7 overnight, when the shelf of the health food store has dozens of the tincture still sitting there from an earlier purchase? A 15 percent increase just by sitting there? Surely, if new merchandise costs the store owner more, well and good, then let the supplier explain why he is charging more. Nothing in the industry supplying vitamins, minerals, or natural remedies has changed much over the past couple of years, except the increased greed arising when the purveyor of the goods sees the demand for his product increasing. In this respect, the suppliers of alternative medical goods are as guilty of profiteering as the suppliers of conventional medical goods. Apart from a purely physical side of the understanding of alternative and natural medicine, there is a moral and spiritual issue here, and let us not lose sight of it.

I maintain that contemporary man's disregard for his spiritual component and responsibility is the root of many evils in our society. We have armies to protect us, police departments to maintain order, and lawmakers to regulate our government, and we accept their need to have an adequate livelihood from that work. But the very fabric of our lives—health—somehow has been allowed to become a major profit-making enterprise, far beyond proper remuneration and fair profit margins for those who risk time and money in the field. To be a physician, a medical researcher, a pharmacist, or provider of health services is truly a noble calling, and the fruits of these labors belong to the world—both for those who can afford it, and those who cannot.

The Twin Threats: Aging and Illness

To the physician, aging is a natural process that can be dealt with, made easier perhaps, but that cannot be averted or stopped. It is simply the result of the physical body breaking down somewhere in the system, and that breakdown is due to wear and tear (meaning usage and time) or illness (meaning damage to the system). Most people accept the fact that aging cannot be averted any more than death can be, though we do not really know who or what decided when or how this should occur in our individual lives. If you are among those who see physical death merely as a progression into the next dimension where your "inner" body continues to function with full consciousness, you can see why there are limits on the durability of that "outer" body, and know that its dissolution is not the end of your *existence*. However, there is a large segment of humanity who does not view life in this way and who considers the physical aspects of life of ultimate importance. These people are not so willing to simply "break down" and will put up as much of a fight as they are able to—to retard the moment of transition, and to improve the quality of life in the physical vehicle as much as possible. There is nothing wrong with doing that, though it should be inspired not by fear of death or illness, but by a sense of living to the fullest in this state of being, even if it must inevitably lead to the next stage of existence, "beyond the veil."

There are numerous books showing ways to halt or reverse the aging process and live a healthier life. Foremost among them is *Secrets of Life Extension* by John A. Mann, a medical technician and researcher. It is by far the most comprehensive and practical study of its kind and I highly recommend it.

Mann demonstrates how certain vitamins and minerals can reverse the aging process by eliminating the creation of so-called free radicals, portions of cells that have broken up and which pose a threat to the rest of the system. Mann postulates that it is possible to extend one's lifespan to 120 years if good care of the body is taken—mind and spirit included.

Some of the best known substances, which are easily obtainable at reasonable cost in any health food store, include beta carotene, selenium, S.O.D. (an enzyme), and garlic tablets to deal with infection, should any occur. The amino acid L-Cysteine is also an important antioxidant, as is RNA/DNA to deal with free radicals.

Without overlooking the genetic factor of physical characteristics inherited from one's parents, we are, nevertheless, individuals who inherit our physical bodies but not our spiritual component from our parents and thus represent a combination of factors to be considered when dealing with individual aging. Thus not all people will age the same way nor be as successful in dealing with it. One of the most misleading factors generally used in today's medical approach is statistics—as if we were all merely numbers, not widely differing individuals with three (not one or two) components. That third component, spirit (anima, persona) does not even figure in those statistics, and yet they are used to prescribe treatments and drugs as if we should all be painted with the same brush. Naturally, it is a shotgun approach to healing: a large portion of those in need of it will indeed fit the statistical norm. But an almost as large number of people will differ in widely varied degrees from that norm, and for them the prescribed treatments will not only *not* help, but may do a lot of damage.

We need to return to treating individuals as uniquely different, and apply the statistically-arrived treatment only after its effects have been considered in the individual case, how it might affect that patient whose history and problems the physician should know and consider. What helps one person may well hurt another, since the overwhelming majority of conventional modern medicine relies on a wide array of drugs, mostly synthetically produced, to deal with the symptoms of the disease first and the cause afterwards. Conversely, natural healing relies on the person's own natural, inborn defenses, on the theory that the weakening or lack of response of those defenses are responsible for the patient's illness. Strengthening or cleaning up those defenses is what holistic healing is all about. It heals the person first and ameliorates the symptoms of disease second.

Aging and illness do not necessarily go together. I watched a 104-year-old Broadway writer and producer named George Abbott give a very fine television interview to my old friend Dennis Wholey on PBS. Not every person will be fit at age 104, or even reach its environs at all, but the fact that some can and do—and so many do not—makes one wonder if we are not missing a very important point about our lifestyle. Some illnesses occur without our understanding why they do, while we understand why many others do and yet do little to prevent them.

My position is basic and simple: once we accept the triune reality of body, mind, and spirit, we cannot expect wellness unless all three are addressed equally at all times. Most conventional physicians will deal with the physical body only, referring what is clearly the influence of the mind over it, to their colleages in psychiatry; if there is a hint of the spirit being involved, modern doctors back off quickly and refer the patient to the brethren in theology. But psychiatrists and ministers in turn have nothing to do with the physical body, and so man is divided in three.

It is no dark secret that stress and worry cause physical reactions in the body itself, mostly involuntary and certainly avoidable.

A recent study undertaken by the Medical Research Council's

Common Cold Unit in Salisbury, England, and published by the prestigious *New England Journal of Medicine*, has found that there was a clear connection between emotions and infections. High levels of psychological stress, for instance, could nearly double a person's chances of catching a cold by lowering resistance to viral infection. While I maintain that we are a triple entity of body, mind, and spirit, I do not for a moment imply that these three aspects of our consciousness are separate in any way, rather that they are wholly interconnected and interdependent. Spiritual activity—beliefs, emotional factors, extrasensory perception aspects—can trigger physical responses in the body, mostly automatic reflexes, with appropriate results, good or bad from the person's point of view. Likewise, mental activity—thoughts, ideas, perceptions—can also trigger biochemical responses, with the results either helping or hurting the individual, as the case may be.

Clearly, then, I propose that we must approach the question of illness—and of the aging process with its deterioration of all three components of our consciousness, not merely the physical one—from the inside out, not from the outside in. By this I mean that bodily complaints should be dealt with by dealing with the person as a whole. Therapy and drugs have their place, but so does imagery, suggestion, and deep-seated beliefs. Some illnesses, of course, are best healed by standard physical medicine: you can't suggest a broken leg to heal itself (though there are incidents suggesting such work by psychic healers). But despite years of research and new drugs ameliorating migraines, a most common form of headache, the best cure is still prevention of the conditions leading to the mechanical reaction known as migraine. Migraine, clearly, is an emotional illness with its physical symptoms ranging from excruciating pain in the head to internal light flashes, nausea, dizzy states and vertigo, and temporary visual distortions. Its origin is always emotional, but in a wide variety of possible causes and stimuli tripping the attacks. Some personal thought patterns, whether or not realistic and based on fact, can do it, as well as external situations, trauma, or a change in temperature. But always it is reacted to by the emotions, not the rational mind, and certainly not caused in any way by the physical body itself, which is the victim, not the originator of the problem.

Meanwhile, another renowned science writer, Natalie Anger, tells us at great length, also in the New York Times, how genetic clues are now being blamed for incidents of migraine. Blaming one's inherited traits entirely for migraine attacks seems far-fetched to me, an old migraine sufferer since age 16 and very much concerned with it. What I am driving at is not so much the discovery of the triggering sequence of events, and how and why we are hurting and suffering from migraines of various types, but a realization, based on years of personal observation, that the real problem with migraine attacks lies elsewhere. What causes these sequences of events to occur in the brain and head, even if the patient is inclined to inherited traits making migraine more likely to occur, are purely emotional states. Anxiety, shock, frustration, fear, worry, over-exertion, and even heavy dreams can all trigger attacks, and they do—I know firsthand. So, inevitably we arrive at the interlinking of physical, mental, and spiritual factors that are together responsible for physical illness.

On the other hand, an Indian-born physician, Usha Mukhtyar, M.D., reports in a letter to the editor in the New York Times (October 2, 1993) that homeopathic treatments have indeed prevented his migraine attacks. Homeopathy teaches that tiny amounts of the same agent causing the disease should be taken as a preventive, or cure. I must confess that the explanation for this process still escapes me, but thousands of people have indeed been helped through homeopathic medicines. While homeopathy has roots in nineteenth-century Germany, there are now homeopathic tinctures and pills freely available throughout the United States, as well as practicing homeopathic physicians, who usually are also medical doctors.

In the same letters to the editor column of the New York Times quoted above, Dr. Seymour Diamond, executive director of the National Headache Foundation of Chicago, Illinois, comments on the latest migraine remedy, sumatriptan. Developed by a team at Brigham Young Hospital in Boston, sumatriptan is said to be helpful and free of dangerous side effects, such as the nausea caused by ergotamin products, the standard remedy for most migraine attacks.

But Dr. Diamond also reaffirms his conviction that "the vascular theory originated by Harold G. Wolff of Cornell University is the most widely accepted for the origin of migraine." Which leads me back to the ultimate remedy: *prevention* by the encouragement of a more resilient emotional reaction to the events and situations that trigger migraine attacks.

*   *   *

One of the most destructive fears besetting the aged and the aging is fear of death. Evidence for a continuance of consciousness beyond the death of the physical, outer body will surely influence one's attitude in the final years of physical life: knowledge, that death is not the end, makes a difference. Is there solid scientific evidence for any kind of life after death? Thanks to modern techniques and a wider view of the universe, the quest for evidence of what the psychical research pioneer, F.W.H. Myers had called "survival of human personality of bodily death" is getting stronger. People who have experienced apparitions of the dead are no longer necessarily accused of hallucinating. Professor Hornell Hart of Duke University, in a survey of reported apparitions, states, "In my view, the apparitions of the dead were indeed who they claimed to be." Dr. Stanley R. Dean, clinical professor of psychiatry at the University of Miami, Florida medical school, says "Sufficient proof has been established for the existence of psychic phenomena, and now the current need is to disseminate the scientific basis of such phenomena." And H.H. Price, Wykeham Professor of Logic, University of Oxford, in discussing whether people sometimes experience apparitions of the dead, in *Light*, a British magazine, in 1959, states, "They certainly do. No one who examines the evidence can come to any other conclusion."

Thousands of such cases occur all over the world, suggesting they are not supernatural, but merely extensions of human consciousness not yet fully understood.

Life magazine, in a 1973 survey entitled "A Crisis in Science" states, "New enigmas in physics revive quests in metaphysics . . . the old-fashioned materialism is now even more oldfashioned . . . its basic assumption, that the only 'reality' is that which occupies space and has a mass, is irrelevant to an age that has proved that matter is interchangeable with energy . . . oldfashioned metaphysics, so far from being irrelevant to an age of science, is science's indispensable complement for a full view of life."

In the same survey, Dr. Gardner Murphy, of the Menninger Foundation, and long-time president of the American Society for Psychical Research, states, "If there was one-tenth of the evidence in any other field of science than there is in parapsychology, it would be accepted beyond question."

Dr. Lawrence Le Shan, eminent researcher and author, writes, "There is more to man, more to him and his relationship with the cosmos than we have accepted. Further, this 'more' is of a different kind and order from the parts we know about."

As we learn more about the nature of man, a breakthrough to the elusive element of consciousness—and its continuance beyond the physical body—seems near. The very scientists who work in the most advanced physical sciences may well be the ones to furnish the final link.

Dr. Werner Schiebeler, the atomic physicist, in a lecture delivered at a Conference on Parapsychology in Constance, Germany, stated "if during séances, entities, phantoms, or spirits of the deceased appear which have been identified beyond the shadow of a doubt to be the people they pretend to be, they must be regarded as something more than the images of the dead. . . . parapsychology has furnished definite proof for the continuance of life beyond physical death."

*　　*　　*

Mrs. C.M. Roche was living in the Boston area with her husband John, who had spent a lifetime working as a machinist at a leather factory. When he complained of chest pain, the doctor diagnosed it as pleurisy and he was told to stay in bed; John was in no imminent danger, and the doctor left. That very night, he complained of pain, and Mrs. Roche decided to keep a watchful eye on him all night long. Suddenly, she saw a "white robed figure" closely resembling her husband in shape, rise up from the bed, and vanish. When she checked on her husband, he had died.

The other question we must ask ourselves when dealing with evidence suggesting that the so-called "dead" can communicate both visually and auditorily with the living is why, and exactly under what conditions? From the vast pool of case material it would appear that in the majority of cases there is indeed some urgency, some need to make the contact, such as letting family know the deceased is well and content, or to address some unfinished business still disturbing the departed one.

A particularly good example concerns a California-based scholar and teacher named Bernard Mollenhauer, whose mother, Frances Mollenhauer, a gifted music teacher, died of a stroke at age 42. As requested in her will, she was to be cremated and her ashes to be placed in a niche at Greenwood Cemetary. Bernard left town after the funeral, sure that everything had been taken care of. But a month later his mother appeared to him, complaining that her ashes had been mislaid. Bernard argued with the apparition, assuring his late mother that the arrangements had been properly made. But she showed him a little table with a wire basket, containing a small copper container. The next morning Bernard wanted to believe he dreamt the whole thing, but, nevertheless, he went to the cemetery and found that his mother's ashes were not where they were supposed to have been placed. They were still in the undertaker's possession, exactly the way his deceased mother had shown them to him. Needless to say, the ashes were properly placed and Bernard never heard from his mother again.

Another example is the case of Don McIntosh of Richland, Washington, who worked as a security guard most of his life, without the slightest interest in the paranormal. But on November 15, 1971, at 6:30 A.M. he woke up because of a feeling of some sort of "presence" in his room. Sure enough, there at the foot of his bed, he clearly saw the face of his cousin and heard him say, "Don, I have died!" Don, fully awake at the time, immediately recognized his cousin's voice, just as the face disappeared. He was puzzled, because as far as he knew, his cousin was well and living a thousand miles away in Ventura, California. Don and his wife discussed the matter, wondering whether they should contact the cousin. But three hours later, at 9:30 A.M., the mail brought a letter from his cousin's wife, informing them that Don's cousin had died of heart failure at 9:30 P.M. on November 8, 1971, a week before the incident had taken place.

Two questions present themselves once we are beyond the evidence for survival and/or communication itself. First, what exactly is it that survives the dissolution of the physical body? Second, is there really such a thing as "the soul," as religion would have us believe? It would seem that we exist in multiple layers: the heaviest, outer layer being the body as we know it, and underneath it a finer, duplicate "body" in which our consciousness resides, and in which it continues the journey onward, once the outer, physical layer is no more. But where is the evidence?

Kirlian photography, developed by a Russian parapsychologist some years ago, has shown the so-called "life force" that leaves a leaf or plant when it dies. If man has an "inner tube" that survives physical death, then that too should be capable of observation. Photographs, taken under stringent test conditions, prove that the so-called "dead" can manifest on photographic film, or even paper, in the presence of a sensitive gifted in that way. The electronic voice phenomenon, EVP, also points to a continuance of consciousness beyond physical death. The evidence is clear, and overwhelming.

We must remember this: wellness is our birthright. Illness is the absence of wellness, not the result of microbe or viral attacks per se any more than aging is the expected overture to death: we do have a choice to live better lives, once we understand what our true nature really is.

FIVE

A Cure for Cancer?

Probably no other single disease has plagued mankind as much as cancer in its various forms, not even the plagues of the Middle Ages or the infectious diseases so prevalent in Eastern countries not so long ago. The insidiousness of cancer is that no one really knows what causes it, and all attempts to fight it are therefore no more than hit-and-miss methods at best. Any illness for which orthodox medicine has no cure also offers opportunities to illegitimate practitioners, those who are quacks or perhaps only self-deluded individuals, those who use quasi-religious methods to cure the sufferers or those who invent complex machinery and delude themselves into thinking that their brainchild does in fact have some effect on the disease. None of this type are even included in this report.

Unorthodox methods of getting at cancer must be divided into two general groups. Those methods that use medical treatment but go beyond that which is currently known in medicine, and those treatments that are based on spiritual healing in its various forms and have no need for medical treatment, either as a component or as the framework for unorthodox treatment.

One of the most promising approaches reached in recent years involves the Waldemar Research Foundation of Woodbury, Long Island. Established in 1947, this experimental clinic is probably most noteworthy because it has developed a virus for treating cancer. The so-called Molomut-Padnos virus discovered at this laboratory has tumor-destroying properties. As yet the virus is not generally available, but medical doctors may refer selected patients to the clinic if they are of the opinion that the particular type of cancer in question will respond favorably to the viral treatment. At Waldemar, viral immunotherapy has been developed with promising results. Immunization against certain types of cancer derived from viral materials together with specific regimen have actually yielded remarkable results in the control and even in the elimination of some types of cancer, though this is not the place to go into statistics, which are readily available from the doctors at Waldemar Research Foundation.

Another success story is that of Dr. Moryth McQueen-Williams, a physician and surgeon and a graduate of Yale University, who has earned a distinguished medical and research record at such centers as Johns Hopkins University, Case-Western Reserve University, and the University of California Medical School.

Together with Kegan Sarkisian, a distinguished research phytologist with a background in physiology and nutritional sciences, and a group of dedicated researchers, Dr. McQueen-Williams has been able to isolate a new compound used in the study of germination in plants and animals—compound KC—which was tested out repeatedly as being nontoxic.

After twenty-five years of biological research, Dr. McQueen-Williams and her associates came to the conclusion, backed by actual test cases, that compound KC would significantly arrest or inhibit all kinds of cancers.

In her report to the U.S. Congress (hearing of subcommittee on public health and environment, September-October, 1971), Dr. McQueen-Williams states:

We believe that cancer, taken as a whole, is a systematic disorder which manifests itself in wild cell aggregates at any time during a lifespan. We believe also that a vertically transmitted genetic mal-coding is responsible for the appearance of the wild cell. Related to this mal-coding are two other phenomena, namely, the intra-uterine lethalities and the various known "birth defects." KC has proven to reverse the aberrant gene-expression in the wild cell, thus reversing the cancer manifestation itself. KC functions in broad spectrum.

Most of the patients treated by Dr. McQueen-Williams as part of her extended experiments in conjunction with various hospitals, are still alive, although many treatments go back as much as twenty years.*

In the 1950s and 1960s the German physician Dr. Josef Issels made international headlines with his cancer cures obtained at his Bavarian Clinic. Although the orthodox medical community has been skeptical of his results, the English weekly *Psychic News* documents some of Dr. Issels' successes.

According to *Psychic News,* quoting in turn from the account of the case published by the newspaper *A. V. Times* published by the British Union for the Abolition of Vivisection, a certain Dr. Schauer, a publishing executive, had been scheduled for an operation for intestinal cancer at a Frankfurt surgical clinic. However, when the surgeon saw that the cancer of the rectum had already developed metastases—that is, secondaries toward the aorta—the man was declared inoperable. Instead of operating, an artificial intestinal outlet was made, and death within three months was expected. Dr. Schauer instead went to Dr. Issels and for several months received treatments from the Bavarian doctor at his Ringberg Clinic. Three years later doctors at the same Frankfurt surgical center removed the artificial intestinal outlet inserted before. Dr. Schauer was declared medically

*Those wishing to learn more about the work of Dr. McQueen-Williams may do so by consulting her many medical research papers or Kegan Research Laboratories.

The exact text of the two doctors' statement before Congress may also be found in a report of the Congressional hearings. Serial No. 92–41, U.S. Government Printing Office, Washington, D.C.

healthy. There was no sign of any rectal cancer. When the surgeon was confronted with these amazing facts, all that was offered in explanation were the words: "Evidently the original diagnosis was wrong—it wasn't cancer after all."

When *Psychic News* asked famed spiritual healer Harry Edwards to comment upon the furor involving Dr. Issels' work, he pointed out that while the Bavarian doctor also used orthodox drugs in his treatments, the recovery rate was so much higher than the other doctors using identical drugs in their treatments. Another factor must have been at work in Dr. Issels' case, Harry Edwards said, pointing out that the doctor had gone only halfway toward solving the cancer problem. He had not shown the cause.

"The primary cause of cancer is psychosomatic," says Harry Edwards. "Frustrations within the whole self in which natural desires, ambitions, and emotions have been thwarted. This promotes the cancer potential. When it develops to the extent to cause a cell to throw off the yoke of glandular discipline, the tumor is born." Interestingly enough, U.S. government scientists have been quietly at work developing techniques to discover "cancer prone" people, according to a report by the science editor of the *New York Daily News,* Mark Bloom. "These 'cancer prone' persons are apparently deficient in natural defensive mechanisms with which to fight the onset of a cancerous growth, according to Dr. Donald L. Morton, head of the tumor immunology section of the National Cancer Institute."

In 1968, in my *Predictions: Fact or Fallacy?*, I quoted a California physician, identified only as Dr. N., concerning the future of cancer research. Dr. N. is not only a reputable physician attached to a major California hospital, a leading psychiatrist, and a highly respected member of his community but a psychic with a long record of verified predictions. All his life Dr. N. has been plagued—if that is the word—by his ESP abilities, and in August, 1966, he said; "A *Dr. Martin* will discover a cure for cancer in 1971 or 1972, and it will be found that the cancer virus is connected with the herpes simplex virus, which appears in common cold sores. Cancer is caused not by this virus, but by the failure of antibodies related to it."

Note the similarity in the names *Martin*, in the prediction, and

Morton, in the science report by Mark Bloom. Even more important, however, is Dr. N.'s reference to a virus as the primary cancer-causing factor and to the herpes simplex as a major link with cancer. In 1966 such ideas were not known to the medical profession. Reality caught up fast. For example, the Houston, Texas, *Medical Tribune* reported on a possible cancer vaccine based on viral theory. According to this medical trade journal, Dr. Maurice R. Hilleman of the Merck Institute for Therapeutic Research at Westpoint, Pennsylvania, mentioned the current activities to find a cancer virus vaccine useful on animals. In particular, Dr. Hilleman mentioned a recently developed vaccine against a chicken cancer called Marek's disease caused by a v type herpes virus. Likewise Mrs. M. N., a laboratory research technician in Canada, called my attention to a report in the *Phoenix* (Arizona) *Star,* linking a virus known to cause venereal disease with the cause of cervical cancer in women and prostrate cancer in men.

By April 1972, popular medical newspaper columnists were speaking of the herpes virus as a cancer suspect as if it were the most generally known medical news. "Laboratory research on herpes viruses is being conducted throughout the world," writes Dr. Theodore R. Van Dellen for the *Chicago Tribune* syndicate, "the tumor forming ability of these microbes is still widely debated." Then in November 1972, new evidence began to emerge linking the common cold virus to cervical cancer.

Even though attention is now being focused on a virus as being the causative agent of cancer, and even though cures as such have not been found, a glaring oversight seems obvious to me at this point; in concentrating on what causes cancer, orthodox medical researchers do not pay enough attention to the question of *how* these substances cause it. The key lies in the method by which viruses, whatever they are, are able to induce perfectly normal cells to behave abnormally.

In this connection information from the spiritual side of life has been of amazing interest in the case of Ruth Plant, a writer and researcher of Jordans, England. I have known Ruth for many years as a professional historian and library researcher, a student of psychic phenomena, and a person of impeccable reputation. She always has had a great interest in healing and over the years has developed her own latent psychic abilities to a point where, while not claiming to be a medium as such, she nevertheless has demonstrated her clairvoyant faculties and her amazing ability to "tune in" on past events or seemingly to obtain information from discarnate entities without especially seeking them. Here, in her own words, is a report concerning a psychic dream which bears on the subject on hand.

"On Saturday, 10th August, 1957, I heard a voice speaking to me quite distinctly in a dream which told me that the explanation of the cause of cancer was this:

" 'When it happens that two quite normal elements in a person come into a *particular relation to one another,* these elements fuse, and touch off the beginnings of cancer. It is not that there is necessarily an excess or minority of either, it is only their relationship to one another that is fatal.'

"I gathered that these two elements were neither of them evil in themselves, so that was why this factor had never been recognized, and the relationship of the components parts measured. If this could only be recognized, and the measuring done, great work might be achieved, both preventive and curative, by breaking up the collaboration before, and even after, it had reached the point of illness.

"The words were spoken very clearly by someone I did not see, and were probably, I felt, from some higher source.

"After this, the dream continued and I saw a doctor from Jordans called Moynihan, whom I did not really know personally, giving a lecture. I did not feel that either he or the lecture were important, like the first part of the dream, but he was somehow an illustration of something, or a link. As he was a relative of the great Lord Moynihan I felt that this dream was probably linked with the latter.

"For many years I searched for the doctor for whom this dream might mean something, feeling that it was an urgent matter to pass these facts on. My doctor friends to whom I sent it were sympathetic, but unable to explain the dream at all. Then I heard a Dr. Holman lecture at an adult college in Shropshire; he spoke on the difficulties of modern living generally, including the prevention of cancer. I wrote him after this, and received a most sympathetic reply.

" 'There is no doubt in my mind at all that the cause, treatment, and prevention of cancer lies in the combination of two perfectly normal constituents of the human body,' he wrote. 'These are catalose and hydrogen peroxide. If not in a proper state of balance the result can be the production of tumors.'

"He also stated that he was a *disciple of Lord Moynihan's.*

"Dr. Holman then went to the U.S.A. and later to Canada to a conference about this. I asked him to come and stay on his way to Canada on 16th August. He left London by plane on 17th August.

"On Friday, 27th July, before I met him, I had a dream of a very thin, energetic man, with prematurely gray hair, in contrast to his young, alive face. His face resembled a portrait I had just seen at Hughenden House, Disraeli's home; his hair was cut in an unusual way; it was not as short as a crew cut, but it stood up and bounced about rather buoyantly when he moved, almost like a schoolboy's.

"I felt he had something to do with cancer research.

"I asked several friends if they knew him, without result, and then mentioned it to Dr. Holman when he came to stay. He told me that it was a clear description of his great friend, a doctor who had died of a heart condition, making him very thin, as I noticed. His hair was just as described. He was of the Jewish faith, hence the link with the Disraeli picture of Hughenden.

"This doctor had appeared to Dr. Holman's wife in a dream when he was dying, and after his death they had felt his presence for three days.

"My great anxiety was to get some more information about this, and I did have one quite long dream which I realized was significant. It was mainly about these two qualities and their relationship to each other, I believe. But, unfortunately, I was at that time very worried about two cats and I confused the word catalase with lazy cats, and thought the dream related to this. Only as I woke up did I become aware of Dr. John Gordon [Dr. Holman's friend] saying to me that I had the whole character of catalase laid before me and stupidly not realized it. He then indicated that he would show me something else at this more waking state of consciousness which would at least show I had been with him though I gathered it would not really be what he wanted to tell us. He then showed me two tall glass receptacles — one had a great deal of stuff in it which, it was explained to me afterwards, was called a media, with a small top which I believe is called a 'culture,' and the other one was vice versa in quality. When I drew a picture of this and sent it to Dr. Holman he said it was an exact description of what he was working on in his laboratory at the time."

If anything, Ruth Plant's interesting dream experience proves the apparent attempt by those who have gone on to help those in the flesh combat cancer. It seems perfectly logical to me that a doctor who has passed on and found the reality of spirit life may wish to continue helping mankind through appropriate sensitives. Since Plant's mind was well schooled and well organized, I can understand that the late doctor wished to use it to communicate with someone in the physical world who might make good use of his rather technical knowledge.

Evidently Dr. R. A. Holman, consultant bacteriologist and senior lecturer in bacteriology, School of Medicine, University of Wales, was such a person. In a brief article in *Mother Earth*, journal of the Soil Association, April 1961, Dr. Holman states: "We now know that catalase is one of the most important enzymes known to man and is responsible for the most rapid enzymic catalyzed processes known in living cells," explaining that the discoverer of catalase, Dr. O. Loew, had already realized in 1901 that the general occurrence of this enzyme in the organized world could not be accidental and must have a specific significance. Dr. Holman continued: "Hydrogen peroxide is formed as a result of many enzymatic reactions and it seems to be general agreement that it is a metabolite normally produced and destroyed by a wide variety of cells. In many living systems there are to be found four very important substances known as haemoproteins. These are (1) catalase, (2) peroxidase (3) haemoglobin, (4) myoglobin." Dr. Loew already knew that catalase protects the cell from the incursions of peroxide (H_2O_2).

Dr. Holman continued, "Because H_2O_2 can be demonstrated in such a wide variety of living things, it is more than likely that there is a specific catalase-H_2O_2 balance for each type of cell whether bacterial, fungal, plant or animal. If this balance is interfered with, either by diminution of the catalase content or by exposure to increasing amounts of H_2O_2, then abnormalities may occur. One is never neutral with respect to H_2O_2; its presence is either desirable or undesirable." Dr. Holman summed up his views on the importance of his work on catalase: "It is obvious that if the balance between catalase and H_2O_2 is upset then all grades of malfunction may appear, ranging from mild disturbances in the behavior of cells down to death. This means that cells can be so deranged that their normal activity is changed, resulting in altered biochemistry and hence disease. Many physical and chemical agents which are deliberately placed on or around or in cells can interfere with the catalase peroxide (H_2O_2) balance and hence induce widespread illness in animals and plants. Perhaps the most terrible scourge of our day is the disease known as cancer, a condition which is intimately connected with a catalase-peroxide (H_2O_2) balance."

In a subsequent article in the *Cardiff Nurses League Journal* of October 1962, entitled "The Cancer Problem," Dr. Holman wrote, "One of the few well-established facts about cancer is that the important enzyme catalase is progressively diminished in the host as well as in the tumor. Catalase inhibition is known to be associated with mutagenic processes and the development of viruses and it is also known that some of the proven carcinogenic agents can inhibit this enzyme." Dr. Holman then pointed out that the widespread distribution of catalase in living cells is essential for the ability of those cells to live in the presence of oxygen. "Numerous workers [Dr. F. Totney, Dr. A. Voisin, Dr. P. Puig, Dr. D. Atansoff] are coming to the conclusion that the key to the cause, treatment and prevention of cancer lies in this altered fundamental biological mechanism."

Dr. Holman readily admits that the environment has always contained some disturbing factors causing cancer in man. The disease has been known for thousands of years. Solar radiation has always been connected with the increase or incidence of skin cancer in certain occupational groups such as sailors and agricultural workers; water, air, and foodstuffs have been found to be contaminated by radioactive materials in some areas as a result of which certain cancers increased in those areas. In urban areas, the increase in soot and poisonous fumes in the air is responsible for the increase in cancer incidence, and civilized living in general is more likely to produce the disease or encourage it than life in a natural environment free from as much industrialization as possible. "If the catalase-peroxide balance is interfered with for a long enough time by physical and chemical agents present in our environment, whether in food, drink, drugs, or in the air we breathe, then we shall see in races so exposed a progressive increase in the incidence of cancer. By contrast, in those primitive communities where such agents are not used or encouraged, the incidence will remain at a very low level."

Dr. Holman is much more concerned with the prevention of cancer than with its cure, following in the footsteps of Dr. Louis Pasteur, who had held that it was more important to prevent a disease than to treat it after it occurred. "The direct treatment by chemotherapeutic and antibiotic agents has not been, and never will be, responsible for its elimination." Dr. Holman's plan for the prevention of cancer is a threefold attack: (1) increase our intake of catalase, (2) increase the manufacture of catalase by our own cells, and (3) curtail the intake of agents which destroy or inhibit the action of our cell catalase.

To increase our intake of catalase we must eat as much fresh food as possible. The heat used in the preparation of food destroys many enzymes, including catalase. Dr. Holman suggests that the consumption of fresh fruit and vegetables should be markedly increased, thus insuring a far greater intake of catalase and the enzyme peroxidase. He notes, parenthetically, that literature is full of references to the fact that garlic-eating people have an increased resistance to cancer. "This is not surprising when one realizes that garlic is very rich in the catalytic systems containing catalase and peroxidase."

To increase the manufacture of catalase by our own cells, we must exercise as much as possible. Physical exercise promotes the intake of oxygen. That, in turn, creates a larger concentration of catalase within us and a resulting detoxification of our bodies.

The curtailment of the intake of agents that destroy or inhibit the action of our cell catalase is of course the most important program of the three, and we ingest many toxic substances. For example, the chemical agents added to food and drink in order to increase shelf life and the dyes, sweeteners, and flavoring agents—all alien agents— may cause cancer. The argument that these chemicals prevent bacterial food poisoning in the consumer does not hold water, in the opinion of Dr. Holman. "It is not only that catalase of the bacteria which is destroyed but also that of the food." And he warns: "The majority of chemicals added to food and drink for preservation, coloration, or sophistication could and should be abolished. Most of the additives are not essential and many are harmful." He also points out that the sodium fluoride added to public water supplies is a potent catalase poison and is cumulative in the body. "Its use is not backed up by sound medical facts, and in any case it does not deal with the prime cause of dental decay which is generally recognized as being due to a sophisticated and chemically adulterated food supply," he says.

Many poisonous chemicals pollute the air we breathe. Large amounts of sulfur dioxide and sulfureted hydrogen, both very powerful catalase poisons, are released into our environment in large quantities as a result of the burning of fuels of various kinds. "It is obvious that the control of air pollution demands our most urgent attention. A good oxygen intake is essential for good health. Some workers go so far as to explain the high incidence of cancer in the human race on the basis of poor or diminished oxygen consumption, and in a sense they are right. Oxygen is essential for the removal and destruction of many toxic agents present on or in our cells, and it is therefore quite obvious that the more actively oxygenated our bodies, the better we shall be able to combat the toxic agents which help to influence adversely our normal cells," says Dr. Holman.

Dr. Holman warns against indiscriminate use of injections to fight infection. Sulfonamides in particular, which have for a long time been known to inhibit catalase, are in some cases proven carcinogens. Likewise, the use of X-ray devices and other forms of radiation, all of which are increasingly used, are known to inhibit the formation of catalase within us. Dr. Holman feels that we must study the safe levels of these practices in order to determine that we are not creating health hazards by the use of such radiation.

Many authors and medical authorities recognize the value of special diets in the fighting of cancer. The German naturopath J. C. Leuchtenberg states, for example, in *The Light That Conquers Cancer,* that the best diet for those suffering from cancer should be fully vegetarian, consisting of food that has in no way been treated chemically. A diet poor in milk and lactic acid but rich in raw vegetables and vegetable juices, sweetened by natural honey, is suggested as an effective way of reducing tumors.

The literature concerning health food and dietary treatment of various diseases is rich and mostly enlightening. But cancer in advanced stages may not easily yield to long-term dietary treatment. The question whether healers can dramatically reduce or destroy cancerous growths is therefore of paramount importance. Some unorthodox healers, fully aware of the difficulty of dealing with this dread disease, and not sure that they can make inroads on it, will frankly refuse to treat patients who suffer from cancer because they cannot promise them anything. It is perhaps the earmark of the genuine healer that he will not promise to heal each and every disease but only that which he believes can be dealt with by the powers within himself or flowing through him. A quack, even one with a medical degree, will promise anything and everything. Unfortunately, there are far too few psychic healers and other unorthodox practitioners who have the power to heal cancer cases.

In the following paragraphs I report on one such pair of healers, a husband and wife team, since a case I referred to them was successfully dealt with by them and since I have access to all the necessary details and medical evidence to report on it for the benefit of those who wonder whether such healings do indeed take place.

*   *   *

One of the brightest young students in my classes at the New York Institute of Technology was a woman named Paulette. She took the spring term in parapsychology and seemed unusually interested in the subject. She believed herself to be psychic. A few times Paulette could not attend classes, and instead of her, the man she was then married to came with a tape recorder on her behalf. Eventually I lost track of her.

To my surprise I heard from Paulette again in late November 1971. She was writing to me from Los Angeles, where she had moved. She wondered whether I was going to teach any classes in parapsychology in the Los Angeles area in the future. Her life had changed drastically, she said. She and her husband had separated, and he had remained in New York. Also, she had changed jobs and was now working for a recording company. She was in fine health, and she had somehow run into an old childhood friend of hers and the two of them had fallen in love.

The meeting between the two old friends had intriguing overtones of having been arranged by fate. Four months after her arrival in Los Angeles, Paulette received a call from a musician named Jim K., asking her to pick up some airplane tickets he was unable to call for. She obliged him and dropped them off at the recording studio. At that very moment a man who turned out to be Ron, her childhood friend whom she had not seen since age sixteen, five years before, also was waiting for Jim K. Paulette and Ron picked up their old relationship and expanded it. Both were still married at the time but arranged for divorces immediately and began to plan their marriage in the near future.

As they were discussing things, Ron discovered that Paulette had not had a physical examination in years and persuaded her to make an appointment for a routine examination with a gynecologist, Dr. Frances Holmes, of Los Angeles.

There was no overt reason for Paulette to seek an examination, no symptoms of any kind, no discomfort, merely the idea of not having had any examination in four years. The appointment for the examination was made on November 1, 1971. Two weeks later, and one week after the initial appointment with the doctor, Paulette wondered whether perhaps she might not be pregnant because of a delay in her normal menstruation. She and Ron had been living together for some time.

However, the results of the routine examination disclosed not a pregnant condition but a Pap three, a fairly high rate of abnormal cells.

In medical terminology the smear test showed "atypia—consistent with severe dysplasia or squamous carcinoma in situ." There are five classifications in the Pap test. The first means negative, the second refers to the presence of various benign changes; Pap three, four, and five indicate the presence of cancer in various degrees. Dr. Holmes confirmed, in a statement dated March 2, 1972, that at the time of the first consultation "a Pap smear taken showed some abnormal cells which were suggestive of carcinoma."

The report also recommended that a biopsy be taken immediately. Paulette, almost overcome with anxiety at this unexpected turn of events, reacted by recalling that there were other ways to deal with a malignancy than the conventional ones. In particular, the idea of a biopsy or exploratory operation did not sit well with her at all, since I had mentioned that psychic healing rarely works where surgical procedures have already been used. Thus, shaken by the disclosure of the test and torn between conventional medical treatment and high hopes for some other, unorthodox help, she telephoned me in New York and asked for my help. Did I know of any good psychic healer in Los Angeles?

The same fate which had brought her together with her former sweetheart evidently had more things in store for her in the future. Ordinarily I would have had to say, regretfully, that I really did not know of anyone sufficiently recommended or established through successful performance, to take the risk of undergoing unconventional treatment at this time. But it so happened that more than a year earlier, in March 1970, a close friend who is deeply steeped in the esoteric had suggested, not because they desired publicity but because of my interest, that I interview a pair of psychic healers in the Los Angeles area, Mr. and Mrs. Krystal.

Thus I was able immediately to suggest that Paulette contact Phyllis and Sidney Krystal. She telephoned Mrs. Krystal and described her condition in every detail. To her surprise, she was told that a personal meeting between herself and the healers was not necessary, nor even desirable—to this day, Paulette and Ron have not met the Krystals—but Mrs. Krystal seemed confident that Paulette could be helped.

Mrs. Krystal told Paulette that she would meet with several of her associates, people with whom she worked in a healing circle, and would call her back as soon as she knew more about the case. A few days later she telephoned Paulette to say that she had gotten an image and that it was to be positive. She instructed Paulette to breathe in and out in a certain rhythmical pattern and to believe that she was getting rid of bad cells through breathing. In addition, every evening just before she fell asleep and upon awakening in the morning, Paulette was to try to picture a circle of blue neon lights—Mrs. Krystal explained that this was a healing light—around the infected area. Paulette was to continue these exercises as instructed indefinitely; Mrs. Krystal told her she would call her again when she and her circle received a different image.

Paulette, somewhat taken aback by the simplicity of it all, was disappointed that the healer did not want to meet her in person, but she accepted the instructions whole heartedly and without question, remembering that I had frequently discussed unusual methods of healing in my classes. At first she had a hard time picturing the blue light, but her fiancé helped her by picturing it for her and as a further aid put a blue light bulb into a lamp, which they kept lit all night long.

After several weeks, Paulette and Ron felt that something was happening. The next morning Paulette received a call from Phyllis Krystal to tell her that she felt something good was happening and to be sure to continue with the exercises. Paulette still went to the regular doctor whenever the doctor thought that necessary, and on December 17, 1971, a second Pap test was taken. The test showed that the disturbance had now receded to Pap two. Instead of recommending an immediate biopsy, the laboratory report, prepared by the same clinical laboratory medical group that had prepared the first report, recommended a follow-up test in three to six months. As the clinical report commented, "Occasional dyscaryotic squamous cells are still present but the changes are less severe than previously noted." Dr. Holmes, in her statement of March 2, 1972, commented that when Paulette was seen again on December 17, 1971, for the repeat of her Pap test, "There was present a rather severe inflammation of the cervix. This responded to treatment." However, the treatment, consisting of a gel prescribed by the doctor, had been discontinued by Paulette after two days because it had caused her discomfort; thus the improvement cannot be ascribed to this particular treatment prescribed by a medical doctor.

Although Paulette's health seemed to be on the upgrade, the couple were still very much worried about the future. With that in mind they made an appointment to see the famed spiritualist medium George Daisley in Santa Barbara, on December 9, 1971. Daisley, a British psychic who resides in the United States, was instrumental in bringing evidential messages from the son of the late Bishop James Pike to the father. To Ron and Paulette's surprise the reading turned out to be something else than what they had expected. Not a word was said about Paulette's state of health. Daisley elaborated about the strange way in which the two had met, though of course he had no prior knowledge of the couple. Finally, Paulette asked whether he received any impressions concerning health. Daisley nodded and pointed at Ron, saying that his spirit informants were telling him that there was something wrong with Ron's left eye and that his glasses had to be changed. The young people were taken aback. Ron requires prescription glasses, and it so happened that the left lens of his glasses had been popping out for several weeks prior to their visit with George Daisley. But they could not understand why so excellent a medium did not pick up the very serious business of Paulette's illness.

Back in Los Angeles Paulette continued with the exercises prescribed by Phyllis Krystal. On January 26, 1972, a third Pap smear test was taken. Would the clinical test show improvement or deterioration state of her health? When the report came, it was *negative.* There were no further recommendations by the laboratory, which commented only, "There is no demonstrable residual atypia." Paulette was free of cancer; her normal menstrual period had returned January 7; she had recovered.

Shortly after this third report, Phyllis Krystal informed Paulette that she had received an image change and that Paulette was now to imagine the circle of blue light enlarging, with the outside ring much darker than the inside. Paulette was to visualize herself holding the ring, like a hula hoop, and jumping through the ring ten times forward and ten times backward. This was to balance out the whole condition of her body. Later, since the doctor's report stated that Paulette was now well and there was no evidence of malignancy, Paulette discontinued the visualization but kept in close contact with the healers. On June 11, 1972, Paulette and Ron were married. Just to be sure, Paulette took another Pap test in August 1972, which again proved completely negative.

I saw the young couple in April 1972. Paulette was radiantly beautiful; Ron was happy and busy working on a new record album; I was curious about their attitudes and about that of Paulette's regular doctor.

"When you had the first treatment with Mr. and Mrs. Krystal," I asked, "did you honestly believe that it would work in getting you well again?"

"Yes, I did, and that was important. I was very positive about it. The healers told me that it was very important in having it work."

"Did you have the firm conviction that it would work *in your case?*"

"I had hope."

"During the treatments, did you ever have any doubts that it might *not* work?"

"No. Never."

"After the first treatment, did you feel that some process was going on within you?"

"I did feel *something.* I couldn't describe exactly what, maybe an enlightening, but I did feel that something was happening."

"Have you told Dr. Holmes anything about the treatment you received at the hands of the healers?"

"I asked her if she believed in psychic healing, and she got very flustered and said that mentally she did, but that on the physical level she wasn't sure."

"Did you tell her about the treatments?"

"I didn't go into detail, because I thought it was useless."

"Didn't she wonder how it was that you were cured?"

"No. I did tell her that I had spoken to a healer, but she didn't go into it any further."

"What, then, is her explanation for the fact that you are well?"

"She didn't say much of anything, but she was definitely amazed."

I of course wanted to interview the healers themselves, to get their point of view on this particular case and perhaps learn more about their methods in other cases, but the meeting was not easily arranged. Mr. and Mrs. Krystal are publicity shy, and only my insistence that the discussion would benefit psychic healing and its understanding by the lay public as well as by some orthodox medical circles persuaded them to meet me. The couple turned out to be soft-spoken, pleasant professional people, impeccably dressed, in their middle ages, almost indistinguishable from any other couple of their class and background.

Mrs. Krystal, who had been born in England, had trained as a teacher. She had lived in the United States since 1937 and since then had taught school, mainly mathematics and art. Mr. Krystal, an attorney in the city of Los Angeles, was, because of his status in the community, particularly reluctant to be identified as a healer. Their children are grown up.

Phyllis was thought to be psychic even when a child, but her family had suppressed this unusual talent. She had rediscovered it within herself some twenty-five years before our meeting. Eastern religions interested her and her husband a great deal, but above all the healing aspects of psychical research fascinated them.

"What was your first instance of psychic healing?" I asked.

"Well, this is rather difficult to answer because there are so many different ways in which we can heal. Some of it is purely mental; we concentrate. Sometimes we don't even meet the person. We can do it at a distance. At other times, if it seems indicated, I put my hands on a person, but it depends on how I get the message *inside me* what I am supposed to do."

Mrs. Krystal could not remember how many people she had healed, what percentage had actually been helped, but she said that there were quite a few.

"I work with other people—I rarely work alone—usually in a pair. On the telephone, usually two people, myself and someone else," she explained.

"How do you work this?" I asked.

"I go into what I call a revery, and some of the people I have been working with also go into a similar state, sometimes at the same time. Then we go back and forth quickly and we see symbolic pictures of the condition and what the remedy would be, and then we concentrate on those."

"But have you met the patient at that time?" I asked. Somehow the method of seeking out an ailment at a distance reminded me of the late Edgar Cayce.

"Not always, no," Phyllis replied. "In some cases I never meet the patient, such as with Paulette."

"But how do you make the contact then?"

"I think that we do contact healing forces. I really haven't the slightest idea as to who these forces are, but I would say that they were personifications to make it simpler for us to get in contact with them. Perhaps an emanation from the Godhead."

"Have you actually identified a person on the other side of life as helping you with this work?"

"Definitely. Yes. But mostly they are personifications of forces."

"When you attempt to heal a person," I asked, "what is the first thing you do?"

"I get in touch with one of the friends with whom I work. There are about half a dozen of us, all women. Sometimes we get together physically and then we go into a meditative state, and sometimes we do it on the telephone. Since we have been working at it quite a while it is very easy for us."

"What is the next step?"

"We have the person's name, and then one of us sees a picture to symbolize what is wrong with that person and what can be done to help. It is very much like an active imagination in a way, except that we do not do it ourselves. It is almost as if it is given to us on a screen."

"Are you given some sort of diagnosis at this point?" I asked.

"Not necessarily; that doesn't seem to be a bit important. It is more important to know what is to be done. Or what we give the afflicted person to do—as with Paulette, some patients are fortunately able to work themselves, and that is always better."

"The patient has to tune in as well?"

"If possible. But of course it is not always possible. Sometimes they don't know what we are talking about, but that doesn't stop the healing."

"It works better if the patient takes part?"

Mrs. Krystal nodded emphatically. "Naturally," she said. "That is why Paulette's healing was such a success. She was very conscientious."

"You give your patients certain instructions?"

"Yes, but only if they are able to understand them and are used to this sort of thing. It would almost get in the way otherwise."

"But could you heal a person without his cooperation?"

"Sometimes not; it doesn't always work out."

"You mentioned the laying on of hands. Is there always healing following this?"

"There's always an alleviation. Actually, there are two different methods of laying on of hands. One person who taught us was a Mrs. Dakota who lived in Hawaii; another, an Indian in Bombay, taught my husband and me how to heal. We have to do exercises at midnight for a certain number of days in order to get ourselves to the point where we can do the healing. It involves meditation and concentration upon our hands. The Indian healer taught us tantric yoga, and by this method we were able to heal. Both my husband and I do it. In some cases I put my hands on a patient and it gets extremely hot and I feel the pain. It builds up to a peak, sometimes as far as our shoulders, and then it generally comes down again. We have to shake our hands and always wash them afterward."

"What about dealing with your own illnesses, if any?" I asked.

Mrs. Krystal laughed rather uncertainly. "I am particularly sensitive to our Los Angeles smog. I haven't found any remedy for it. But as with any other kind of illness, either I or my husband or one of the other people I work with will tune in on it and meditate."

"Do you do this work merely for your own gratification or to help others?"

"We practice yoga and self-development, and along with it goes the helping of others in many ways. One of those ways is through healing."

The Krystals never take a penny for their help, do not seek new patients, are not interested in glory or publicity.

Good news travels slowly when it comes to cancer. Unfortunately, Dr. Holman's findings, though published thirty odd years ago and available both to the general public and the medical profession, have remained totally unknown to anyone I have talked to in this field. In view of the fact that the still widely accepted view on combating cancer is to destroy cancerous cells by any means, no matter how damaging this may be to the body, it is not surprising that anything suggesting a totally different approach would not find much credence.

However, even in 1993 we are no closer to a cure than when Dr. Holman made his discovery. Dr. Herbert Shelton in "The Healthway Advisor" newsletter stated that "cancer is an evolutionary endpoint in a long chain of pathological processes. Not only is it hard to cause, but it requires a lot of causing!"

A study of the effects of vitamin therapies on cancer deaths has recently been undertaken by Chinese and American doctors in Linxian Province in China. The effect of daily doses given patients of beta carotene, vitamin E, and selenium over a five-year period proved these significantly healthier in respect to cancer than those not receiving them. Dr. William J. Blot of the National Cancer Institute, one of the people involved in this study, is quoted by the *New York Times* of September 15, 1993, as stating that the results were significant, in "that they offer a hopeful sign that vitamins and minerals may be effective in reducing cancer, and they help us target priorities for future research."

Not long ago, it was discovered that the inner bark of the yew tree, growing principally in America's Northwest, contained a component capable of curing, or at least reducing, ovarian cancer. Unfortunately, it involved destroying many trees to cure relatively few patients. This drug, taxol, has also aroused interest from the American pharmaceutical company Bristol-Myers, which discovered an alternate source in the yew's tree's needles, by extracting from needles and branches a compound of equal effectiveness, without requiring the destruction of the entire tree. In addition, the clippings will not only come from the Pacific Yew, but also from the more plentiful yew trees growing wild in Europe and Asia. In Germany, yew farming has begun in earnest at a tree farm in Cologne. Their product, patented as taxotere, will be exploited jointly by Bristol-Myers and the French drug company, Rhone-Poulenc-Rorer.

Early studies on taxol also suggest it may work with breast cancer and malignancies of the neck, head, and lung. By January 1993, the Federal Drug Administration approved taxol.

One of the most dangerous cancers for men is cancer of the prostate. Despite years of research, we do not really know why it occurs, except by indirect reasoning. Enlargement of that organ occurs in the majority of all men after age 65, sometimes even after 50, and it is due to the following causes. The production of the male hormone testosterone declines after age 40 as a matter of natural aging, though in varying degrees. When testosterone is diminished in the prostate, the other hormones, which continue to be produced, take up more space in the organ and thus cause its enlargement. Benign enlargement of the prostate does not necessarily lead to cancer. But it is wise to counteract this enlargement if possible as it will eventually cause interferences with the urethra and urination. Fortunately, there are ways of doing this, the latest being a pharmaceutical product called Prostar. However, this will mask the percentage points of a prostate protein called PSA and thus may prevent the early detection of cancer in the prostrate. On the other hand, a natural plant remedy derived from a berry called *Serenoa serrulate*, commonly known as saw palmetto berry, does just that: it prevents enlargement and even reduces it in many cases. Another natural vitamin called zinc picolinate, which is extremely easy to assimilate in the body, especially when taken with vitamin B_6, will also prevent or reduce the enlargement of the prostate.

When there are changes in some of the cells that would indicate the threat of cancer, men need to be very alert to prostate cancer, as "the silent killer" has no symptoms per se.

Recently, through the good services of a friendly doctor, I

became acquainted with a plant remedy that seems to work in men the way taxol works in women. Like the saw palmetto extract, this too was known to American Indians for centuries as an aphrodisiac, a connection that makes sense when one realizes that it is, after all, the prostate which manufactures the male seminal fluid. The remedy comes from a woody plant growing in the Central American rain forests, a plant which winds itself around tall trees. It is the root and woody portion of this plant called Smylax, or Coculmeca by the Indians, which, when taken with alcohol of some sort (red wine, for instance) will act upon the prostate in the following manner. PSA— prostate specific antigen—is the substance which can be an indication of trouble in the prostate if it rises beyond the level considered normal in the blood, viz. 2–4 points. When it reaches levels beyond 10 points, that usually indicates trouble. The PSA will go up, slowly in older men, less so in younger men; but it never goes down. Nevertheless, the plant remedy I am reporting here has done precisely that: affected the blood level of PSA downward. Unfortunately, the plant remedy is still in the experimental stage, as I am trying to determine just how much one should take, and how much of it might become available to those seeking it.

Various vitamin and mineral treatments are being used today to fight or prevent cancer of every kind. Dr. Linus Pauling believed in megadoses of vitamin C as a preventive. Many doctors deny that there is anything to that. But the fact remains that a fully balanced nutritional diet maintained at all times can indeed prevent cancer. Unfortunately, few people have such a diet or even know what one consists of. More on diet and health will be covered in chapter 7.

But again I must emphasize that the energies spent on the cure of cancer—whether traditional medicine or alternative and natural ways—pay too little attention to the likely cause of cancer. Doing so would entail the acceptance of a medical anathema: the existence of a triple layer of existence in man—the physical outer body, the mind operating through the physical brain, though by itself of a much less physical nature, and finally, the inner body and seat of spirit, the persona, that part of us that is indeed immortal.

This means that our emotions, reactions to events in our lives, desires, feelings, troubles, and frustrations, are all primary factors in causing cancer: Controlling and balancing them for a harmonious lifestyle prevents the cancer. Environmental sins, bad nutrition, and toxic substances that enter our bodies irritate the system and make it prone to cancer development. These, however, are the secondary culprits, not the first. If we cannot completely harmonize our existence, and our triune nature breaks down now and then, making use of natural substances will remedy the problem without causing harm through so-called "side effects," as do synthetic substances, which, after all, are poisons alien to the system.

Oftentimes people of relative obscurity are doing the very best work in the cancer research field. Dealing with cancer is a voluble and controversial subject, especially since medical establishment groups are firm on insisting that there is not a cure, and continue to recommend the traditional therapy: chemotherapy and radiation. Though the establishment must by now realize that these delay but do not cure cancer, and oftentimes destroy the patient's own defense system, which might have worked better had it been left alone.

So it is with great respect and real excitement that I close this chapter by reporting two more avenues that seem to provide hope. Nicholas J. Gonzales, M.D., has developed a highly concentrated nutritional program that saves lives, to put it simply. Individualized diet, a substantial number of supplements, and what he calls "detoxification," make up his program. The supplements consist of vitamins, minerals, enzymes, and glandular concentrates; a cancer patient may be on as many as 150 capsules a day. In addition, detoxification consists of coffee enemas, and other procedures to cleanse the body of metabolic wastes. While none of this is exactly new, and the catalogues of nutritional supply houses have them all available, it is Dr. Gonzales' evaluation and application in each individual case that seems to make the difference. Dr. Gonzales can be contacted at 36 East 36th Street, Suite 204, New York, New York 10016; (212) 213–3337.

William Fischer is a German-born publisher of health books in

Canfield, Ohio, whose publications include *How to Fight Cancer and Win*, and *Miraculous Breakthroughs for Prostate and Impotency Problems.* Both books cover the field extensively, including all that should be avoided, and all that is beneficial for the patient if illness strikes. These books can be ordered from the publisher at Box 368, Canfield, Ohio 44406; (216) 533–1232.

SIX

Diet and Biochemical Healing

Such trite generalizations as "you are what you eat" have a great deal of truth in them; the food we take in determines our state of health to a large extent because the fuel determines the performance of the engine. It is not so much the amount of food or even the combination of foods we eat but the quality of the ingested nutrients that is significant. There is hardly a well-read or reasonable individual alive today who is not aware of the struggle going on between the forces of unadulterated foodstuffs and those who wish to close their eyes to the increasing number of chemicals added to foods in order to preserve them for longer periods. The matter is no longer one of concern to the esoteric fringe: it has been aired publicly and many books have been written on it.

My reference to diet in connection with healing is more in the nature of the preventive attitude toward foodstuffs in the long run rather than of any specific prescription. In partaking as much as possible and as much as is practicable of pure foods, one is automatically excluding the variety of diseases that crop up in time if one eats adulterated foodstuffs containing preservatives and other additives, such as color and artificial flavors.

Certain categories of foodstuffs are altogether damaging to health: the various cola drinks, the majority of sodas, anything containing large amounts of white sugar—ordinary ice cream—white bread, and many more. Anyone familiar with health food standards will be able to avoid these foods and thus prevent much disease that would ordinarily come his way in time.

But there is much more to the health aspect of proper foods than the simple avoidance of certain foods and use of others. It is not just what you eat but the state you are eating it in that counts. Food that may be totally harmless when eaten in a relaxed state may suddenly act up and cause gastric pains if the person eating it is upset or emotionally unbalanced at the time. Digestion and absorption of foodstuffs is a highly complicated process, involving not only the gastric tract but the mind as well. A number of lateral processes are vitally important in the proper disposition of the foods taken into the body—including the glands of the body and the production and release of enzymes. If the emotional apparatus is upset, the nervous system is automatically and immediately affected. As a result, irregularities of the glandular functions may occur, in turn leading to malabsorption or gastric upsets.

Ideally, a few minutes of total withdrawal from one's problems are advisable prior to eating a meal. If that is not possible, a few deep breathing exercises of the yoga method would be helpful in relaxing the diaphragm and various other muscles of the body that may be tense as a result of stress. Above all, it is vitally important to put a divider between the moment of activity and the moment of food intake. For example, "grabbing a sandwich" instead of lunch while discussing business is very harmful. By creating an intermediary period, no matter how short, between the mentally active process of daily living and the calm, well-regulated intake of food, we insure ourselves against chemical upsets in the body. After we have eaten, we must insure the continuing digestive process by observing a few moments of calm reflection or rest. A brisk walk after dinner helps prevent obesity, but this walk should not be taken while the mouth is still filled with half the dessert. It is all a question of timing, of pauses between one activity and the next.

As Edgar Cayce abundantly made clear in his writings, certain combinations of foodstuffs are chemically incompatible in the human system. By themselves and taken individually they are perfectly harmless. Brought together within the body simultaneously they can create damage or at the very least ill health. A good example involves coffee.

Cayce was not particularly in favor of coffee as such, but he suggested that those who needed this stimulant at all cost should at least avoid taking it with cold milk or cream. He recommended that coffee be taken black or with hot milk. The aromatic acids in the coffee that are so harmful to the stomach lining will be "bound" by the hot milk but not by the cold.

Sugar, especially white sugar, in one's tea is harmful to the functions of the liver; honey is not. The reason is that sugar represents a refined product turning into starch within the body while honey, an invert sugar, does not. Taking milk products together with fruit is not recommended. In this respect we should be aware that some of the dietary laws of ancient religions, such as the Semitic, are not so much divinely inspired as they are the result of contemporary health problems. By warning the Hebrews against the absorption of pork, Moses merely turned a health factor into a religious command, realizing that it would be obeyed more as such than as the former. The custom of eating either milk products or meat and cereals also is a health-based religious command. The ancients knew very well how certain foodstuffs would combine chemically in the body.

Those able to accept vegetarianism will find that the absence of meat does in no way interfere with their balanced intake of food, provided they learn to enjoy certain milk products and protein-rich nuts and soybeans. Recent discoveries have shown that the incidence rate of cancer is highest among people eating a great deal of meat. It is my firm conviction that all meat, being a secondary food supply, carries within itself the danger of infection and must be considered the cause of many illnesses.

When illness has struck, for one reason or the other, a proper diet can restore good health even in the most severe diseases. Diet can be used to exchange the toxic elements in the system with healthful ones. This exchange takes time—the replacement cannot be done overnight—and to be effective demands that the affected individual must adhere to a very strict diet and cannot deviate from it. Instead of drugs and synthetic medicines, natural remedies are resorted to. The largest number of these remedies comes from herbs and other plants, concocted in such a way that the natural characteristics of the plant are completely preserved (in contrast to the synthetic putting together of chemicals).

Today the remedies prescribed by D. C. Jarvis, M.D., from Vermont, are widely used. In a popular work entitled *Folk Medicine*, Dr. Jarvis lists the most common complaints and the natural remedies prescribed by him. A similar book, containing remedies for many common diseases, is Richard Lucas's *Nature's Medicines*, which has a foreword by Dr. Harry Benjamin. Mr. Lucas's book is on the shelves of many medical practitioners today because of its practical listings and commonsense approach to even the most unusual and esoteric herb remedy. Lucas quotes actual cases that have been helped by this type of prescription, and his recommendations are supported by solid evidence of previous healing successes.

Putting exercise and diet into their proper perspectives in the healing picture and warning against the currently fashionable drugs, reducing pills, and other remedies so glibly prescribed by the average practitioner, Marylou McKenna's valuable *Revitalize Yourself* is another recommended book of recent publication. Carroll Righter, the venerable astrologer, speaks of the relationship between astrological factors and health and diet in *Your Astrological Guide to Health and Diet*. He explains the relationship between certain birth signs and certain diseases common to these signs and the dietary precautions people born under those sun signs should take to avoid illness. Finally, I recommend a little pamphlet by Lionel Stebbing, "Honey as Healer," in which the immense and varied healing properties of honey are stressed.

Some basic dietary truths are age-old, although the people who make use of them are not aware of the reasons for their preferences. A case in point is the liking for garlic by people of "older nationalities," especially in Eastern Europe and the Orient. Chewing the bulb of garlic is considered to offer protection against various forms of disease and infectious illness. Only recently has it been discovered that garlic is the only substance known to medicine capable of combining with viruses, thus destroying them. For that reason the intake of garlic is probably the best remedy for the common cold and other respiratory infections. Richard Lucas calls garlic "the bulb with miracle healing powers." He quotes an older source, Dr. W. T. Furnie, who wrote of it in 1897, "It is stimulating, antispasmodic, expectorant, and a diuretic. Its active properties depend on an essential oil that may be readily obtained by distillation."

We have had much of this knowledge available to us for the last hundred years. Yet we have largely ignored it and searched for artificial means of dealing with the diseases of body and mind. In rejecting the natural means to heal, man is foolishly disregarding the wisdom of the ages for the mirage of modern machinery. Because he puts together chemicals in a way that allows him to see everything happening as a result of his own power and decision, he feels that he is progressing toward a better understanding of the human body. Accepting existing natural cures, frequently without fully understanding the mechanics involved, requires a degree of faith in a universal balance that many modern practitioners lack. Yet, as has been proven again and again, the natural way of healing is the best way because man is a natural creation, just as are the herbs and plants used for healing. The synthetically produced pill or drug, in contrast, does not share man's vital force field. It is in fact a dead substance. Introduced into a living organism, it can do more harm than good.

One of the greatest healers in recent times, opening exciting new horizons for natural treatment of disease, is the French medical doctor Jean Valnet. Dubbed "Dr. Nature" because of one of his early works on natural healing techniques, Valnet has written extensively on the several forms of natural healing he champions. The Valnet methods consist of treating the entire patient, not the area in which the complaint lies. In this respect his methods are similar, although not identical, with the homeopathic methods used by certain German practitioners. Valnet is a "regular" medical doctor who has learned to improve on this orthodox knowledge from the unusual sources that have opened up to him during his career. In 1972 Dr. Valnet's *Phytotherapie,* subtitled *Treatment of Illnesses Through Plants,* appeared. Both well-known and exotic plants are listed in the book with their properties, side effects, if any, and the use they can be put to in healing. Exact prescriptions on how to get the essential part of the plant from them, the amount to be used, and the methods of application make this book an enormously valuable adjunct to any medical library.

In his *The Treatment of Illnesses Through Vegetables, Fruits, and Cereals,* based upon an earlier edition along the same lines with much new material added, Dr. Valnet lists many well-known and many other little-known food plants and fruits and gives their particular properties and the use they can be put to. Far better than any cookbook, this work deals with the very essence of foodstuffs at our disposal and teaches us how to get the most out of them. With each food is an indication of the diseases for which it is usable and the way in which it is best applied.

Using foodstuffs and plants in the treatment of disease even in the excellent and in many ways unique manner devised by Dr. Jean Valnet is still within the generally known area of natural medicine. But the doctor has also developed a third approach to health and the treatment of illnesses. His latest book, *Aromatherapy,* subtitled *Treatment of Illnesses Through Essential Oil of Plants,* is immensely popular in France. The term "aromatherapy" has passed into the common language, and numerous articles have been written about this exciting new approach to health.

Using essential oils containing, in concentrated form, the most potent properties of the plants from which they come is an ingenious way of introducing powerful remedies directly into the body of the patient through the pores of the skin rather than into the stomach, where they must undergo various chemical attacks before they are assimilated and utilized, through the orifice of the mouth. The method also lends itself to certain cosmetic treatments on the border line between health and personality improvement. Dr. Valnet does not object to this aspect of utilization which his discoveries have found. He considers the concern for cosmetic well-being an extension of general health and as such an integral part of the homeopathic concept of treating the entire person rather than a mere part of the body. The way the practitioners see it, cosmetic treatments merely restore the *appearance* of health, while the Valnet treatment is genuine healing by which skin and other bodily conditions are actually dealt with in a therapeutic fashion. The results are due to healing, not to coverup or purely cosmetic manipulations.

With the help of Sylvia Maria Brown, a Californian deeply involved with unorthodox healing studies, I met one of the students and practitioners of Dr. Jean Valnet's methods. Madame Micheline Arcier has practiced aromatherapy for many years in England and recently set up a treatment clinic in Beverly Hills, California. When I met her, I was able to learn firsthand what aromatherapy is all about.

Since the essential oils are introduced into the body through the skin, it is only natural that skin care is an essential part of the treatment involved. But it would be wrong to assume that aromatherapy is merely another advanced form of skin care or conventional beauty treatment. We are dealing here with an authentic and fully developed form of unorthodox healing, administered either under the direct supervision of a medical doctor or following strict rules laid down by Dr. Valnet himself.

Madame Arcier met with me at the Continental Hotel in Hollywood to discuss her work with Valnet's aromatherapy.

"The treatment we give is partly for relaxation and partly to help skin conditions," she explained. "Those are the two main problem areas we deal with. Our work is unique in that it involves the complete care of the whole body; with one treatment we work on body and face."

"How exactly do you approach this 'wholeness' of treatment?" I asked.

"May I give you a typical example. Mrs. Hicks comes to me with some problems. I would take about two hours with her. My assistant records her medical history, while I examine her psychological situation, her family background, her way of life. After that, I do the examination and treatment; by giving a treatment I find out with my hands what I already know from the question period."

"What do you do with your hands?"

"I apply pressure on the nerve points."

"Is this similar to acupuncture?"

"We have a few common points with acupuncture, but we do it *with the thumb*. I find out exactly what the reaction of the body is. A treatment starts on the back of the head, going right down the spine level; we work on the nerve ganglia all along the spine. The ganglia are responsible for messages to different organs; we call this *reflex therapy*. If the organ is not in good condition, congested or tired, the back becomes 'like a map' and you can read what is happening in the body by seeing the reactions on the back. For instance, if the kidney is badly infiltrated, we will see a red mark. We also see the conditions of muscles and tissues. Women have great problems with tension; 80 percent of all women, young or old, who come to me, do."

"What do you do next?"

"I tell my patient what I have found, and then we start treatment. Sometimes people find it difficult to understand that by working on the lower lumbar and coccygeal region, you also work *at the same time* on their feet. This is very helpful sometimes in conditions involving bad legs where you can't touch them. But you can stimulate the blood."

The hands stay on the body for about five minutes. By touching the person's body the operator also learns more about that particular person's reactions to touch and pressure and indirectly gives indication of bodily conditions. The application of aromatic oils, specially prepared for each individual case by Madame Arcier, comes immediately after the massage. She follows the Valnet prescriptions as to which oils are useful for specific maladies. For instance, sandalwood is recommended by the doctor in cases involving kidney conditions or food poisoning. Sage is used for rheumatic conditions because it helps eliminate toxins. The oils used for people in need of slimming down are the same oils used for kidney infections, Madame Arcier explained, since stimulation of elimination is the goal in both cases.

Oils used are never standards; they are individually prepared like prescriptions depending upon what Madame Arcier has discovered during the examination. She then combines the necessary ingredients to make an oil that is likely to yield results in the particular case she is treating. None of the oils are synthetic; all are pure and of natural origin.

Once the oils have been applied to the skin, the operator continues with the pressure point treatment. There are some other movements, such as lifting of the patient's body, finding out the condition of certain muscles, and in many cases vibration of the spine. All this is done by hand, of course. No machines of any kind are used in the Valnet technique. The reason for this insistence on manual operation lies in the need to adjust pressure and relaxation to every inch of tissue in the patient's body.

Patients return for additional treatments in about five weeks' time. If the condition for which the patient consulted the therapist has not improved, Madame Arcier may change the treatment or prescribe different oils, depending upon the needs of each individual case. In addition to the essential oils and herbs, the treatment includes oil baths and diet, and eventually exercise is added to the recommendations.

I asked Madame Arcier whether her technique had ever helped a medical condition where standard medical procedure had failed (though she never deals with the seriously ill unless a medical adviser is in attendance). She recalled the case of Michel J., a patient of Dr. Valnet. This man had a problem involving ingrowing hair in his beard which created continual infections. Because Madame Arcier has for many years specialized in skin conditions, working closely with Dr. Valnet, he referred this particular case to her. The man, twenty-eight years old, worked as an attorney, and his public appearance was of prime interest to him. From London, Madame Arcier evaluated the condition and sent the man some special oils; one oil to soothe the condition and another to be used as an antiseptic. By the next mail she received confirmation that her treatment had worked. As soon as the infections had died down, the patient was able to have the excess hair removed by electrolysis. The condition never came back.

Although Madame Arcier is careful not to undertake any medical treatments, she does so out of fear of being accused of malpractice rather than for lack of confidence in her treatments. She was trained in a school supervised by a medical doctor, studied aromatherapy with Madame Maury, a specialist in the field, and with Dr. Jean Valnet. Among her own contributions to this field is a special treatment for pregnant women. Because pregnant women are particularly vulnerable to poisonous influences, essential oils placed on the skin must be right for both mother and expected baby. Most practitioners of skin care are not aware of these problems. Dr. Valnet declared her treatment for pregnant women both harmless to the child and useful to the mother.

Her treatments are not physical alone. She explains, "The action of the scents on the brain has been extensively studied by continental scientists and practical experiences show the value of essential oils in achieving calming or uplifting results." Micheline Arcier's headquarters are at 4 Albert Gate Court, 124 Knightsbridge, London S.W. 1.

Diet is as important to the proper functioning of our body—our "vehicle"—as is good gasoline to the running of a car. As we move toward the year 2000, one would think that poisons in the form of preservatives would have been removed from our foodstuffs and that proper nutrition would have become commonplace. Not so. Processed foods abound, manufacturers thrive, and under the guise of better business methods, those who provide our foods play down the dangers inherent in preservatives of any kind, claiming that they are necessary to ensure that the food does not spoil. The truth is, it is strictly a matter of prolonging the food's shelf life, which spells larger profits and a better return on their investment.

I personally will not eat or drink anything that has any kind of chemical preservatives in it (fortunately, they must be listed by law). I wouldn't want to eat bread containing calcium propionate "to retard spoilage" and I would not want to drink cider containing "only" .5 percent of sorbitol to prevent it from aging. It is all about prolonged *shelf* life . . . not yours or mine! Products, particularly grain products like breads and cereals, which state categorically "no artificial preservatives" have to really mean it, and they do. As long as you keep them refrigerated properly you will have no problems. In the case of some cereals, natural sugar content will act as a preservative even outside the refrigerator. Preservatives (chemicals) are meant to kill off bacteria forming in the food or juice during the process of aging that leads to spoilage. Along with those undesirable bacteria being knocked off, all good bacteria is eliminated as well. Pasteurizing the milk in the nineteenth century was a necessary precaution to prevent smallpox and other infectious diseases cows might pass on to humans. Today, "flash" pasteurizing orange juice and apple juice keeps them from turning "hard" (prior to becoming alcohol), but also makes every nutrient in them worthless and dead. Freshly-pressed orange juice and cider will keep a week when refrigerated: why drink dead juices full of unwanted sugar?

It has been commonly known among health-conscious people that foodstuffs which are by themselves alright, may cause illness if taken together with other foodstuffs. After all, the absorption of food and drink into our physical system is a chemical process and chemical reactions and interactions will occur. At the same time, those who wish to avoid gaining weight will also benefit from the following diet suggestions.

For breakfast, try to stay with fruit and fruit juice, and do not eat protein foods at the same time; carbohydrates are alright. For your midday meal, have a salad or other vegetarian food, and no fruit. For your main meal, vegetable protein and carbohydrates, such as legumes and pasta are best.

This brings me to another matter which may not be as easy to accept by the majority of people used to a mixed diet. Contrary to what you may have heard about the need for adequate daily intake of protein, our need for protein is much less than generally thought, and differs greatly from individual to individual, depending on energy needs. There are also complete vegetable proteins available, such as soybeans and most legumes, as well as high protein content found in tofu and tofu products, derived from concentrated bean curd.

When it comes to treating cancer the natural way, a vegetarian diet is of vital importance. Would it not be sensible to start with a vegetarian diet anyway, rather than wait until illness necessitates it?

I have been a practicing vegetarian since age 11 and have been inside a hospital only twice in my life for a few days only. My state of health surprises the average physician, especially when they find out that I am a strict vegan, one who does not use any kind of animal products. In the following pages I will explain why I feel a vegetarian diet is an insurance for continued good health and a longer life. Those who say they eat meat, poultry, or fish "only" once a week are in my view no different than those who claim to smoke cigarettes only "once in a while." It is still unhealthful behavior. Those who say they "only" eat red meat but no chicken, or those who do the reverse, are not vegetarians at all. Of course, we all must find our own way to survival and good health; I have long found mine.

According to a July 1992 *New York Times* report on "eating well" by Marian Burros, as of July 1992, twelve million Americans consider themselves vegetarians, an increase of 20 percent over the past ten years. Naturally, there are all sorts of vegetarians, ranging from partial to totally vegan, but the fact is, more and more people realize that the consumption of meat and animal products is not healthy.

"Man may have heart attacks because he was born to be a vegetarian but decided to eat meat," three Brooklyn researchers said recently. Man's digestive system simply cannot handle the fats in meats, the researchers theorize. The fats are deposited in the walls of the arteries until the blood vessels clog up. Meat-eating animals do not have the same trouble, Drs. William S. Coleens and Efstratios Vlahos say in an article on vegetarianism published in 1973 by *Town and Country* magazine. Dr. Coleens is quoted as saying that he was so certain of the bad effects of meat, that he would not swallow any.

The upsurge of vegetarianism in the Western world is the product of nineteenth century emancipation and a humane outlook on the part of individuals, who then became the spiritual and intellectual leaders of the vegetarian movement and in turn spread their philosophies to larger segments of the population. There was no deep seated, "grass roots" movement for vegetarianism prevalent in Europe prior to the second half of the nineteenth century, although individual poets and writers may at times have pointed out the horrors of slaughter and the dangers of meat. Probably the most prominent of these writers is the late George Bernard Shaw. Throughout his life he admonished his fellow man to forgo the use of meat, both on moral and on health grounds. He predicted blandly that he would live to a ripe old age, and when he finally died, his coffin would be followed by a procession of various farm animals whose lives he had saved by abstaining from eating their meat. As it happened, Shaw died in his mid-nineties, and never suffered any great debilitating illness during his long life. Shavian vegetarianism is pretty much the most common form of this philosophy in the Western world today.

Essentially there are three types of vegetarians, and three motivations for being a vegetarian. The three types of vegetarian are the vegan, the lactarian, and the ovolactarian. The vegan and his variant, the fructarian, abstains from all animals, animal products, eggs and milk products, even from the use of vitamins and additives, and lives therefore mainly on vegetables, fruits, and nuts. Vegans are firmly convinced that any form of processed food is detrimental and prefer their food raw, whenever that is possible, rather than cooked. They maintain that sufficient vitamins are contained in the vegetables they eat so that vitamin pills are not necessary for the diet.

Dr. Jean Mayer in an article in *Family Health* (February 1973) says, "There are large numbers of our contemporaries who seem to have become vegetarians out of fear. The vegans in England who avoid all animal products are apparently motivated largely by the belief that animal products cause cancer. In this country there is a somewhat more sophisticated belief that meat and poultry are full of hormones which will cause cancer. Fish is said to be preserved in antibiotics, which will sap your ability to fend off germs, milk is full of DDT, and eggs are saturated with mysterious unnamed chemicals. Not one of these claims is true, but all of the proof in the world can't seem to change the attitude of this type of vegetarian about animal foods."

Since this article appeared in February 1973, one can only assume Mayer was ignorant of statements an article in the *New York Times* of

September 29, 1972, headlined, "Dietary Factors Linked to Cancer of Digestive Tract." In this special article by Jane E. Brody, it is stated that, "Worldwide changes in the incidence of cancers of the digestive tract are pointing to meats, alcohol and a deficiency in the trace element molybdenum in the diet as possible causes of these major cancer killers. Dr. John W. Berg, epidemiologist at the National Cancer Institute, told the Seventh National Cancer Conference, 'Much to our surprise, six different meat items were found to be associated with a high bowel cancer risk' and he explained that Argentina and Scotland, which use a lot of meat, have high bowel cancer rates not much different from that in the United States. He is quoted as emphasizing that this did not mean that eating meat caused bowel cancer, but it would mean that something in the meat or added to it was the culprit. At present, the doctor explained, science had no explanation for any such causative relationship. Studies are now being conducted among vegetarians, who eat no meat, and Seventh Day Adventists, who eat little meat, to seek further confirmation of his findings."

That unwanted or unneeded hormones can cause cancer in humans is well known among doctors. And it is a fact that much meat and poultry in the United States is injected with hormones in order to make the meat more valuable. It is also a fact that these hormones go right into the human body with the consumption of such meats. DDT has been outlawed in the United States for the very reason that Dr. Mayer said the British vegans were afraid of it. Animals eating grass sprayed previously with DDT, or for that matter with any other insecticide, store the poison in their system and it goes into the milk and thence into the human body. Not only are these claims or fears rational, but they do not even cover the entire range of dangers existing in the consumption of meat or fish products.

However, vegans are by no means representative of the majority of vegetarians in the world today. They are, in a sense, the conservatives among vegetarians, preferring a very strict diet to one of convenience. The majority of vegetarians is either lactarian, meaning they partake of milk products, or ovolactarian, meaning they partake of milk and egg products.

Those who are lactarians find that their diet is well-balanced and generally there is enough of a variety of foods available to them so that no problem of nutrition exists. This is even more the case with ovolactarians. Since the majority of desserts, for instance, contain eggs, and since eggs are added to a number of other dishes as well, an honest lactarian or vegan will not touch a piece of pastry containing eggs, even if one egg has been used in 500 lbs. of pastry. It is not the amount of the unwanted product that counts but the principle behind it.

Both lactarians and ovolactarians take vitamins with their food although they insist on the vitamins being of natural or organic origin. In cities especially, the need for additives such as vitamins is particularly great. However, if one lives in the open country and has access to fresh vegetables or even grows one's own, vitamins are no longer required in most cases. This is so because the vegetables coming onto the market in the city are generally two or three days old, by which time the vitamin content has either shrunk or been completely eliminated. Only freshly cut vegetables or freshly collected fruit maintain the high vitamin content originally put into them by nature.

The majority of vegetarians, who are either lactarians or ovolactarians, are also interested in health foods and will buy their products at health food stores, although it must be remembered that health food and vegetarianism are two different things. Likewise, faddish diets such as the macrobiotic diet have nothing to do with real vegetarianism. The macrobiotic diet, formulated by a Japanese school of philosophy in recent years, consists primarily of selected fish products and some vegetables. It differentiates between that which is grown close to the ground and that which grows above the ground. Ultimately more and more foods are eliminated from the system until the dieter lives on brown rice alone. While such a diet may be suitable to some selected individuals living a quiet contemplative life in the Far East, it is totally unsuitable and perhaps even dangerous to a Westerner. I have seen people try the macrobiotic diet for a number of months, until their health was in such a poor state that they had to discontinue it. Some of the reasoning behind the prohibition of certain vegetables seems unwarranted. More than anything, the macrobiotic diet is an implementation of a religious belief and not based on health motivation or on moral concepts. It is closely associated with Zen Buddhism.

There seems to be some question in the mind of the outside observer concerning the prohibition of eggs and egg products by some vegetarians. The argument goes like this: An egg is not an animal, especially an unfertilized egg. Why should it not be consumed? The answer of course is that an egg does represent a comparatively high state of development toward the animal life, whether fertilized or not, and while eating an unfertilized egg does not deprive a chicken of its potential life, it does in fact represent the consumption of an animal-like product, made up of materials similar to the chicken itself once it is born.

The fallacy that fish meat is less undesirable than meat derived from beef or poultry from the vegetarian point of view is another myth; neither is fish meat any less poisoned than other meat, since our rivers and lakes are polluted; and while a fish may not have a voice to cry out against being killed, its anxiety at the moment of death is just as great as a farm animal's capable of venting its fears. Thus the problem of adrenaline accumulated just before the moment of death, comes as much into play with fish as with other forms of meat. This applies equally to seafood, crustaceans and, in fact, any kind of animal meat, whether of a higher or lower order.

It does not apply to plants being ripped from the soil or cut off because plants are a different kind of organism, devoid of blood, and do not respond the way animals do. But in terms of taking life, of course, plants do represent a life force also, and if one were to carry vegetarianism to extremes, one would not eat salads or vegetables, but live only off fruit and nuts, since these two categories alone permit the host, that is the tree, to function after the fruit or nut has been taken, without harm to the host organism. The truly perfect vegetarian, therefore, is not the vegan, but the *fructarian*, a person who eats only raw fruits and nuts and nothing else. A diet based on these two categories can be entirely sufficient, but is very difficult to maintain in organized society.

What is a vegetarian? Twenty years ago a vegetarian was a man, usually bearded, who walked the streets wearing strange clothes, had an unkempt fanatical look about him and quite obviously did not belong to the mainstream of society. Vegetarians were oddballs, rebels, weirdos. For some time there was a vegetarian party, headed by the editor of a small vegetarian journal, which attempted to place their candidate in Congress. But the Vegetarian Party did not succeed any more than the Townsend Party succeeded in placing their pension reform candidate into the White House. Political vegetarianism is dead. Fanatical vegetarians are comparatively few in number; middle-of-the-road vegetarians exist by the millions.

Whatever the motivation, a vegetarian is, or should be, an individual living a balanced life—if anything, in better health than his fellow man partaking of meat; more peaceful and understanding than his meat eating cousin; and on the whole, a more advanced person than the nonvegetarian.

VEGETARIAN GUIDELINES

1. I shall not eat the meat, or meat products derived from animals, whether large or small, whether flesh, fowl, or fish.
2. I shall not use products containing chemical agents likely to hurt my state of health.
3. I shall not destroy the food I use by overcooking, but eat whatever is palatable and digestible in its raw state.
4. I shall not drink alcoholic beverages (with the exception of small amounts of wine or wine-derived drinks occasionally), and I shall not smoke or use drugs at any time.
5. I shall attempt to clothe myself without the use of leather, to discourage the use of animal skins for clothing and shoes.
6. I shall always remember that mine is a peaceful Way of Life and not to impose it on others, no matter what, unless they wish to embrace it.

A vegetarian should also use health foods whenever that is possible, perhaps even more so than the meat eater. The reason may be that his system, more delicate since it has been deprived of the bombardment of harmful substances inherent in meat, may be more vulnerable to chemical agents than the meat eater's. Although the steady intake of harmful substances found in most commercially produced foodstuffs tends to accumulate and eventually cause illness, it also creates a certain toughness in the system, by which the nonvegetarian's body is able to withstand the onslaught of chemicals somewhat better than his vegetarian cousin's. In the long run, of course, the body of the nonvegetarian will succumb to illness where the vegetarian will not.

Sometimes people wonder how some foodstuffs such as almonds and nuts can be designated as organically grown. How would they differ from ordinary almonds and nuts? Again, the difference lies in the soil treatment, the lack of spraying of trees and bushes, and the cautions observed in harvesting and packaging of the product. When a substance is inherently harmful to the body, whether it is produced under high or low standards, substitutes are suggested by the health food users. For instance, chocolate is certainly not a useful substance for long-term use. It causes tooth decay, constipation, and in some cases acts as a stimulant at times when stimulation is not wanted. The health food industry has therefore created a similar substance from the fruit of the St. John's Bread tree called carob. Carob, when treated with raw sugar, tastes and looks exactly like good chocolate. Caffeine-free coffees are part and parcel of any health food store. Substitutes such as fig coffee or malt coffee are also suggested for those who want to avoid the intake of ordinary coffee.

A vegetarian may drink coffee, tea, or cocoa, but a wise vegetarian will restrict the intake of these substances to minimal amounts. He would be better off without them. But there are times when a stimulant is required. Fortunately, there are other stimulants which do not create the same health hazards as *caffein* or *tein*. *Gota Cola* and certain East Asian teas offer stimulation without a kickback. Extracts of ginseng root are also useful in this respect.

In the United States, the burden of supplying organic foods lies with the health food stores, whether individual stores or chains. Lately, some large commercial outfits have actually gone into chains, such as MCA. In Europe, especially in Germany and Austria, health foods are generally carried by a large number of pharmacies, termed *reform pharmacies*. They do not carry fresh vegetables or meats, as some American health food stores do, but they do carry a large selection of cereals, additives, breads, carob products, and other products capable of being stored for considerable periods of time without deterioration or need for preservatives.

The trouble with maintaining health food standards is that you have to think of side effects not generally associated with the food products themselves. The water you use to cook vegetables in, or only to steam in, may be polluted and chemicals may enter the foodstuffs by that route; or the water you drink may be strongly flavored with fluoride or other chemical agents, and these poisons may enter your system directly by drinking it or by washing your foods with it. Ideally speaking, therefore, health foods should only be washed or cooked in chemically free water.

In the United States bottled water derived from safe and natural wells is being used extensively in lieu of drinking water taken from the tap. It is a sad comment upon life in modern times that we can no longer drink the water of our water system with impunity. Not only does ordinary tap water, especially in big cities, have a horrible taste, but it also contains all sorts of unwanted toxins. Some of the New York City water, for instance, is derived from the Hudson River, one of the most polluted streams in the world. Despite assurances that pollution elimination plants are in operation and that the water is in fact totally filtered of these harmful agents, the doubt remains as strong as ever. Most vegetarians and health food users have long since switched to bottled water, chiefly derived from mountain sources, such as the Mountain Valley wells or some particularly clear wells in the mountainous regions of Arkansas.

Naturally, buying one's table water adds to the budget. But even this is not always a guarantee of obtaining the very best. In an article entitled "A Study of Bottled Water Finds Some Samples Dirty," the *New York Times* on March 2, 1973, pointed to the fact that "An Environmental Protection Agency investigation of selected segments of the bottled water industry indicates that the water is often dirty . . . In what was conceded to be a small survey, covering about 5% of the companies in the field, E.P.A.'s water supply division examined the operations and product of 25 concerns in Connecticut, Ohio, Texas, and California. Fifty samples of their output were put through laboratory analysis. Of the fifty samples, according to a pending E.P.A. report, four contained coliform organisms, a standard indicator of the possible presence of disease causing bacteria. Coliforms are usually of human or animal intestinal origin and are often associated with sewage. Another sample contained an excess of lead that could not be traced to the water's origin. In addition, there were instances of discrepancies between the samples' chemical contents and label listings . . . In many cases, bottling was not performed under sanitary conditions."

Obviously, the bottling industry, shaken by this negative report, is taking measures to police itself more fully. The health food industry is by no means perfect. There are bad examples even among the well-intentioned. But as the health food industry grows it becomes more and more aware of its responsibilities to the public, and it also comes at an increasing rate under the supervision of certain federal inspection agencies. Under those circumstances standards are likely to be sufficiently safe to eliminate the element of risk at least to the point where the intake of health food is nearly always safe. Exceptions due to improper handling or processing may of course occur, but if I had a choice between taking this very small risk or taking the very considerable risk of using ordinary foodstuffs, I would bet on the health food approach.

When Dr. Louis Pasteur discovered the process known as pasteurization, he was justly hailed as one of the pioneers of medicine. In pasteurization, a heat process kills harmful bacteria in the food or liquid subjected to the process. Because nineteenth century cows suffered greatly from tuberculosis, pasteurizing the milk was a safety device which eliminated the dangers from bovine tuberculosis in humans. From that day onward, all our milk has been pasteurized except, of course, small quantities called *certified milk* available in the

United States, or some milk taken by the consumer on the spot, where the quality of the milk is known to the farmer and the cows supervised constantly for possible signs of disease. But nutritionists discovered, as time went on, that in pasteurizing the milk, the process also killed all nutritional values, especially the vitamins in the milk. Thus, along with the bad bacteria, the good bacteria so necessary to the body were also being eliminated, and what resulted was an entirely safe and pleasant drink without much nutritional value left.

Consequently, some people prefer so-called certified milk. That is milk which has not been pasteurized, but which comes from cows constantly under medical supervision, produced under highest cleanliness standards and tested continuously. Such milk is not homogenized either, meaning that its natural balance of skim milk and cream are maintained precisely as nature provided it. The removal of fatty substances from milk disturbs this balance and so-called skim milk can be harmful to those drinking it because of the calcium content imbalance found in such milk products. When raw milk is taken directly from the farmer one may, of course, boil it and cool it. Although this will also eliminate harmful bacteria, it is not as destructive to vitamins as flash pasteurization by much stronger heat processes. Flash pasteurization, incidentally, is also being widely used nowadays to make apple juice and other fruit juices free of spoilage. Thus such beverages can be stored almost indefinitely. They never lose their flavor and they have nothing else to lose, having already lost their vitamin content at the beginning.

Much is being made of the need to control pests and the alleged danger to fruit and vegetables from insects. However, the only danger to the crop from insects is the destruction of part of it. Insects do not poison the fruit or vegetable they touch; they merely eat it. If one is willing to accept a certain percentage of loss, due to insects, and eliminates the damaged fruit or vegetables, using only that which is free of insects—which is usually the bulk of the crop—one has not only a clean and safe crop, but a strong natural fertilizer as well. Using the damaged fruit or vegetable as the base of the next season's crop, one is in effect recycling part of the crop and thus maintains a stronger bond between soil and that which grows upon it.

Although some health food enthusiasts will not agree with me, I am opposed to any form of fertilizer derived from the excretions of animals since they are bound to contain harmful germs. I am also opposed to most chemical or artificial fertilizers since alien substances are added to the soil by them, much of it on the surface where it can be absorbed into the plant or vegetable. I am, however, in favor of natural fertilizers such as part of last season's crop, which in spoiling will provide the soil with sufficient chemicals to improve the following season's crop without adding anything harmful. In this way one is more closely following the natural rhythm of things, since that is exactly the way it happens in nature. A tree may die and fall to the ground, but eventually it is absorbed by the soil and helps to stimulate other trees' growth around it.

Vegetarians are likely to turn to organic remedies for illness rather than to the man-made variety. But even beyond the organic label, the vegetarian will look to esoteric forms of healing agents whenever he has the opportunity to do so. Not all vegetarians are well read in this field: the herb remedies of the Welsh physician, Dr. E. Bach, author of *The Twelve Healers* and J. Lucas' *Folk Medicine* are, however, gaining wider acceptance every day. The vegetarian's attitude toward what he eats evaluates not only nutrition, but healing properties as well. For instance, garlic is an excellent seasoning agent, and an equally excellent purifier and remedy against colds. Lemon juice, while supplying seasoning to a salad, also supplies a bowel movement when necessary, and parsley not only decorates any dish rather nicely, but destroys mouth odors as well. The intake of celery is said to counter incidences of arthritis. Honey is both a purifier and a sweetening agent, and the pectin in apples and other fruits counteracts poisoning in the system.

There is almost no food which does not have a healing property in addition to its nutritional value, provided it is a natural food, grown without any chemical fertilizers and not treated in any way. There are, of course, any number of plants found in nature which are not of nutritional value but which have therapeutic properties, such as gold seal and myrrh, both potent purification agents and astringents. Vegetarians in general tend to look to natural remedies as contained in existing plants whenever they are aware of them, rather than to synthetically produced condensed patent medicines which their doctors may prescribe for them simply because they do not know enough about natural herb medicines. Being a vegetarian certainly helps to be aware of what exists in nature, and there is almost no disease, in fact no disease at all, that does not yield to some existing herb or plant. The difficult thing to know is what fits which disease, and if we spent only a fraction of the time and effort on modern medicine on the understanding of nature and her therapeutic aspects, we would all be a lot healthier for it, vegetarians and meat eaters alike.

Many vegetarians will carry their attitudes to the dentist as well. They object to the use of injections, such as the injection of procaine products or of so-called laughing gas, which is nowadays used very sparingly because of its inherent dangers. In some people novacaine, the most common form of procaine used, may also cause toxic reactions or prolonged discomfort. Vegetarians are more likely to accept self-hypnosis or hypnosis by the dentist in order to avoid the need for novocaine injections.

It should also be noted that vegetarians, being more sensitive to the toxins contained in most ordinary foods, will react quicker and more strongly to the presence of alcohol in their systems. In other words, a vegetarian is a cheap drunk; he may get "high" on half a glass of wine. The majority of vegetarians will not take any alcohol, although middle-of-the-roaders such as lactarians or ovolactarians do take wine with their meals in moderate quantities. Although hard liquor is generally refused by all vegetarians, occasionally a small quantity of cognac or brandy is permitted.

The state of the body while eating or drinking is of great importance to what happens to the food or drink taken in. If the body is tense, and vital muscles not relaxed, the food will be processed erratically—in spurts, as it were—and consequently the all-important timing of the process will be interfered with. The same, of course, happens when one eats or drinks too quickly, swallows the wrong way by swallowing some air as well as the food or liquid, or in general interferes with the normal, measured flow of the intake of food or drink into the system. Vegetarians do not rush their meals, but allow their bodies to be in a fully relaxed state prior to eating or drinking. This isn't always possible, but a few minutes before mealtime some form of relaxing exercise can do wonders. Here are some don'ts when it comes to eating, whether you are a vegetarian or not.

1. Don't eat or drink after running.
2. Don't eat or drink when overheated or frozen. Permit your body to assume the temperature of the environment, or as much of it as it is able to in a short time.
3. Don't eat or drink immediately following a coughing or sneezing spell. Your muscular apparatus may be in a state of disarrangement and will require several minutes to adjust itself to normal.
4. Don't eat or drink when emotionally disturbed or immediately after you have had a traumatic experience of any kind. The reason for this is that your acid glands are in an abnormal state of activity at such times, secreting far more acid than is necessary for the proper digestion of food and drink. Emotional upsets automatically activate certain glands in the body, especially the acid producing glands in the stomach, and the sweat glands. It is therefore unwise to burden the glandular system with the job of digesting food or drink at a time when they are strained by emotional stimuli passed along the nerve fibers.

There are a number of exercises designed to relax the bodily mechanism prior to the intake of food or drink. Deep breathing three or four times in a row, followed by a sighing type of sound will help start the body to relax. Bending down slowly and then raising the body again a few times can also be useful. Breathing exercises are particularly useful since they perform two functions simultaneously: they relax the muscular apparatus and they expel toxic substances from the lungs and bloodstream. Probably the best of all exercises are various forms of yoga. This applies equally to simple breathing techniques as to the more complicated postures which are held for a certain period of time. In this respect, yoga is the opposite of calisthenics or gymnastics. In the latter, great efforts are made for a number of rapid movements, whereas in yoga the movements are slow, and emphasis is on holding certain positions for a period of time. The underlying philosophy is also quite different: in calisthenics and gymnastics, the body is being thought of exclusively. With yoga, body, mind, and spirit are dealt with as one.

Even more important than the physical state before eating is the mental state of the individual. Mind controls body, mind triggers bodily reactions. To come to the table with one's mind filled with problems, with worries, with unresolved conflicts, is to invite trouble. Vegetarians know very well that an untroubled mind digests a great deal better than a troubled one. This is especially necessary to the non-meat eating segment of the population since the breaking down of some vegetable tissues, especially when eaten raw, requires a greater effort than the digestion of meat or other animal products. We should recall that the cow has four stomachs aligned in succession, through which grass passes until it finally turns into milk. Humans do not have such a handy arrangement. They have one stomach; larger though it may be, all work is done in it. Consequently, anything affecting the texture and the stomach lining, such as emotions, must be very carefully controlled.

Nothing is more likely to upset the digestive process than considerable amounts of alcohol prior to eating. This does not mean that the French aperitif has no value. A small amount of wine can, in fact, stimulate the appetite. The emphasis here is, as with so many things, on the amount. Vegetarians do not take alcoholic beverages to start their meals. They prefer fruit juice, preferably acid ones, since that will help the digestive process. Unfortunately fresh fruit juices are almost nonexistent in conventional restaurants.

One of the chief differences between eating vegetarian-style and being a meat eater is the bulk of food necessary to satisfy the hunger of the eater. Even if large amounts of protein, such as legumes or soybeans are included in a meal, a vegetarian meal does not satisfy the appetite as much as a meat meal will. This has to do with the cellular structure of meat and vegetables. Vegetables contain much more water than meat. Under the circumstances, a much larger amount of vegetables would have to be consumed in terms of bulk and weight to effect the same sensation as with a smaller amount of meat or meat products. Since the stomach cannot hold this excessive bulk, it is not possible to make up the difference with vegetables. Consequently, vegetarians get hungry again much sooner than meat eaters. In a way, however, that is a blessing in disguise.

Many medical authorities have held that more frequent meals, during which less is consumed, are preferable to three very large meals a day, because they strain the bodily apparatus less than the three large meals.

Some medical authorities warn against snacks before bedtime, because such snacks allegedly cause bad dreams, or at any rate cannot be properly digested and lead to weight gain. If the snack is small and consists of comparatively easily digested foods, this will not happen. This myth belongs in the same category as the one blaming a cup of coffee for sleepless nights. As a matter of fact, one cup of coffee tends to induce sleepiness, because the caffeine widens the arteries and capillaries. A second or third cup, however, would indeed keep the subject from falling asleep.

False beliefs as to which foods are good for you and which are not, are just as damaging to good digestion as are undue haste and pressures. Whether through autohypnosis, suggestion, or hypnosis administered by competent operators, a state of serenity is of the greatest importance where digestive difficulties have been encountered. Vegetarians know that thoughts are real things, and that the proper thoughts while eating can help good digestion. Therefore, vegetarians need not permit indigestion under any circumstances.

Being a vegetarian has many advantages. No matter what work you are in, living by vegetarian food standards is likely to give you more energy, better health, and a more even-tempered approach to the problems facing you. Statistics have shown that areas heavily indulging in meat-eating, such as the greater Chicago area, for instance, are also high on the list of crime-ridden and violence-plagued areas. Perhaps excessive meat-eating makes man violent and aggressive. This does not mean that vegetarians are docile and peaceful. It does mean, however, that a vegetarian is less likely to allow his aggressive natural instinct to rule him than his meat-eating cousin. Apart from the minor inconveniences of not always finding satisfactory food supplies at work, and being forced to bring one's own lunch to work, being a vegetarian definitely results in greater clarity of vision, not so much of the physical eye, although that, too is involved, but of ideas. The absence of toxic substances in the food makes for clearmindedness and for a consciousness of one's own health, far beyond that which average people demonstrate. The vegetarian concept is a clean way of life, and somehow this cleanliness permeates all departments of a vegetarian's work life, whether in terms of actual physical cleanliness, orderliness, or arrangement of ideas.

Even when a vegetarian plays, he has more zest, more of a sense of humor than his frequently dyspeptic colleagues.

On a purely physical level, sexual endurance is of course greatly favored because of vegetarian dietary ways. Despite the frequently voiced claim that the absence of meat proteins weakens the physical structure of a vegetarian's body, any vegetarian protein will be more than equal to his meat-eating colleague in matters of sexual endurance. This is so because much of the vegetarian food is beneficial to the muscular strengthening, to the cleansing and continual rejuvenation of tissues, to the strengthening of nerve fibers through the intake of minerals and vitamins. And since most vegetarians do not touch alcohol at all or only in very limited quantities, and do not smoke, they have none of the problems associated with these two habits so common to meat eaters.

Part II

NON-PHYSICAL

HEALING

Mind Over Matter

Up to this point I have dealt with physical substances and treatments, whether derived from conventional medical practice or alternative techniques. But the *mind* plays an important, if not pivotal, part in health and healing. This was known long before Sigmund Freud, but it was expressed in terms of religion, superstition, and folk beliefs.

While it is true that pain, illness, and bodily malfunction can affect the mind and cause it to react adversely (instead of mind controlling it), it is equally true that we would not be aware of these undesirable states if it were not for our mind signaling it to us consciously. The power of the mind to heal, or to deal with illness with positive results is far greater than most people realize. Physicians, however, usually dismiss the powers of mind as a healing factor in favor of prescribing a pill.

What the mind does do is set in motion purely physical reactions and consequences within the physical body. There are two approaches to mental healing that can work, though by no means in all cases nor always as a substitute for physical medicine. Hypnosis and outside suggestion is one approach, auto-suggestion the other. Each affliction must be evaluated as to the best way to deal with it, but a great many illnesses can indeed be controlled by the mind.

In recent years hypnosis has become more and more accepted by the medical profession as a valuable tool in the treatment of nervous disorders, personality problems, and deep-seated anxieties. Unfortunately, it has also been abused by stage hypnotists for the amusement of the masses and on occasion been dealt with as a kind of parlor game by people who know nothing about it—or not enough, at any rate, to be cautious in its application.

In hypnosis the conscious mind is temporarily shelved so that the unconscious may take over. Actually, hypnosis is a two-way street: material is brought out of the unconscious of the subject or material is placed into the unconscious by the hypnotist. Many misconceptions about hypnosis continue to be believed by the uninitiated, sometimes even by medical doctors or other professionals. For one thing, one cannot be hypnotized against one's wishes; stories along the lines of the famed Svengali and Trilby relationship, a fictional account of the total dependency existing between a subject and a hypnotist, are simply fictional. Indeed, the majority of those who wish to be hypnotized cannot be hypnotized because they are unable to relax sufficiently to "go under." Frequently people will request hypnosis in order to rid themselves of certain bad habits, such as cigarette smoking or excessive drinking. Many of these individuals cannot be hypnotized because their desire is not sincere but merely a social coverup and what they hope for is failure rather than success.

The one in five people I have found to be good subjects for hypnosis are generally emotional yet stable individuals, people who are trusting and like to rely on guidance, especially guidance given by professional people. They are individuals who like to talk a good deal, have artistic or cultural interests, and are frequently either liberal or flexible in their views of such things as morality, social customs, and politics. People with fixed ideas, prejudices, preconceived notions, fears, or those very much set in their ways are less likely to make good hypnotic subjects.

The personality of the hypnotist plays a major role because hypnosis is 90 percent good relationship between hypnotist and subject and 10 percent suggestion. This relationship need not be an intimate one, but it should be friendly and personal rather than clinical and impersonal. For that reason medical hypnosis, undertaken by medical doctors in connection with certain treatments, does not always succeed as well as hypnotic treatment by hypnosis specialists who get on friendly terms with their prospective subjects.

There are three basic degrees in the hypnotic process. First-degree hypnosis, sometimes called suggestion, consists of verbal relaxation, with the subject either in a chair or prone on the couch. At this stage, the subject hears and remembers everything said by the hypnotist. The first stage of hypnosis is used when minor problems are to be taken care of, such as general nervousness without deep-seated factors, minor bad habits, fear of impending exams in school, or uncertainty about meeting the boss and other forms of everyday occurrences.

In the second stage of hypnosis deeper levels are reached. Here the patient does not always remember everything said to him yet acts according to the commands if such are inserted into his unconscious mind. I always use the second stage of hypnosis during a second visit by the same subject in order to make sure the process is orderly and no shock results. The second stage can be used to suggest the discontinuance of bad habits, such as smoking or alcoholism, and in reverse strong suggestions can be inserted into the unconscious mind of the subject when the second deepest level is reached. It is up to the hypnotist to program the subject to forget or to remember the instructions given under hypnosis.

In the third or deepest stage no memory of what is said to the subject or by the subject to the hypnotist should remain. If there are traces of memory just the same, then the third stage was not complete and a new attempt should be made to bring the subject down to that level at another time. The third stage of hypnosis is used when serious emotional disturbances are to be dealt with. This, however, should never be undertaken by a hypnotist unless a medical doctor has approved the attempt, or when conventional psychoanalysis has failed. Only if third-stage hypnosis is undertaken for other reasons, such as psychical research, especially regression into alleged earlier lives, need a medical doctor not be present.

Under no circumstances should anyone undertake hypnosis with known mentally disturbed individuals or with those suffering from serious illnesses at the time. Hypnosis should also be avoided when the subject is very tired, with women during the menstruation period, and with children unless special conditions make it advisable.

Hypnosis works through the power of suggestion. In removing temporarily the conscious mind with its editing and deliberating faculties, the hypnotist lays bare the unconscious mind, which is uncritical, wide open for suggestions.

Hypnotherapy consists of two avenues of approach. First, the hypnotist reaches down to the third stage—in degrees, of course—to probe the unconscious of the patient for any suppressed hostilities or other disturbing thought material. Since it is the conviction of those practicing healing that wrongful thought processes can cause illness, it stands to reason that suppressed negative and destructive thoughts are just as dangerous as those brought up to the surface and exteriorized. As a matter of fact, in bringing them to the surface and airing them, the hostilities and other wrongful thoughts are taken from the system of the individual concerned. Cleaning out, so to speak, the unconscious of the subject does not, however, by itself restore the proper health balance. For that reason the properly trained hypnotist will insert certain positive suggestions, anything pertaining to a particular case, ranging from thoughts of love where hostility was prevalent before, to specific instructions on wholesome habits or living patterns. If the patient suffers from physical illness as well, healing processes can be stimulated by suggestions implanted in the unconscious.

Normally, the patient will not be aware of these suggestions, but they will work, even though the patient is not conscious of the stimulations and the hypnotist will not disclose them until full recovery has been accomplished.

Hypnotic regression can also be used in the research of potential former lives. If reincarnation material can be brought to the surface and if it is authentic material capable of some verification in conventional sources, the knowledge of such conditions can benefit the subject because the patient is made aware of certain conditions in past lives as having caused his health predicament in the present one. In this respect hypnosis is used as an adjunct to the better understanding of karmic law and indirectly contributes toward a stronger stand in the present life in dealing with the ill health caused by mistakes or omissions in a previous one.

Hypnosis is, further, very useful if the subject is psychic or capable of "dissociation of personality," a term used to describe trance mediumship. By suggesting that the patient allow his own personality to step aside temporarily and create a kind of void within the body (although linked with it through the so-called silver cord), the hypnotist allows spiritual forces to operate the body of the patient directly, thus opening the subject up to treatments by these entities in a much more effective way than if they were consciously aware of this intervention. This process, of course, works only if the subject has strong mediumistic abilities. On numerous occasions, spiritual entities have complained, through their mediums, of their inability to "get through" to certain individuals in order to perform healing because of that individual's resistance or because of a natural tendency to hold on to the conscious mind. In this respect hypnosis acts as a gateway, loosening the bonds between conscious and unconscious minds rather than as a direct healing factor.

Those unfamiliar with the various techniques of hypnosis may shrug off results as being imaginary or, if the disease yields to hypnosis, will hold it to have been imaginary to begin with. But this is simply not so: hypnosis triggers definite actions in the personality of the subject. Hypnosis also allows outside forces to enter the etheric body of the patient and to adjust it so that the physical body may fall in line with it.

By itself hypnosis does not heal. But hypnosis causes actions and reactions in the sick person which in turn heal the individual. These actions and reactions either would not normally take place or would take a much longer period to become effective. In many ways, hypnosis is a short cut to action. Visualization techniques form part of hypnosis. For instance, if the hypnotist suggests to the patient that he see himself wholly well, when the patient is obviously not so in the present condition, then the hypnotist is stimulating the patient to project a recovered image of himself. By doing this, the hypnotist performs a service similar to that of the psychic or unorthodox healer, without possessing any of their psychic energy gifts. The difference lies in the method: the healer applies forces from within himself, whether or not they are inspired by an outside power; the hypnotist merely stimulates forces within the patient and makes them work for him. Both methods may result in recovery.

There are some physical ailments or injuries where the conscious effort of the patient will not be sufficient to "straighten things out." On the other hand, it may be medically desirable for the patient to make a certain effort toward this end, such as in the case of muscular spasms or vascular cramps, to name a few such conditions. Under hypnosis, the patient can easily perform the necessary exercise, which he could not undertake while conscious, partially because it would be a painful effort and partially because of fears. Upon bringing the patient out of the hypnotic state and through appropriate suggestion, no residue of pain or discomfort would remain.

Just as described earlier as a method of healing oneself, the blocking of pain from wound or injury to nerve center in the brain can also be accomplished by the hypnotist. In suggesting that pain does not proceed along a certain nerve strand, and that it is in fact wholly blocked from reaching the control center in the brain, the hypnotist automatically shuts off the sensation of pain in the hypnotized patient. Even after the patient comes out of the hypnotic state, pain will not return. But the hypnotist must be careful to parallel these suggestions with constructive suggestions to initiate the recovery or healing of the wound or injury itself. Since pain is frequently necessary to alert the subject to an existing difficulty, eliminating pain is in no way the same as a cure. It should only be undertaken hypnotically when a cure is also being used simultaneously.

Auto-suggestion, on the other hand, is not always easy when the patient is so disturbed by the affliction that the necessary sense of assured authority required to make it work cannot be attained under those circumstances. But if the patient understands what the powers of suggestion can indeed accomplish, that positive conviction and attitude alone will ensure success of the suggestions. With auto-suggestion, the affected part of the body, or condition, is addressed as if it were a separate entity; suggesting that it cease to act in the manner causing pain or illness, it helps to image the affected part, or function, and "seeing" it change before your "inner eye," so to speak. This method works particularly well with nervous and emotional problems, which in turn would have triggered physical disturbances purely psychosomatic in nature. Headaches, tension syndromes, vertigo, tiredness, panic: these are some of the problems the mind can often successfully relieve where otherwise a chemical agent would have been resorted to.

Auto-suggestion is particularly helpful when sleeplessness is the problem. Sleep is not only a vital necessity to "recharge your batteries," but it is actually the "other half" of your existence: you are either awake or asleep. Sleep and dreams go hand-in-hand, and since the bonds of consciousness are loosened in the sleep state, certain experiences are possible which cannot occur when you are fully awake. Symbolic dreams, valuable in psychoanalysis, and even prophetic dreams, implying the presence of extrasensory perception abilities, are among the most important experiences we can have. Experiments conducted by the Dream Laboratory of Maimonides Hospital in Brooklyn, New York, under Stanley Krippner, M.D., have shown that people go through various patterns of REM, or rapid eye movement, while asleep (or adream, as I prefer to term it). It follows that experiences encountered in the dream/sleep state are of a separate but very solid reality, and are not to be dismissed as mere "smokepuffs," as our ancestors would have it. Because the conscious mind is temporarily turned off, the unconscious portion of our mind is able to unfold freely. While the conscious mind obeys logic and rationalization, the unconscious is not burdened by such restrictions and can freely travel beyond space and time, even in total circumvention of the laws ordinarily governing these dimensions. Sometimes, the resulting experiences seem confused, even silly, but on occasion they are revealing: problems not solved while awake, find solutions, and insight into conflicts, even foreknowledge of future events, is possible on awakening. One of the most common sleeping "problems" affecting people in this "age of anxiety" is the inability to fall asleep and sleep soundly the required hours. An entire arsenal of sleep-inducing drugs is available to the insomniac; some by prescription only, because the physician knows only too well that these drugs are habit forming and ultimately dangerous to the sleeper.

A far safer (and cheaper) way to control sleeping habits is within the grasp of every person. Assuming that you want to doze off at 10 P.M., start preparing your self a half hour before by visualizing (in your mind) an alarm clock with the hands set to 10 P.M. Then change your train of thought at once. This is very important. Don't dwell on the sleep command. Five minutes before 10 P.M., say to yourself (aloud if you wish), "Wouldn't it be nice to fall asleep at 10 P.M.," and again visualize the clock set to that hour. Again, change your train of thought. Promptly at 10 P.M., no matter what you are doing, whether reading a book or just resting, you will begin to doze off. If it does not work at first, set a new time half an hour later, and repeat the process. Only this time insert another thought: "It doesn't really matter, if I fall asleep or not, there's no danger at all if I don't, but I might as well," and again change the direction of your thoughts. And this time, prepare to be in Morpheus' arms.

Religious Healing

The basic difference between religious healing and psychic healing and other forms of unorthodox healing is the insistence on the part of those who do the healing, and usually also on the part of those who are healed, that the power comes directly from God or at any rate from divine sources, and that both healer and recipient of the healing are merely instruments of that divine power.

For religious healing to occur, a religious attitude on the part of both healer and patient is essential. While it is true that many psychic healers, who use the life forces within themselves to heal, are also religious people and never fail to emphasize that they would be nothing if it were not for the power of God to heal through them, they also admit that the power itself comes from or through their physical organisms and minds. Since such healers also consider their personalities, both physical and spiritual, part of the Godhead and ruled by it, they are in a way indirectly committed to a form of religious healing. But the true religious healing requires no intermediary gifted with extraordinary powers. Anyone may be chosen by the deity to perform the seeming miracles. Sometimes the deity heals the afflicted person directly, without even the intermediate role of a channel or healer. Sometimes, as in the case of Lourdes and other sacred shrines, certain environments are necessary to effect a cure.

Religious healing is not necessarily Christian in origin; the Jewish religion accepts divine healings, as do most other world religions. But Christianity, with its emphasis on the Holy Trinity and, at least in the Roman Catholic version, on certain elements of mysticism, is particularly well suited for divine healing. In every religion, however, the religious healer leaves the matter of whether or not a patient is to be cured up to God. Thus the healing becomes a matter of *arbitrary choice* on the part of God. With religious healing, the patient is encouraged to apply for help and to direct his request either to God or to one of His intermediaries, a saint or holy man. There is no guarantee that the prayer will be answered in the affirmative. Whereas the psychic healer stands on his record of past healings and accepts his gift on a scientific basis as well as a matter of faith, the religious healer merely voices the patient's request, leaving the execution of the request to the higher power.

It is obvious that the acceptance of the existence of such a higher power—God, the deity, on the universal law—is necessary on the part of both healer and patient. It is difficult to explain the successful cases of religious healings on any other basis, and if I offer suggestions as to the methods followed by various forms of religious healings, I do so not in order to deny the divine origin of the entire process but merely to point out how divine power manifests itself; for even the will of God, in order to be effective on a physical level, must perform certain physical or mechanical functions. Nor, of course, do I wish to suggest that a scientific explanation in any way eliminates the need for a spiritual or religious cause. Dividing the art of healing into "medical science" and "religious intervention," as happens today all too often, is by no means a desirable state of being. "Division leads not to progress but to confusion. The fruits of division are dissension, intolerance and waste," writes the celebrated American philosopher Manly P. Hall, in his marvelous work, *Healing: The Divine Art.*

*   *   *

Having discussed the necessary attitudes one must bring to bear if one is to understand religious healing, let us now look at some case histories.

Probably the best-known of all religious healing centers is the Roman Catholic shrine at Lourdes, in the south of France, close to the Spanish border.

In 1858, a fourteen-year-old girl named Bernadette Soubirous, her sister Toinette, and a friend, Jeanne, went into the woods to look for things of value, such as old bones or rags that they could sell for pennies. At a grotto near the Gave de Pau, a tributary river of the Pau, Bernadette saw an apparition.

"I saw a lady dressed in white," she recounted. "She was wearing a white dress and a blue sash and a yellow rose on each foot the color of the chain of her rosary."

Thus the story of Lourdes began. The details are common knowledge, having been written about endlessly and even filmed, so suffice it to say that after the twelfth apparition of the "Lady of Lourdes," on March 1, 1858, a woman named Catherine Latapie bathed her injured hand in the spring discovered by Bernadette and recovered the use of two fingers that had been paralyzed before.

This was the first recorded cure at the shrine. The following day, when Bernadette returned to the grotto, there were, according to police figures, 1,650 observers with her. This time the message was to tell the priest that people should come to the grotto in procession and to have a chapel built there. By the time of the fifteenth apparition, on March 4, 1858, Bernadette had become somewhat of a local celebrity and people sought her out even after she had left the grotto. Evidently the healing power traveled along with Bernadette even when she had left the grotto. A blind girl named Eugenie Troy was kissed by Bernadette on her way from the grotto and was restored to sight.

As the apparition appeared to Bernadette on further occasions, controversy continued to rage, with the authorities generally tending to be critical of Bernadette's story. But while the debate continued, an event of great importance for the future of Lourdes transpired. The two-year-old heir to the French throne, Prince Eugène Napoléon, suffered a sun stroke at nearby Biarritz. The Imperial governess decided to seek supernatural support for the boy's recovery at Lourdes. By that time the grotto had been barricaded and declared off-limits to all, in order to play down the importance of the shrine. But after meeting Bernadette and being instructed where to look for the Lady, the governess went to the grotto in the company of her two daughters and a nun to get some of the miraculous water of the spring and take it back to the Imperial prince. Sprinkled with the water, the boy recovered almost instantly. As a result, Napoleon III ordered the barricades at Lourdes removed and opened the gates wide for the subsequent cult centering around the miraculous shrine.

It would take pages even to list the many cures effected at Lourdes between 1858 and the present time. When the grotto became an accepted institution even by the generally anticlerical government of France, and when the treatments were carefully supervised by the medical profession, thousands upon thousands of people came to Lourdes and many went away cured. Controls have since been tightened and cures of purely nervous diseases declared inadmissible as evidence of the water's healing power.

In recent years an average of ten so-called miracles have occurred each year. But the number is misleading, since many other healings, less spectacular than those accorded the extraordinary position of a so-called miracle, may also have occurred at Lourdes. In any case, there are miracles enough to demonstrate religious healing. Dr. Alexis Carrell, for example, the man who created the "artificial heart," observed how a cancer dried up before his very eyes and fell off the patient's hand in a matter of moments.

Moreover, the miraculous healings at Lourdes are by no means a matter of the past. In August 1972, a case involving a six-year-old girl from Glasgow, Scotland, Frances Burns, made headlines. The little girl had been suffering from cancer for three years, and had been given up by English specialists. As a last resort, she was brought to the shrine at Lourdes. On her return the doctors declared her cured of the malignancies.

On August 6, 1967, I met a lady in Paris who had herself demonstrated dramatically what a healing at Lourdes can be like. On June 30, 1936, Madame M. Etienne, of Paris, was alone in her apartment when in a cooking accident a large portion of her body was burned. For a year she stayed at the hospital Bechat. During that time she received forty-three separate skin grafts. Despite the skin grafts there was doubt that her legs could be saved, since most of the burns were in that area. In particular, her right leg seemed to be beyond salvation. But she refused to agree to the amputation, hoping against all odds that she could have her right leg. As she was lying in her bed, unsure of her hopes for a future, a Catholic woman suggested she get on the "White Train" to Lourdes—since, as she put it, "in her situation she might as well."

When Mme. Etienne arrived at Lourdes she was placed in the hospital on the ground floor of the establishment situated inside the grotto. There she was to stay for four days, after which she would return home whether or not a cure had been effected. On the last day she was particularly depressed, wondering what would now become of her. The doctors had carefully examined her and ordered cold compresses put upon her, standard treatment for third-degree burns. Other than that, no remedies were given her. At the morning Mass on the day of her scheduled return to Paris, Mme. Etienne prayed in silence, asking God to make her well again. It was almost a challenge. Then, as she was being given communion, she noticed something very strange going on within her. Suddenly she felt rather well. But she didn't say anything to the officiating priest or anyone at the hospital. Routinely she was brought back to her bed after taking communion and instructed to lie quite still. She was dressed, for shortly afterward she would be taken to the train on a stretcher, to go back to Paris. To the attendant's amazement, however, she asked for her slippers and proceeded to put them on her feet, ready to walk on her own, something she had not been able to do for more than a year. The walk from her bed to the train would take somewhere between five and six minutes. As she crossed the outer office of the hospital—on the arm of the attendant, to be sure—she was stopped by the hospital staff, who insisted on having her examined. But there was not enough time for that, and Mme. Etienne insisted on being taken to the train. She slept most of the journey home, taking a taxi at the railroad station and returning to her own apartment without any difficulty whatsoever. Afterward her doctor confirmed that she was completely cured, her skin perfect and only a few marks to show where she was burned.

"Was the healing instantaneous?" I asked her.

Mme. Etienne nodded emphatically. "Immediate. The priest was raising the host, and I was thinking how cold I was, when all of a sudden I felt this gentle warmth go through me."

A few years later she contracted an infection on her leg, leading to an ulcer. When the doctors saw it, they cautioned her as to the possible seriousness of the infection, in view of the fact that it had occurred in the same area where her burn had been. To everyone's amazement, however, the ulceration healed quickly, leaving no further difficulty behind. It was as if the entire area had been covered with some invisible, very special protective shield. When she returned for another examination a year after her cure, and submitted to the thirty-two doctors comprising the medical establishment at Lourdes, one of the doctors told her, "What a pity you didn't see us before you left, so that we could have certified a miraculous cure in your case." Since then Mme. Etienne has gone back to Lourdes in gratitude, every year, just so she can stand in the grotto and tell God how glad she is He listened to her.

*   *   *

Though perhaps the most famous, Lourdes is not, of course, the only place where religiously inspired miraculous healings take place. St. Anne de Beaupré in Canada; Knocke, called the Irish Lourdes; the shrine of the Madonna of Guadalupe of Mexico; and many lesser known holy spots throughout the world claim to heal the sick miraculously. Then there are the singular miracles, the ones attached to holy persons that, by Catholic law, are elevated to the position of saint.

Thus in June, 1968, a Papal Court considering sainthood for the late Pope John XXIII heard the amazing case of Sister Caterina Capitani of the Sisters of Charity of Naples, who claimed to have recovered from a critical illness after Pope John had appeared to her on May 25, 1966, in a vision, dressed in a white tunic and saying, "Don't despair, my child. You will be healed."

A little Belgian boy named Herman Wejns, who died in May 1941, worked as a miracle worker for five of his ten years. Despite his young age, he spoke like an adult and, being a devout Catholic, frequently helped the people of his village in times of distress, especially during the German occupation. After his death many were healed in his name—people who would go to Herman's grave in the cemetery, pray, and await a miracle.

Rabbi Solomon Friedlander of 2176 Grand Concourse, Bronx, New York, is a healer of some renown. He is the eleventh generation of a family of Hasidic rabbis, belonging to an ancient sect that believes in possession and other forms of psychic phenomena. The number of those who have been healed by the "miracle rabbi" include one Harry Kalinsky, who suffered a skull fracture in 1955. Although his physicians thought he would not last the night, he survived after intercession by the rabbi, whom his mother had telephoned for absent healing. The rabbi asked for the patient's name and a photograph and predicted full recovery. Two months later the patient walked out of the hospital, completely recovered.

Cecile Diamond, fourteen, suffered from inflammation of the brain and according to physicians had only one chance in a hundred of survival. The rabbi saw her in the hospital and placed an amulet in her hand, praying for her. The child felt better the following day and left the hospital cured.

Healing runs through almost every religion. The Church of Ireland, a Protestant denomination, speaks of the church's ministry of healing in its pamphlets; in the United States, the revivalist ministry of David Nunn of Dallas, Texas, calls its publication the *Healing Messenger*. These people try to heal both spirit and body at the same time but expect religious loyalty in return. At Lourdes and other shrines no one cares whether the patient is a believer or an atheist. Nor are there ever any charges for services rendered.

If one would consider an alternate explanation for what happens at Lourdes and other shrines, one would have to come up with something truly tangible; for the argument for divine intercession is indeed formidable. The fact, however, is that no tangible explanation has been offered. On the other hand, if we accept the possibility of psychic healing in a religious setting, all sorts of interesting theories suggest themselves. For example, no one, to my knowledge, has pointed out the amazing similarity between the grotto, enclosed as it is on three sides, and the spiritualist's cabinet in which manifestations take place under controlled conditions. Could it be that the grotto has a similar effect on the patients, and that the healing power is really the psychic power brought down to the sick by various spirit forces detailed to heal and help them? In some cases perhaps the life force in the patient himself joins up with the force being sent down to him to make the healing possible. Instantaneous psychic healing is not uncommon, as the process involves a "burning out of diseased areas of the aura," and replacing those areas with fresh power particles from the healthy portion of the aura.

There is no doubt in my mind that an extraordinary process occurs at Lourdes when healings take place, but not necessarily a supernatural one. Whether the vision seen by Bernadette was indeed the actual Mother of Jesus Christ or some other spirit is not even important. I do not doubt that Bernadette saw a vision as described; what it was at this point can be merely speculation. What is hard fact, however, is that many desperately ill people, unable to find help through orthodox medical sources, were cured and are being cured at Lourdes.

Individual religious healers are of course legion; many of them simply believe that their faith can not only move mountains but also remove physical illnesses from those who come to them for help. Yet if honest prayer alone could heal people, then everyone praying honestly would be a healer, but that is simply not so. Consequently something other than the religious prayer, something beyond the healer's own faith, must be at work when such unorthodox healings occur. Quite likely a combination of personality factors, peculiar abilities on the part of the healer involving a strong life force in his body, strong emotional cooperation from the patient, and ultimately the bond of combined prayers that do not only invoke the deity to help but also evoke the powers within the healer to get into action.

Garrie Taylor, nearly seventy, is by profession a real estate salesman, by avocation a free-lance missionary in the field of spiritual healing and a professional dowser. In his area of Pennsylvania, the town of Zelienople, he is renowned for his accurate dowsing ability as to water, oil deposits, and maps.

Taylor did not realize he had psychic healing power until he reached the age of fifty. Then he suddenly became interested and read all he could put his hands on. In 1957 a friend brought a young man in terrible pain to Taylor because no doctor or dentist could apparently discover the cause of his pains. The patient was a welder by profession. The pain was in his mouth, but X-rays taken that same morning showed nothing amiss. Taylor took the young man to a quiet room and started to pray for him. When Taylor had asked the Holy Spirit to descend upon everyone present, the young man walked out of the room and lay down on a sofa in the living room. Taylor was then impressed to pass his hand over the man's face. As he did so, he felt a great surge of heat coming from the face. Immediately, the young man felt that Taylor had accurately pointed out the area of his troubles and went back to his dentist, who took another set of X-rays and discovered that, in the short time since the earlier dental consultation, an abscess had formed in the roof of the man's mouth. The dentist was now able to treat the matter, and two days later the young man was well.

"I practice spiritual healing without touching the person," Taylor explains in his quaint Pennsylvania Dutch way. "I believe in Father, Son, and Holy Spirit and that Jesus is my personal savior and that eternity is always now and that God is the center of everything everywhere at one and the same time and that I am part of God."

On one occasion he had agreed that he would pray for a friend living in Missouri and that the friend would tune in on Mr. Taylor's prayer at a certain time of the day. Taylor kept his part of the bargain, but at the appointed hour the man's cows got loose and he had to try to get them back into the stables, thus being unable to sit quietly and tune in on the healer. Suddenly the man felt himself filled with the power of divine healing and was instantly cured of his condition, even though he had not tuned in on Mr. Taylor.

"When I pray for the sick our Lord shows me in my own body where the affliction is; I then relinquish the ailment of the person to God and then I relinquish the area in my own body to God," Taylor says. "I see everyone as perfect pure spirit."

Another case involving Taylor was that of a doctor who himself was ailing. The doctor's disease, phlebitis, had prevented him from lying down to sleep for a long time. Unable to walk, he spent most of his time in a large chair. Although the doctor had not called upon Taylor's services, the healer, who was a school chum, decided to pay him a surprise visit anyway since he had not seen him for many years. The patient was not exactly happy to see the healer, because he was not a believer in that sort of thing and knew only too well what Taylor was up to. But Taylor, remaining polite, eventually was asked to come in. Taylor asked the doctor's permission to pray for him, which the man answered by reminding him that he was going down to hell anyway, but to go ahead and try. Earnestly, Taylor began to pray, "I am perfect pure spirit. There can be no congestion in body, mind, or soul, where there is only peace; or where there is only tranquility, serenity, peace." He then asked the Holy Spirit to descend upon them all and heal the man in front of him.

Something happened to the nonbelieving doctor, for he began to cry, explaining that this was the first time he had been without pain in nine years. That night he was able to lie down to sleep in the normal way. The next morning the doctor was able to get into his car and drive for nineteen hours straight to St. Louis to his mother-in-law, also sick, in order to bring her back and have her treated by Garrie Taylor. Taylor obliged carefully and relieved her of whatever her trouble was.

Taylor passes his hands over the afflicted areas and prays at the same time. A neighbor who had an accident in his garage, cutting off a thumb and sawing through some of his fingers of his hand with a power saw, had been in a veteran's hospital for four months, but the pain was still unbearable. Taylor passed his hands over the man briefly and then walked out. He did not see the man again for four months, but when he did the patient no longer wore his arm in a sling. When Taylor inquired how he was, he explained that the pain had now gone into his little finger but that he was otherwise fine. Taylor gave him another treatment, and when he checked him out half a year later, the man was well and able to use his hands as if nothing had happened.

Maurice Olinkiewicz operated a light factory in a loft on lower Broadway in one of the oldest parts of Manhattan. He emigrated from Poland in 1913 when he was ten years old. For more than fifty-five years he has lived and worked in lower Manhattan, and during all those years he has had many psychic experiences, from premonitions to visions of the dead to being visited by the ghosts of those who lived at one time where his factory now stands. None of these things faze him. He accepts them as perfectly natural, but he has learned to keep his mouth shut about them, unless he talks to someone who understands such things.

Many years ago something happened to change his outlook on life completely. Olinkiewicz thinks that God wanted to show him that he need not be afraid of anything and therefore sent these strange experiences to him. Having had his encounters with ghosts and visions, he decided that God wanted him to help people through his psychic powers. Being devoutly Roman Catholic, however, he could see these powers only as part of prayer.

"I pray for people to get well. There was a black woman of about thirty-seven years of age who lived across the street in that hotel over there," he told me once, pointing through the window. "She would come out of the hotel day after day and start to hit her fists against a lamp post. She was a mental case." One Saturday afternoon she stood in the center of the road, trying to direct traffic. The healer saw this from his window and realized that she might get killed at any moment. He started to pray for her: "Please, Lord, make this woman calm." A moment later something came over the woman; she walked out of the road, quietly, and back to her hotel. The following morning she came out again as she had done so many times before; only this time she was quiet and dignified. Olinkiewicz inquired at the hotel about what had happened to the woman when he failed to see her sometime after and was told that she had gone home to her people since she felt well again. Olinkiewicz likes to look out the windows of his second-story factory and watch the traffic below.

A week after the original incident with the black woman he noticed a man with a brand new crutch having difficulties trying to cross Broadway. Olinkiewicz began to pray for him, asking God to make the man walk without crutches. As the healer watched, the man walked another block to Mercer Street, then, suddenly, took his crutch and threw it into the gutter.

So many people got well as a result of Olinkiewicz's prayers that he began to wonder whether he had some special gift. As yet he was not ready to accept this, being extremely modest and simple. Further proof came as a result of a visit by a real estate man, Joseph Medynski, of Ramsey, New Jersey, who had heard of Olinkiewicz's abilities as a healer. Medynski went to see Olinkiewicz at his factory in September 1971, to ask the healer for help with his wife, who suffered with cancer of the lungs. A medical specialist from England had recently given her no more than three months to live.

Olinkiewicz promised to pray for her every day. He did not see the man from New Jersey again until two weeks after Christmas 1971. When he saw him come up the stairs, he feared the wife had died despite his efforts. "I have big news for you," Mr. Medynski said cheerfully. "A week before Christmas I received a call from the hospital to come right on over. I feared the worst, but when I got to my wife's room, she was sitting up." He questioned his wife's doctor and learned that he could take his wife home now. The reason? On examination it was discovered that the cancer had disappeared. Medynski offered Olinkiewicz money, but the healer refused to take any. He never takes anything for his efforts.

Perhaps the most dramatic case of instantaneous healing occurred at a most unlikely time and place. In April 1971, Olinkiewicz was riding the subway when he noticed a young girl sitting across from him who was evidently blind. With her was her seeing-eye dog. When Olinkiewicz realized that the girl was blind, he started to pray for her, so that she would see. Although the healer prayed in silence, a man sitting next to the blind girl looked straight at him and smiled as if he were tuned in on Olinkiewicz's silent thoughts. Suddenly the dog jumped up as if someone had stepped on his tail. But Olinkiewicz continued to pray for the blind girl to see. After three minutes of this, the blind girl started to look in his direction. Little by little her eyes opened up and she started to see. Amazed, she looked at her hand, and then at her dog and then turned around looking at the passengers.

When the train stopped, she started to get off, at first following her seeing-eye dog in the direction he was trained to take her. But seeing the crowds going in the opposite direction, she insisted on following the crowds. Soon she disappeared among the people leaving the station. Olinkiewicz never talked to the girl. The girl never talked to the healer. Yet he was able to help her see.

Olinkiewicz was looking out the window of his house into his little backyard one night not long ago when he noticed a lily he had grown blinking on and off like a light. It was around 11:30 P.M., and the yard was lit only by the moon. As he kept staring at the lily and its strange behavior in amazement, he saw the figure of what to him appeared a saint of some sort on top of the tree, with hands outstretched toward him. He pointed it out to his wife, but she could not see the vision. On another occasion Olinkiewicz had seen a cross in a circle in the sky, a blue light that signified healing to him. He has looked out the window into the sky and seen the Northern Star, surrounded by many other stars blinking on and off.

Eventually so many people came to Olinkiewicz for help that he had to organize his healing activities in some fashion. He composed a letter in which he promised to pray for the afflicted provided the patient would also pray and believe in God. Nowhere is there any mention of money or even free-will offerings. Olinkiewicz is truly

God's man. "I accept requests for prayers regardless of religion, nationality, or race. We are all God's creation, so don't hesitate to write to me," he adds, giving his factory address, 681 Broadway, New York, New York 10012.

Mrs. L. C. is in her late thirties, divorced, and works as a nurse in a general hospital in the Midwest. She has had many psychic dreams that later proved to be significant. Since she is a religious person, she believes in the power of prayer to heal people. On one occasion, she decided to pray for the recovery of a particularly ill patient in the hospital. This woman had been unconscious for three weeks due to deterioration of the brain, and the doctors had given her up.

On the night of June 20, 1968, as she was praying for her patient, Mrs. L. C. suddenly felt a deep heat, a very warm feeling going over her body, and she fell into a kind of trance. In this state she saw Jesus Christ, surrounded by a glistening bright light, touch the body of her woman patient in the hospital. At that instant she was released from her trance and quite herself again. The next morning, prior to her going to work at the hospital, she told her family what had transpired during the night. To her disappointment the woman patient did not seem any different that morning, nor the following day. But on the third day after Mrs. C. had seen Jesus Christ touch the woman's body in her vision, the woman woke up and rose from her bed. Later she told the nurse that on that particular night when Mrs. C. had prayed for her—of course unknown to her—she had felt deep heat go through her body.

Kathryn Kuhlman was a slight, gentle woman whose appearance belied her fervor on the platform. Thousands say they have been cured in her meetings, and thousands more always awaited her appearance in their areas with great eagerness. Mrs. Kuhlman herself disclaimed any healing powers whatever, always putting it down as the work of God and taking no credit for the cures. But this is often merely a way of shifting the burden of proof. All evangelists do this, and despite the healings effected during her services, Kathryn Kuhlman was more of a religious preacher than a true faith healer. Even more so is the famed Billy Graham, whose healings are never anything but spiritual and very denominational. Evangelists like to invoke Jesus and let "Him" do the work; more esoterically minded healers would refer to God rather than to Jesus.

It is a moot point whether anyone gets healed at an evangelist's meeting through the power of God, singling him out for a healing, by the prayer and personal power of the evangelist, or by the energy reservoir of a feverish mass audience, or all three together.

Undoubtedly, there are cases of mass hysteria and individual "hysterical hypnosis" induced by a combination of religious fervor and verbal stimulation. In the end, the majority of such cases draw largely upon hidden power reservoirs of the patients themselves, opened up through the devices of religious healing.

It seems to me that the available energies from a religiously oriented crowd, working in unison as it were, would furnish the energies to burn out diseased areas of a person's aura and allow healthy aura particles to flow in and straighten out the etheric body. Whether this effect is achieved by intellectual means, by experimental means, or by the invocation of divine powers is really beside the point. The fact remains, however, that religious healing works often enough to make it a responsible form of unorthodox healing.

Even today in the 1990s, faith healing is as prevalent as ever. Whether the preacher officiating is able to invoke divine powers directly, or whether his fervor stimulates the existing inner powers of the patients to heal themselves, is a moot point; if it shows real results, so be it, regardless of origin.

Unfortunately, greed does not halt before religious pretense. A number of popular faith healers have not only not cured anyone, but have been shown to be fraudulent manipulators bent only on fleecing the gullible faithful.

Gurus in colorful garb from India are being worshiped like saints, given money, fancy cars, and being listened to when they decree that their followers must not do this or that—such as engage in sex or eat meat—or that they must observe the rituals and so-called prayer services of that particular sect or guru. None of this has the slightest connection with true spirituality, but people tend to want to belong to groups of equal outlook, and some find in this discipline a degree of comfort.

True spiritual healing requires no intermediary but works only if the person addresses himself or herself directly to the godhead. Whatever one's religious beliefs or community, there *is* help to be had in this fashion, and rarely in the other one.

Metaphysical Healing

Prior to the popularity of the term "New Age," the philosophies and techniques of metaphysical healing were referred to as the "occult sciences," even though they are not sciences by conventional standards, and the term occult does not cover all of them. I use the term *metaphysical* to describe these methods because they go beyond the physical approach to healing. Either way, however, we are dealing with a truly mixed-bag of the very good and truly effective, and much that is neither helpful nor damaging, and some that is pure bunk and self-serving. Purely commercial-minded entrepreneurs with neither proper training nor proper intentions head expositions and seminars and offer a variety of "health activists," leaving it to the public to take its chances. In each case, there are some truly worthwhile practitioners involved, and a lot that sounds, at best, vague. So it is indeed the buyer who must beware. Having said this, I do recommend the examination of many of these catch-all expositions and weekend happenings, because some may very well be helpful to the seeker.

For instance, the Whole Life Expo Workshops held twice yearly in New York and Los Angeles, have always had a sprinkling of well-known lecturers or practitioners among what appears to me well-meaning unknowns. Another entrepreneurial event is the New Life Expo which offers such things as free spinal exams, free samples of holistic remedies, a free music concert, alternative medicine, environmental discoveries, and psychic phenomena. Among participants of repute are nutritionist Gary Null, author and health authority Deepak Chopra, and perennial flower child Timothy Leary. The new Life Expo is run by Mark Becker strictly as a business, though he does offer new avenues to personal health, and does not claim any kind of critical appraisal or evaluation. Becker also publishes *New Life Magazine* at 40 West 72nd Street, New York, New York 10023.

The concept of psychic and unorthodox healing has always been part and parcel of all occult teachings, no matter what specific philosophy was involved, whether Western or Eastern in origin. No esoteric concept is imaginable unless the healing of body, mind, and spirit is also involved. The separation of material and spiritual things, or of body versus mind as it is practiced in Western thought and orthodox medicine, is totally alien to the occult sciences, which view man as a whole, the components of which are inseparable and indivisible.

Wrongful thoughts create illnesses, and thought processes reverse the conditions. Such matters are entirely in the hands of the sufferer—no one is forced to think wrongfully, and once the mistakes are realized, a person is capable of reversing the trend.

There is no superior power in operation to prevent one from seeing the light and doing something about one's condition. The act of acquiring knowledge, of looking into a problem of health, of initiating a process of healing, is a voluntary act on the part of the patient. The results of this act are not necessarily guaranteed: he may or may not succeed in locating a proper healer, and the healer may or may not succeed in helping the condition. In the case of self-healing, the sufferer may or may not succeed in his efforts, even if he applies himself thoroughly and according to the proper techniques. According to the law of karma, free will is that which we exercise upon our own judgment, whether motivated by emotional or logical factors. What we accomplish by our own decision will of course affect the final outcome—in various ways, depending upon the abilities and powers of the individual to carry out a determined course. But the condition requiring some action on our part is not entirely of our own making. According to the philosophy of reincarnation, of which the law of karma is a part, conditions are in existence independent of us. We move toward them or become involved with them in order to react to them, rather than the other way around. According to this widely held belief, illness may result from wrongful thinking, or from a variety of causes as in accidents, but the causative factors were brought together by the law of karma, which required such a condition to exist at that point in our lives.

Generally unaware of this influence around us, we then proceed to deal with the situation as it arises and in the best way we know. Thus we control the *outcome* to a large degree; we do not control the *incident*, which is determined by a superior law and order.

We may ask ourselves, why do some people become ill in certain ways, while others living under similar circumstances do not. To say simply that wrongful thinking in this particular case has caused disease is not sufficient. Why did such and such an individual think wrongfully, thus causing disease? Why was he not led to sources of information that would have prevented his wrongful thinking while someone else, under similar circumstances, was helped to find the information that would prevent his having wrongful thoughts? What determines the fate of the individual, the destiny that begins and ends with the state of health?

According to the philosophy of reincarnation, widely accepted in the Eastern part of our globe and among many esoteric people in the West as well, one's previous incarnation and what one accomplished during it determines progress in the current one. One works out through ill health what one committed in a previous lifetime. For example, crippled individuals or those with birth defects are believed to have been culprits of one kind or another in another lifetime, causing others to become crippled or injured in similar, though not necessarily identical, ways.

This belief postulates a law of retribution in which the wrongs of one lifetime must be worked out by the right doings of another. The problem is that the average person is not aware of his previous lifetimes and thus has no way of focusing his actions in such a way that he can undo the wrong of a previous incarnation *consciously*. He must do so purely out of his own initiative, intuitively. By doing something correctly in the current incarnation, without knowing why one does so, the individual cancels out an ancient debt.

On those rare occasions when people have snatches of memory of previous lives, they are permitted this "bonus" because a previous lifetime had been cut short or been tragic in some other way. To the extent of these bits and pieces of information they are able to check back upon earlier incarnations and learn, perhaps even profit, from such memories. But unless these individuals work with a reputable hypnotist to regress them and dredge up from their unconscious the deeply embedded memories of past lives, they will be unable to make much practical use of that information. By and large, people do not recall previous lives, and those purporting to supply "life readings," going into great detail over dozens of former lives, are perhaps only dealing in hopes, if not outright fantasies.

Genuine reincarnation memories are of the kind that contain names, places, and details that are capable of verification in historical records. Fantasy reports on previous lives frequently include fanciful countries, nonexistent names, or conditions that cannot be properly checked out. This is not to say that some of these life readings do not contain true information as well, but one must use extreme caution in accepting material from earlier incarnations, especially if one tends to base one's present activities upon them.

In accepting karmic causes for specific diseases, we are not necessarily forced to live with them as incurable or unalterable. The fact that the disease exists in this incarnation only means that something caused it to be in a past lifetime: what we do about it in this life is our own concern, and we are quite free to do everything within our power to relieve the condition.

Simply by having the condition in the first place, karmic law has been satisfied. Once that is so, an individual may use esoteric or orthodox methods to rid himself of the condition without affecting karmic law in the least; for it is no person's destiny to suffer with or without cause. To suffer with cause is unnecessary if one recognizes the cause and does something about it, and to suffer without cause, when there is no recognizable reason for it, is even less acceptable, for in such cases the absence of any notion of guilt makes the healing effort so much more plausible.

Psychic healing, of course, is in itself part of the occult sciences; the majority of mediums, whether professional or amateur, have some healing gift and are able to perform healings—largely because the force that makes healings possible is the same force that makes psychic phenomena in general possible. It may be utilized to make communications between the so-called dead and the living available to those seeking them, or it may be used in one of several ways as the driving power behind physical phenomena, clairvoyance, psychometry, and the entire range of ESP phenomena. The choice is the user's.

Although astrology is not strictly part of the occult sciences, it is frequently considered an allied art and those interested in psychic phenomena are nearly always also interested in astrology. Basically, however, astrology relies on mathematical considerations, on conclusions drawn from certain positions in the heavens and on earth, rather than on any intuitive, emotional processes. However, astrology has long held that certain planets "rule" or influence and dominate certain parts of the human body and mind, and if we accept the validity of astrology on the basis that it represents cosmic radiation primarily from the nearby planets, the sun, and our moon, then this concept does acquire scientific validity. Cosmic radiation bombards our earth at all times, is measurable, and can be evaluated as to possible results. Some cosmic radiation is definitely harmful whether of natural or man-made origin. Other radiation is beneficial, and astrology has pinpointed these effects and placed them in the appropriate relationship to the human personality.*

*Those who wish to acquaint themselves with exact data for each and every part of the body according to the twelve zodiac signs will find profuse and detailed information in such works as Carroll Righter's *Your Astrological Guide to Health and Diet*. Sybil Leek also has written extensively on the relationship between health and astrology.

Basically, there are two relationships to consider when one deals with the astrological impact upon one's health. First, the astrological chart of the individual at the time of *birth* reflects the strength and weakness of the individual, the areas in which he or she *may* expect trouble, and the areas in which he may not. Certain planets "rule" certain parts of the body; thus the parts of the body so ruled will be strongly affected when these planets are in certain positions. If the positions are in a "friendly position" to the rest of the person's horoscope, then beneficial results will prevail and that part of the body will feel fine. Conversely, if the planets are badly related, illness in those areas is possible, though not necessarily inevitable. (Nothing in astrology is ever inevitable—especially if the person, by being forewarned, looks out for potential difficulties and tries to avoid them.)

Second, the "aspects," or relationships between individual planets, the sun, and the moon *at certain times* in the current life of the person involved, also have a lot to do with the state of health at that time. While the natal chart—the horoscope at the time of birth—reflects permanent and basic conditions in the organism, the temporal configurations in the heavens relate to the state of health at specific times in the life of the individual.

No one should follow the advice of a brief newspaper column on what to do on a certain day, as such material is neither scientific nor accurate. But careful scrutiny of an individual chart drawn by a competent astrologer for the person involved will disclose certain trends existing at certain times. One should study these conditions and then make one's decisions as to what one might do under those "transits" and what not. A calm, rational approach to astrological data can be utilized to preserve one's good health and prevent accidents.

Somewhat on the fringes of the occult sciences are the various forms of yoga. These teachings of Indian and Tibetan philosophers are very ancient and very basic. Hatha yoga, dealing with the physical body, is particularly valuable to those living a life according to esoteric concepts. Hatha yoga should take the place of ordinary calisthenics or gymnastics. The principal difference between this yoga and all other forms of exercise is simply expressed. In ordinary

exercise, body parts—muscles, limbs, and breathing apparatus—
are used rapidly or consecutively in order to test their abilities. Doing
twenty push-ups in the morning leaves one exhausted. Running as fast
as one is able is equally ill advised in many cases. Lifting weights
beyond one's capacity may be dangerous. Playing tennis or handball,
if one is not really used to it, causes undue strain on ligaments, wrists,
and ankles and results in fatigue rather than in a strengthening of the
bodily apparatus.

In yoga, on the other hand, emphasis is not on performance but
on the holding of certain positions for as long as one is able. By taking
on certain carefully designed positions and staying in those positions
for a few seconds, gradually adding seconds until one accomplishes
the maximum suggested by the teacher, one gives the affected muscle
or limb a chance to expand without also using up precious energy.
The secret of Hatha yoga lies in the calm and deliberate holding of
positions. At the same time emphasis is put on the right frame of mind
accompanying these positions and breathing at a comparable rate is
also very much emphasized. Breath is the essence of life itself: many of
the yoga exercises stress improved breathing techniques because the
oxygen introduced into the lungs materially affects the operation of
the body during the position.

Calisthenics and other forms of gymnastics as well as most
ordinary sports pay no attention to mental or—heaven forbid—
spiritual attitudes during the performances. Yoga, on the other hand,
is effective only if mind and body coordinate their activities completely. By stressing this duality of purpose, yoga recognizes and
utilizes the interaction of the physical and etheric bodies simultaneously and for mutual benefit.

Lastly, certain pagan religions, such as Wicca, stress healing
among their most urgent goals. In Wicca, healing those present in the
circle or those at a distance is accomplished by a community effort
called the raising of the "cone of power." Energy is drawn from the
participants through singing, chanting, and dancing in unison. As the
energy potential becomes higher and higher, and just when it reaches
the zenith of its power, the community is ordered to stop abruptly,
usually dropping to the floor. By this abrupt action, the energy cone is

released and sent forth in a predetermined direction. I have seen this method work repeatedly and know that energies thus produced and sent out to an ailing person can affect the state of health of the individual.

Such practices do in no way involve miracles or even strong belief on the part of the recipient. They are primarily scientifically acceptable transfers of energies raised by a group of human beings for a single purpose. In some ways, this is a form of telepathy, except that thoughts of well-being are transmitted together with raw energy to burn out the diseased parts of the patient's aura.

Most likely some other emotionally tinged religions, such as the Holy Rollers, who work themselves up to fever pitch through religious singing and dancing, accomplish their healings in similar fashion. In either case, it is not necessarily the deity descending personally and touching the sick who performs the healing, but the religious practitioners themselves through the use and channeling of their bodily energies. The deity concept serves primarily as a focal power.

If the seemingly miraculous results are later ascribed to a supernatural agency, in a manner of speaking and indirectly that is correct; for if it were not for the concentration point represented by the deity symbol, the outpouring of energy would not have been accomplished.

Finally, some individuals wonder whether their illness may not be due to *psychic incursions*, that is, a kind of possession by external spirit entities, who bring with them an ailment from their own physical past.

It is perfectly true that mediums, especially the trance variety, take on the passing symptoms of the dead individual speaking through them or the sufferings and memories of illness that occurred in the life of the person using the medium at that moment. But these reenactments serve primarily to identify the individual and to exteriorize past sufferings in this way. After the trance state ends, nothing of the symptoms remains and the medium rarely remembers what went on while in trance.

Ordinary individuals may become hosts to possessing entities in various ways, usually by permitting the contact either consciously or unconsciously, but the health condition of the possessor does not become a major factor unless the takeover is complete—in which case the host personality is in deep trouble all around and needs a good exorcist.

People who are sensitive may enter a place where sickness has been prevalent in the past and feel the "bad vibrations." This is a kind of psychometry, and a change of location usually ends the discomfort. True psychic incursions of the succubi or incubi variety (demons of either sex to the kabbalistically inclined) do not invade healthy, self-possessed individuals.

As long as these methods lead to tangible results, and help people, well and good. Where I draw the line is with a number of self-styled prophets and alleged descendants of space aliens, who call themselves "star-born" and offer hodge-podge philosophies concocted from ancient Egyptian and Babylonian material laced with homegrown nonsense. They usually adopt fanciful and exotic sounding names, and manage to create enough excitement to have a following, docile and all-believing in the supernatural powers of their guru. Naturally, those followers want to contribute to their guru's upkeep, too! Most of these latter-day prophets really believe in what they preach. While by themselves they are not dangerous, the beliefs created in the minds of their adherents can sometimes prevent people from seeking medical or psychiatric help where they might indeed find solutions. While they are usually harmless, the public should be aware of their true nature as cultists, not proven healers.

TEN

What Exactly Is Psychic Healing?

In the 1990s, a lot of what we used to call "New Age" ideas are suddenly coming back again, allowing us to look at them from a more mature point of view. We look at claims of extraordinary healing feats not with a believer's uncritical fervor, but instead with a single question on our mind: Will it work for me?

It is important to keep in mind that even so-called "non-physical" healing is not just wishful thinking. Energy coming from the physical body of the healer is involved, unless the healing is a case of "spirit intervention" where a discarnate friend or relative helps someone in the physical world get well. That, too, has happened and is well documented. But even this kind of intervention is not pure nothingness. The etheric body in which we continue our lives in the next dimension is certainly an energy field as well, even if it differs from the one a healer on the physical plane may deal with.

What we should guard against is to fall into the bottomless pit of metaphysical thinking, the belief system that does not require hard evidence so much as faith and belief. Not that the latter is wrong in providing a positive attitude, so very important to expedite success in any kind of healing. But parapsychology is not metaphysics—we do require reasonable proof.

On one extreme, we have traditional researchers (and doctors) desperately trying to explain seemingly puzzling phenomena by purely physical answers, never for a moment allowing the possibility that the third human element, *the spirit or persona*, might be the causative factor. In late September of 1993, Dr. Richard Jed Wyatt, chief of the neuro-psychiatry branch at the National Institute of Mental Health in Bethesda, Maryland, tells the world that his team have located "a specific local area of the brain active during a cognitive process in a living person with schizophrenia." He is talking about the so-called Broca's area, the speech center in the brain, and its connection with another area, Wernicke's area, which is the hearing center. All this has to do with a new explanation why schizophrenics "hear voices," or, as the *New York Times* writer Daniel Goleman writes late in September, 1993, "hearing voices, the hallmark symptom of schizophrenia" and goes on to state about the latest findings supporting "a leading psychological theory of auditory hallucinations, which proposes that when people with schizophrenia hear voices, they are unable to recognize them as their own thoughts, and so perceive them as words spoken by someone else."

However, years of hard evidence regarding multiple personality and auditory phenomena research undertaken by parapsychology suggests that at least some of the so-called cases of schizophrenia aren't that at all: rather they are genuine cases of possession, where discarnate entities manage to obtain entry into the unconscious of a living person and become entrenched in that person's mind. I myself had several such cases, notably one the late Eileen Garret, President of the Parapsychology Foundation, had sent to me after conventional psychiatrists had failed to dislodge the several entities and voices this young woman was hearing. Through hypnotherapy and other approaches, notably what in parapsychology is called the Rescue Circle, I was able to get rid of the unwanted voices, which had belonged to people who had died and who had somehow found entry into the young woman's mind. She was able to return to her home and lead a normal life.

If some medical people had their way, they would want to commit all mediums—trance or clairvoyant—to institutions for being schizophrenic, which of course they are not. But until medicine acknowledges the existence and importance of the "third" force—the spiritual dimension—it will fail to come to grips with the real causes of multiple personality and "voices," never learning to differentiate between genuine cases of mental illness, and psychic phenomena.

This also holds true with organ transplants. If indeed we are triune in nature, replacing the physical heart in a patient leaves its etheric counterpart out of it. The patient's own, damaged etheric heart (an energy field) remains, and now the healthy new physical heart is implanted within it—the match cannot ever be good. Proof of this is the rather high failure rate of organ transplants.

Also, reports of people changing personality traits after transplants persist. Last year (1993), Richard Hopkins wrote in *The National Examiner* how "used hearts give new owners strange feelings," citing the case of a California truck driver named James McCarthy whose interests switched from football and beer drinking to a sudden infatuation with music and cultural interests after he received the heart of a deceased music teacher.

Psychic healing works because of the triune nature of life. Whereas conventional doctors treat the physical body in the hope of healing it from the outside in, psychic healing takes place on the etheric body first, from the inside out, and as a result, the physical outer body falls in line and is healed.

Next to the warning functions of ESP, probably the most valuable asset is the gift of psychic healing. A person is nothing if not well and healthy, and well-being is the most important of all states whether we are in the flesh or in the nonphysical world.

Psychic healing is as old as mankind itself. It is the treatment of ailments, both physical and mental, by the powers of the spirit, or, at any rate, by forces that have not yet been recognized as being physical in the ordinary sense.

Much of the early psychic healing was done mainly by priests or lay priests, and it was thought necessary to surround the application of such healing with a certain mystery in order to strengthen the patient's belief in it, and thus strengthen his will to get well.

To this very day, it makes a great deal of difference whether a sick person trusts his doctor or not. Faith cannot move mountains perhaps, but it can surely rally the body's own defense mechanisms.

In psychic healing, no medicines of any kind are used, and it is not necessary that the patient be a believer for the cure to work. Certainly faith helps—and also strengthens the resistance to disease—but true psychic healing, which is often instantaneous or very nearly so, does not require such state of mind on the part of the subject. There are several kinds of what in England is often referred to as "unorthodox healing"—as if there were an orthodox death and an unorthodox one—depending on the method used.

Spiritualism, which is essentially a religion—or a cult, if you wish—calls it spiritual healing and claims that God works through the hands of the healer as he touches the body of the patient.

Harry Edwards, who has certainly cured thousands by the mere laying on of hands, falls into this category. Of course, he has had failures, too, but the fact that he has had successes in large numbers is the more remarkable fact. Some traditional physicians like to explain such cures away by speaking of unexpected remissions. But many of the diseases that have been helped by healers like Edwards, the Brazilian miracle healer Arigo, or the latest Philippine psychic surgeons are simply not the kind that would disappear by themselves.

The nonspiritualist healer refers to his craft as psychic healing in that it utilizes some force present in his body to destroy disease in another person's aura and body. The theory behind this is simply that when the healer concentrates his psychic energies in his hands and lightly moves them above the affected area of a sick person's body, he "burns out" the diseased portion of the aura or magnetic field. Healthy energy then rushes in to fill the gap, and the moment the inner body is restored to perfect health, the parallel outer body cannot help but fall in line. The disease clears up almost at once or as fast as the cells can keep pace with the orders from the etheric within.

I know this works, and it works principally among people possessed of great magnetism or power of personality—people whose life force seems very strong, so strong, in fact, that they can spare some of it to heal less fortunate human beings. In a modest sort of way I have been able to heal an aching joint or a headache or two. I merely concentrate my thought energies on the afflicted area and pass very gently over it with my hands, without, however, touching it. If the patient responds properly, he will report a hot sensation in the affected part, far beyond the normal bodily warmth emanating from a hand passing an inch away.

Dr. John Myers, the great photography medium, was also a fine healer. I have seen testimonials from people who had been given up by orthodox doctors only to be rescued at death's door by Myers. The energy streaming from his hands has shrunk tumors and has restored health to a number of people in recent years. Myers reports on this himself in his writings, but the statements from his cured patients speak even louder. He has never charged a penny for his services. Another successful practitioner is the famous London healer Fricker, who runs two clinics around the clock. He has achieved remarkable cures. Fricker is not a spiritualist, but rather religious in his orientation. He feels that God is working directly through him. Be this as it may, he has cured people who were not helped elsewhere.

I have had a session with Fricker for a minor but incurable ear ailment I have had for many years. One session is hardly enough to hope for cure, of course, and Fricker told me so immediately, but I did have an odd sensation when he placed his hands over my ears. It was as though a strong electric current were flowing from them into my head. Great warmth seemed to come from them and I felt relaxed and a bit numb. The ear noises were slightly less loud for a day or two, and then they returned. But something *did* happen, and I am sure that Fricker would eventually have succeeded if I had been available for more sessions.

Many people who are otherwise not in the least interested in ESP or psychic phenomena may have the gift of healing and not realize it until someone tells them of the strange sensations experienced when their hands were put on them or passed above them. Just like other forms of the extra sense, the power to heal can be increased through use. Once recognized, the gift should be used often.

Fricker himself was a total disbeliever before he went to a healer not long ago. There he was told that he, too, had the gift of healing. Skeptical, he did not do anything about it until an emergency occurred and a girl in his shop became ill. With no doctor on hand, Fricker put his hands on her and she recovered.

Probably the greatest healer of modern times was the late psychic Edgar Cayce. Several books have been written about this remarkable man, and a film may soon be produced to acquaint the public with his accomplishments. Gina Cerminara's *Many Mansions* and Thomas Sugrue's *There Is a River* are the best of the books about Cayce, and Jess Stearn, in his book *The Sleeping Prophet*, also writes with much insight and compassion about the man.

Cayce's son, Hugh Lynn Cayce, now heads the Virginia Beach Association for Research and Enlightenment (ARE), which is also referred to as The Cayce Foundation. To this day, this group has a curriculum of lectures both in Virginia Beach and at its New York branch dealing not only with Cayce's work as a healing medium, but with his even more remarkable readings of people's past incarnations.

A little-educated photographer by profession, Cayce knew none of the answers to anyone's problems when he was awake. But in trance, ostensibly asleep, he was taken over by experts in medicine who could instantly diagnose a person's illness at a distance, prescribe the proper remedy, and *never fail!*

From these astounding cures by the thousands, Cayce went to predictions about world conditions in the future—one of the less pleasant ones being about the destruction of parts of California and New York City at some future date.

Cayce's trance statements were all carefully written down by his followers and are available in published form for anyone to study. As for the reincarnation aspects of his work, they may well be as authentic as all his other accomplishments, but they are more difficult to prove in the conventional scientific sense.

To give briefly even a rudimentary account of the remarkable powers of Edgar Cayce would be to do an injustice to his memory and the Foundation now practicing so much of what he preached, for Cayce was a deeply religious man who thought that God had given him his unique gift to help the suffering. The facts are readily available for those who wish to study them, but Cayce himself, unfortunately, is no longer healing the sick.

There is always hope, of course, that another Cayce will come along some day whose mediumship will be the healing kind.

To heal oneself psychically, one must learn to let go of the outer world so that the inner world may come to the fore and take over, at least temporarily, the functions of life. A broken leg may not be easily healed by psychic energy, but many other ailments can be. In fact, I am convinced that disease is a state of disharmony inflicted on a person either by himself or indirectly by others. Even then, he is to blame for allowing such conditions to persist. Bacteria and viruses certainly exist, but they are always present in the human system. Could it not be that these latent disease causers are impotent while the personality maintains in the body a proper physical, mental, and spiritual balance?

If this delicate balance is upset by wrongful thinking, negative emotions—ranging from fear and anxiety to hatred and destructiveness, from frustration to depression and boredom—then the body must fall ill. Conversely, proper thought will restore the state of good health.

This brings us to the great question of this age—*the art of proper thinking*. It is nothing less than the key to happiness, health, and success in all spheres of human life.

A thought is an electromagnetic impulse, a small piece of energy, created in the mind (not the brain) of a human being, which carries an image—visual or auditory—or an idea. If the thought is merely created for the creator himself ("I was just thinking"), then the impulse may *go* out from the mind in every direction and possibly be caught by any receiving mind close enough to catch it. By "close enough" I do not mean only physically close, but also emotionally close.

For example: let us say you think of a beautiful red rose, because you happen to like this image—because you like red roses. They mean pleasure to you, and thinking of them is a sensation that pleases you. Someone standing next to you might suddenly say, "I like red roses, don't you?" or something to that effect. He may not even be aware that the thought did not originate with him and that he was merely verbalizing something that came drifting into his unconscious. Or again, a loved one far away may suddenly have a thought of red roses while also thinking of you. She may write you about it and on checking the time the idea came to her mind, you will find that it coincides with your own original thought about the red rose. This, of course, is telepathic communication. It may be possible because of physical or emotional closeness. But without the existence of the thought process, telepathy could not exist. We could not communicate with each other or even with ourselves.

Nothing becomes real until we think it is real. By themselves, objects, or even other people, have no reality for us. They do not exist as far as we are concerned until we formulate a thought of them. At the same time, anything we can express in thought is *real*, whether it actually exists in the physical, material sense or not.

This is why, in the thought world into which we all pass after death, life is so much more real than in the material world. Over there, as you think, so you are. If you think you are young and handsome, why, that is how you are, not only to yourself, seen through your own etheric eyes, but to others looking at you with theirs!

Thoughts, originating in the mind, are a true creative process colored by emotional connotations. They are made up of electrically charged molecules that travel outward the moment they are put together as a "thought." They keep traveling, indefinitely, but on the way gradually lose potency, since radiation from the original thought keeps going out in all directions, and thus ultimately the thought will become weaker and weaker as it travels farther and farther.

If, however, a thought is created and directed specifically at another mind with the desire that the other person receive it, such thought is much stronger and less likely to stray all over the map. If the receiver is attuned—that is, emotionally fit to receive—then thought transfer will take place directly. This may even be successful if the receiver is asleep and the thought is implanted in his unconscious mind. It is clear that the discipline of the sender is most important, and such thought discipline can be attained by proper training and by proper attitudes.

Some scientists still refer to the brain as the seat of thought creation, which it assuredly is not. The brain is merely the transformer, the switchboard, and the storing house of thought impulses both sent out and received. It is the mind that operates and controls the brain; the mind is the real place of origin for the thought process. Even animals have minds—though far less complex than ours—for they have as yet not attained our degree of evolution.

It is a moot question whether God created man in one fell swoop or whether man slowly climbed from the monkey state. In either case man is a divine creation, as is all of nature in its miraculous ways. Even the intricate biochemical processes that have caused life as we know it are a miracle. To attempt to formulate the exact theological truth is not my purpose. I do know, however, that the power in man is *thought*, and only thought.

Granted that we cannot all be brilliant and that human personality varies greatly, I maintain that any normal, reasonably well-balanced human being can influence his own life by *proper thinking*. Not only can illness be reduced to the natural processes of aging, but healing depends very largely on the frame of mind of the one to be healed—not a state of belief, but of optimism in all matters. The trick in self-healing, even in so small a matter of a cold, is to suggest to your own body that it rally and drive out the invaders, function properly, and enjoy the healthy life it is capable of. This power to suggest to your body, even to parts of your body, works. I have seen it work. Verbalizing a problem is no mumbo jumbo. It is a realistic process with tangible results if properly carried out in a positive state of mind. By that I mean that trying it while thinking that it might not work is as bad as not doing it at all. You must be honestly convinced that it will work, and work for you it will.

But cure of many illnesses, especially the large group of psychosomatic illnesses—those caused by emotional and mental processes and only exteriorized by the physical body—is merely the beginning of practical use for thought power.

In the material world, most individuals face superiors or business partners of one kind or another at various times in their lives. To help themselves reach a successful conclusion of such meetings, proper thought images should be set up ahead of time. By thinking that one will bring the other person around to one's own views—be it to do with a sale, employment, partnership, or what have you—one need only set up a thought pattern showing that what one desires has already happened. Then, when the confrontation occurs, quietly repeat the thought while awaiting the outcome. It does not always work, but it works often enough to be worth trying. When it fails to work, a contrary thought pattern may be at work in the mind of the other person, stronger than yours and thus able to set your desires aside. But you lose nothing in trying and may gain everything by firmly assuming that it will work.

Words are the key instruments to action. Thoughts are the souls of words.

Disciplining your thoughts so that they will always remain in constructive channels is achieved by maintaining a firm grip on your own mind.

Try not to allow negative emotions, such as hatred, destructiveness, envy, jealousy, or depression, to enter and clutter a clear mind. They do nothing for you except salve the ego, and ego is nature's way of putting you on guard. When you find yourself feeding the ego with false pride or with self-pity because of failure, it is time to pull back and do some actively constructive thinking instead—for it uses up energy, too, and leads absolutely nowhere.

When you're turned down in some enterprise, beware of feeling: (1) self-pity, (2) hatred for the one who turned you down, or (3) a sense of frustration which you cover by changing the direction of your drive. Instead, analyze why you have failed *this time*, regroup your mental forces, and come back for another day as soon as you can with the firm and unaltered conviction that you will ultimately win out.

Fear and anxiety are sure to defeat any project. Fear is the absence of necessary information, and anxiety is a state in which fears are allowed to dominate your life. You, the individual, are fully and solely responsible for bringing them on. Your own faulty thought processes have allowed these bad idea patterns to slip into your healthy mind.

Once you recognize your own guilt in permitting this, you have won half the battle. *Anything you bring on, you can also take away*. Repeat this to yourself a few times and you will realize how quickly you can act. Command your mind to cast out the fearful thoughts and replace them with fresh thoughts of self-assertion and confidence. Then plan again, and this time you may be the winner.

Your own state of mind is as much recognized by those you deal with as if it were written all over your face. Thoughts form a person's atmosphere—the aura that surrounds him—and anyone even slightly sensitive can feel it if he is uncertain or apprehensive. These negative thoughts communicate themselves to the other person and help defeat you. By the same token, positive, confident thoughts of accomplishment also come across the gap between you and the other man and may well help you win him over to your way of thinking.

Negative emotions and evil thoughts are responsible for much hatred and destruction in this world of ours. It is all well and good for the clergy of every denomination to preach the Ten Commandments or their equivalent on Sunday and tolerate or even support the crimes being committed daily in the name of nationalism and political power.

The taking of life, whether human or animal, is never an act that can be defended. Even if you kill in self-defense, you have saddled yourself with an unfortunate deed, though it may have been an unavoidable one in the physical sense. But to conduct large-scale warfare for the purposes of imposing political systems on people whose main desire is to live peacefully cannot be excused on any grounds whatever. This is as much true for the one side in our world-wide conflicts as it is for the other.

We can only hope that future generations will eventually learn to channel their thoughts in such a way that the negative thoughts leading to violence cannot intrude. For if one individual can overcome this weakness, so can others, and a veritable mass movement toward the practice of positive, spiritually valid thinking alone can save us from the self-destruction that is sure to come if we persist in our current thought patterns.

I wish that our schools and universities would teach young people the *art of proper thinking* the way they teach them semantics and chemistry. And I wish they would teach them how to verbalize properly, how to restrain negative thoughts, and how to apply thoughts so that they will serve us best.

If these are not vitally important subjects, I don't know what are. For surely thought rules all activity and all creative processes. We must not leave the teaching of proper thinking to such esoteric sources as schools of yoga and cultists. We must allow all of our people to partake in the broadcast sense of the techniques that can make their lives so much healthier and happier, and by doing so for the individual, create a better sum total, a better world to live in.

A vast number of people have been healed either through their own powers or through the powers of others who were not even aware of the fact that they had them. For example, in many instances the power of healing is intimately connected with religious belief or sudden enlightenment. Some of these cases I have listed among the religiously inspired forms of healing, but it is at times difficult to know where to draw the line between purely psychic and religious healing, because a religious belief can trigger psychic abilities through a combination of positive attitude and the actual activation of dormant powers within. Then, too, the difference between a person quietly meditating upon another and sending healing thoughts and an individual praying to God for the same purpose is merely one of semantics and attitude, not of hard and cold facts. Both types of healing are, of course, paranormal and unorthodox.

Frequently the healing power comes together with other forms of psychic expression such as ESP or clairvoyant dreams. Jean L. of Redding, California, has a long record of psychic ability, including astral projections and experiences with deceased relatives, especially her late father. When her children were down with stomach flu, complaining about cramps, she found herself holding her hands slightly above the stomach area and saying something to the effect that the bad germs would be drawn out of the stomach. She then swiftly moved her hands upwards with great emphasis so that the germs could come out.

Mrs. L. does not know what made her do this, but the fact of the matter is that the children said that they could feel the germs leaving and quickly recovered. Mrs. L. thought that her success was due primarily to suggestion, but she has been equally successful at relieving pain and illness by similar methods on other occasions.

Mrs. Virginia A. C. of Framingham, Massachusetts, also has had a number of psychic experiences. At the early age of ten she found herself greatly upset because her mother was suffering from pain in the hip and from a weak back. Virginia wanted to stay home from school so she could be with her mother, but her mother would hear nothing of it. As the little girl walked down to the bus stop thinking how nice it would be if someone could assume the pain of another person to give them some relief, she suddenly felt her hip hurt very badly and she started to cry. At that instant she realized that she had assumed her mother's pain. By the time she had reached school the pain had gone away. When she returned home, she asked her mother how she felt. The mother informed her that a strange thing had happened; the pain had suddenly left her shortly after Virginia had gone off to school.

Mrs. Lucile M. B. of Los Angeles, California, has experienced almost the entire range of psychic phenomena over the years. On February 24, 1968, she was sitting quietly at home meditating on healing. It was about 8:30 P.M., and she felt at peace. Suddenly her eldest son Edward burst into the house, bleeding heavily from wounds about his head. He had been attacked by five thugs on a dark street and beaten with chains and broken bottles. After Mrs. B. and her husband had taken the boy to the hospital and had gotten him patched up, she wondered how the boy could have been so badly hurt at the very time when she was meditating on healing. Several days later he was able to tell her exactly what had happened. Although he had felt the weight of the chains and the force of the blows, he never felt any pain at all during the attack. According to doctors at the hospital, the boy could have easily been killed. Nevertheless, he had felt nothing because his mother was sending him healing thoughts at a distance.

Mrs. Virginia Cameron, formerly of Cincinnati, Ohio, and now a Florida resident, has been interested in psychic phenomena for many years. Presently she is lecturing on the subject at a local college as part of an adult education program. Mrs. Cameron is a critical individual, inclined toward acceptance of phenomena but at the same time careful not to base her findings on simple belief. She herself has developed a respectable amount of ESP over the years and is currently testing that faculty whenever there is an opportunity.

Among those attending the regular sessions of the Parapsychology Forum in Cincinnati were a number of amateur mediums and healers. Virginia has for many years suffered from the pains of arthritis, a disease for which there is no known cure. A Mrs. Mildred Barton and Virginia were discussing a case of healing over the telephone on March 11, 1970. Mrs. Barton was telling Virginia Cameron about a Cincinnati policeman who had been wounded in a gun battle and who had been the subject of a prayer Mrs. Barton had sent in a letter to his mother. Unexpectedly, the policeman had recovered without the often-accompanying infection which follows gunshot wounds. When Mrs. Barton offered to repeat the prayer for Mrs. Cameron, she gladly listened. It was 11:30 A.M. when Mrs. Barton started to read. Mrs. Cameron was holding the telephone receiver in her right hand looking at her left wrist, which was resting on her knees. The joints of her fingers were then swollen, painful; her hand felt cramped. As Mrs. Barton continued, Virginia's left hand became rosier and warm as if an extra blood supply had flowed into it. The right hand continued to ache, but pain receded quite rapidly from the left.

By 2:00 P.M. there was no pain in the left hand, and pain was receding from the right hand as well. The slight deformation in the joints was still present, but there was no discomfort. By 8:30 P.M. pain was absent from both hands. Occasionally, Virginia felt slight twinges, and thinking that the pain was returning, she took the salicylate ordered by her physician. This remedy eases the pain but does not erase it and the relief is short-lived, about two to three hours. At 10:30 P.M., pain and discomfort were still absent from both hands. Customarily Mrs. Cameron is awakened at least once a night by cramping and stiffness. This did not happen that particular night.

There was no real discomfort until well into the following day when it began to return. By 8:30 p.m. the discomfort was at its usual intensity, but Mrs. Cameron had been free of all pain for a considerable period of time. This development could not be ascribed to ordinary remission. In her own experience, pain came and went, but the absences of pain were related to clear, warm weather. March 11, in contrast, was cold and damp; March 12, even worse (Cincinnati experienced a blizzard at that time). Even though the arthritic condition returned eventually, Mrs. Cameron is convinced that something happened to it during the period when Mrs. Barton's efforts were effective.

Mack Brockman of New York City is a retired printing pressroom foreman in his late sixties. His bouts with the occult are few and far between but remarkable in some instances. When he was in his early thirties, he suffered from a most acute sacroiliac condition. The sciatic nerve was jammed against the base of his spine. He had been to the best doctors in New York City and was told that his case was hopeless. After eight months of suffering, the morphine no longer helped, and he could hardly sleep. He began to contemplate suicide. One night, at 1:00 A.M., when he was sure that his wife was fast asleep, he went to the roof of his six-story apartment building to do the inevitable. As he was about to jump off, his late father's apparition manifested quite plainly in front of him, pushing his hands toward him and telling him to stop. At the same time the apparition informed him that everything would be all right with him.

Brockman simply passed out on the spot. When he woke up hours later, he was covered with sweat. Still shaken, he went down to his apartment and lay down on the couch. He awoke again and saw his wife sitting next to him, informing him that he had slept for eight hours straight. It had been the first time in eight months that he had really slept. Brockman got off the couch. His pain was gone. Instead of being bent over, as before, he stood up straight without the slightest discomfort.

Frieda Peternell St. Clair is a middle-aged housewife living near Chicago, Illinois, and the mother of four children. Her late father was a professional spiritualist medium who died when she was only sixteen years old, so she did not really come much under his influence. Her husband is not interested in the occult, and she never pursued psychic interests. However, she experienced so much pain after the birth of her third child that she found herself in a state of despair and started to cry. In this condition she sent a prayer out toward her late father to help her, asking him to make the pain go away.

All of a sudden a strange feeling came over her. Fully awake, she saw a white, luminous spiral over her bed, making a strange, humming noise as it moved up and down over her slowly. At the same time she could see, out of the corner of her eye, three or four spirit forms standing in front of the closet in the room, one of whom she recognized immediately as her father. She was frightened by this unexpected experience and tried to let out a scream, but she found she had no voice and seemed completely paralyzed. After what to her seemed a lifetime, but was in fact only a few moments, everything went back to normal again. She let out a bloodcurdling scream, and her mother came in, wondering what had happened to her. She explained her experience but was assured that it had only been a bad dream. Too exhausted to argue, Mrs. St. Clair went to sleep. The next morning she jumped out of bed and walked into the living room. There was absolutely no pain or discomfort left.

Rachel Kadan of San Diego, California, suffered from arthritis for years. It had gotten so bad that she could not lift her arm without excruciating pain. Then one night in February 1968, she saw a large brilliant gold-and-white light at the foot of her bed. At the same time she was told things she did not quite understand or remember. Confused by the strange flow of words, she said she would rather have her arm healed than listen to such language. With that she felt herself bodily lifted out of bed as a shock went from the bottom of her feet up through her entire body to the top of her head and back again and once more up to her head. It felt as if a tremendous amount of electricity had been sent through her body. For three days she didn't dare try her arthritic arm. When she did, she discovered that her pain and disability had completely disappeared. They never returned; she is able to use her arm even in extremely cold weather.

Olga Atherton of Yorkshire, England, has on several occasions been healed by what she describes as a great healer. He saved her life after a heart attack, when she did in fact pass out of the body, and he has cured her of a slipped disc, dislocated hip, and appendicitis. This shadowy figure has appeared before her three times in her life. She saw his face as that of a young man with a bronzed complexion and brown eyes. Miss Atherton does not understand why this entity has decided to help her. She feels that her life has been a failure; she is poor, lives alone, and considers herself a very unimportant person. Nevertheless, whenever serious illness has struck in her life, this shadowy entity has appeared and she has been cured.

Cases of spontaneous healing, either by parties known or unknown, are legion. A large percentage of these cases cannot be explained on the grounds of spontaneous remission or other natural causes. There is a large residue of cases where only paranormal intervention remains as the sole explanation for the improvements manifested.

ELEVEN

Who Are the Healers?

Now that I have worked with, investigated, and submitted myself to a variety of declared psychic healers, and heard their explanations as to what constitutes their "gift" and how and why it works, I have been able to come to my own conclusions about it. What is involved in all healing of this type is energy, whether you call it bio-energetic force, body magnetism, or any other fancy name. It is physical energy—measurable—and it depends on the healer's ability to gather enough of it within his own body to be able to transfer it through his hands onto the patient, usually passing several inches above the patient's body because a psychic healer heals the aura or etheric body first, before touching the skin and physical body.

Conventional medicine has still not come to terms with the worst diseases. New attitudes are slowing beginning to develop, but we are far from cognizant of what I would like to call "the new medicine," where body, mind, and spirit are equally dealt with by our physicians.

To be a medical doctor you have to go through medical school for upward of five or six years, be an intern, and then you can practice medicine. Even if you are the greatest natural born healer, if you plan to be a doctor following the traditional form of medicine you have to reconfirm your inner promptings by formal training and actual experience in the field.

No one in his right mind would consult a physician unless that physician had a degree in medicine. Yet there is no guarantee that a degree in medicine will result in the restoration of good health or in any kind of change in one's condition. The degree merely reassures the patient that his prospective physician has been taught the fundamentals of orthodox medicine, perhaps even something about human personality if he has had psychiatric training, and that he is reasonably competent to deal with him. The degree in no way evaluates the man's ability; nor does it contain a magic formula for health. Orthodox medical doctors with the same amount of training and the same opportunities to test their training have given totally different forms of therapy to their patients. Quite obviously, the training and the knowledge of orthodox medicine are not by themselves a great equalizer among physicians: something intangible enters the picture, something involving the individual personality of the doctor, the way he thinks, the way he administers medicine, the way he deals with the problem of illness. Not without good reason have old-line physicians emphasized their excellent bedside manners, meaning of course their psychological approach to the patients. Much more than the actual training goes into the making of a good physician.

The psychic or unorthodox healer is under no such obligations. His training may be nonexistent. In fact, the majority of psychic healers have only a smattering of knowledge of medicine; nor do they pretend to be medical doctors in any sense of the term. *Healers are born.* The innate ability to be a psychic healer certainly is part of the individual personality. Only the development of the gift of healing is a matter of time, effort, and opportunity. Some latent healers go through life as ordinary people, without the slightest interest in anything of the kind. Often, however, latent healers, suddenly and dramatically, discover that they are healers, that they have the gift of helping others overcome illness.

To some of these the call comes rather late in life. Why this is so is hard to tell, except that perhaps they themselves were not quite ready to become vehicles of the power that heals until they had reached a certain stage in their personal development. Many healers do not know how their power works, what it is, or where it is from. They accept it and use it and are grateful that they have been chosen as vehicles of the power. Others try to explain it by saying it is the gift of God, or that a specific saint, master, or dead physician inspires them and tells them what to do.

Nearly all healers start out by discovering their gifts accidentally, often over matters concerning friends or relatives, and then develop them by using them on other people. When their abilities become known outside their immediate circle, they begin to be called upon by strangers, and before long they feel that they are ready to set up shop in some way, to heal those who want to be healed. At first, this may be merely a part-time occupation, in the evening, after hours; some may not take money for their ministrations, while others will take what is euphemistically called "free-will offerings." Eventually, however, some of the successful healers turn professional, though they are careful not to claim any medical treatments or to promise absolute success to their clients, being well aware of the legal difficulties they can get themselves into. Most psychic healers in America charge fees for their time rather than for their services; there is no law against anyone's being paid for time used in the interest of others, and so long as the healer stays within the letter of the law, he or she is not likely to have difficulties with the authorities.

Unfortunately, most laws are totally inappropriate in respect to genuine psychic healing. They lump together patently fake quacks with authentic healers, just as the archaic laws of some states, such as California and New York, still do not know how to differentiate between a Gypsy tea leaf reader or fortune teller and a researcher in parapsychology. In time, no doubt, these inequities will be straightened out.

For the record, *no* psychic healer ever caused anyone any physical harm; the application of unorthodox healing has never worsened any illness. The claim, put forward by orthodox physicians hostile toward psychic healing, that a patient who consults a healer instead of seeing a conventional physician is in fact allowing his illness to progress instead of doing something about it does not really hold water. In the first place, good psychic healers do not seek to subvert orthodox doctors. It is not necessarily an either/or situation. In the second, the majority of people consult healers only after conventional physicians have let them down, either directly, by telling them that they can do nothing for them, or indirectly, by promising them help when in fact they cannot deliver it. Only a tiny fraction of those in ill health seek out healers *first*, before trying the orthodox route to salvation, because, unfortunately, the majority of the population is not as yet psychically oriented.

Indeed, while this effectively destroys the opposition to healers, this factor tragically limits the effectiveness of the healer. People are far too hesitant about consulting healers. One of the purposes of this work is to acquaint the broad masses with the possibilities of finding good health outside the traditional edifice of medicine. In the case of radical surgery particularly, prior consultation with a competent healer may very well prevent the necessity for surgery altogether. Of course one must deal with the time element. In some diseases prolonged lack of conventional treatment can allow the disease to progress. But one of the strong points of psychic healing is that generally a total cure, and if not a total cure then a substantial improvement, is instantaneous, or at least much faster than conventional treatment will lead the patient to expect. Thus a comparatively small risk is taken in consulting a competent healer prior to allowing radical surgery to take place. In view of the sacrifices involved, an enlightened patient is justified in attempting the unorthodox route first—so long as he is sure of the services of a truly competent and acknowledged psychic healer.

The proof of the pudding is in the eating. Some healers go through the motions of their art and fully believe that they are healing those in need of help. Suggestion plays a certain part in these unorthodox healings, but not beyond the patient's full cooperation in wanting to be healed and in believing in the healer. Once such a relationship is established, something has to happen between healer and patient that is not under control of the patient. If a healer has extraordinary results and his percentage of "hits" is beyond expectations—that is to say, the majority of his cases are successfully concluded—inevitably his or her reputation will eventually spread until the name becomes a household word in the esoteric field: among those who accept psychic healing as a reality. If the healer is a modestly successful individual, perhaps someone using his art only intermittently, the name may not mean very much outside of a small circle of friends and admirers. Nevertheless, such unknown healers may suddenly become successful ones because the gift of healing has a way of coming and going in spurts. In the United States and elsewhere there are plenty of examples of both kinds of healers.

Among the modest and sincere healers of my acquaintance who practice the art of laying on of hands is a woman named Ella Morris who works at Riverside Church in New York City. A well-known New York medium, the late Betty Ritter, had for years practiced spiritual healing through prayer and the laying on of hands. William Linn, another spiritualist and minister of his own church in New York City, is a good psychic healer, using essentially similar methods to Betty Ritter.

Sometimes spiritualists get together for a healing circle in which as many as eight individuals take part, with the patient within the circle. The concerted efforts, partially prayer and partially the sending forth of healing energies from their bodies and minds, are supposed to cleanse the patient of illness, working through the aura and thence into the body itself. One such healing circle that I tested, in the home of the Reverend William Linn, proved to be an extraordinary experience. For about fifteen minutes I felt wave upon wave of energy surrounding me, and I left the house with a feeling of renewed vigor and at the same time of great calmness.

A London medium, Mary Rogers, is active in spiritualist circles in that city, and does an excellent job of psychic healing with her hands. I have subjected myself to her ministrations and felt the surge of power coming, as it were, from her fingers onto my neck and thence into my body. Healing is never an attempt to deal with one particular area of the body but is always meant to be general. Illness is indivisible, health is indivisible, to the psychically oriented person.

On the boundary between unorthodox healing and natural treatments lie the methods employed at Buxted Park, Sussex, England. Maintained by Heather and Ken Shipman, independently wealthy English people, Buxted Park relies on osteopathy and nature cures as well as on such esoteric methods as naturopath treatments and color therapy.

Buxted Park is a magnificent country mansion, dating from 1725, standing on high ground overlooking a lake, a river, and a park. Other forms of unorthodox healing, notably psychic healing and the laying on of hands, are not part of the regular routine at Buxted Park but are encouraged when and if a proper medium is in residence there.

Healing does not require a person to be an adult. Twelve-year-old Bonnie Campbell-Best of Winchester, England, acquired a certain reputation for putting her hands on people and curing them of various diseases. Bonnie's father is a professional faith healer, and she discovered her ability shortly before her ninth birthday when a patient of her father's came to the house looking for relief from back pains. Since her father was away at the time, the little girl impulsively placed her hands on the woman's back, the way she had seen her father do it. To her surprise the patient looked up and confirmed that all pains had disappeared. This encouraged the little girl to try her hands with others. Her success with various forms of illness, such as a twisted arm, throat cancer, and the problem of a little boy who had been unable to speak, encouraged her to continue treating those who came for help. When Bonnie's father realized that his daughter had a greater gift than he had himself, he encouraged her to look in that direction. Neither of them charge for their services but accept free-will offerings.

A German lawyer, Dr. Kurt Trampler, telepathically diagnoses the diseases of patients he never meets or sees. He is not a healer in the sense that he uses his psychic abilities to deal with the illnesses themselves, but through his telepathic powers he enables medical doctors to get to the cause of a patient's illness quicker and with more guidance than by probing in the conventional way. Dr. Trampler has been tested by teams of investigating scientists and found to be amazingly accurate in his diagnoses.

There are far too few outstanding healers in America today, but one of the most unusual healers I have met is Betty Dye, a housewife living near Atlanta, Georgia, who is the mother of several children, the wife of a slight, soft-spoken man who works for one of the major oil companies, and a medium. Not just a woman with a prophetic vision of the world to come—and a fine record of past predictions come true—Betty Dye has the power of spiritual healing. Gradually, as she became more and more aware of her psychic powers, principally through predictions and involvement in various cases of murder or mysterious disappearances, she also developed her powers as a psychic healer. Thus, after much consultation as to the direction her developments should take, and perhaps also influenced by the fact that the spiritualist churches seem to offer protection from law enforcement authorities who still look askance at psychics in some parts of the world, Betty Dye studied for the spiritualist ministry and in due time received her certificate, making her a bona fide spiritualist minister and member of the association, not that, as she herself is fully aware, membership in a spiritualist association has anything to do with her ability as a healer per se. "Please get the idea across very firmly," she told me during one of our meetings in Atlanta, "that healers do not have to be ordained ministers, church deacons, or special ones within the church. They are surely not the only ones God gives the healing power to." To Betty Dye, who comes from a devout Southern Baptist background, the power to heal stems directly from God.

But what about her record?

James Douglas DePass, of Atlanta, an author and officer of the Atlanta Theosophical Society, consulted Betty Dye in December 1970. In response, Betty Dye went into trance, during which one of her controls, who identified himself as a doctor in physical life, diagnosed Mr. DePass's ailment as being connected with the stomach. Betty Dye had not been told anything about the visitor's problem.

The entranced medium then laid her hands on the affected areas of the patient. His pains left him by the end of the first sitting. During the trance, Betty Dye felt completely unattached to the proceedings and at one time grew very dizzy. She has a vague memory of what was spoken through her, but during the treatment itself she seemed to be "outside" her own body. Both the patient and the medium feel extreme heat during the laying on of hands.

Betty Dye feels that the power comes directly from her spirit guides and the thoughts and words expressed by her during trance are merely filtered through her as a vehicle. The voice speaking through her at such times is that of a man who has far greater knowledge and vocabulary than she has in her ordinary condition. The medical doctor who acts as her control speaks with authority and sincerity and apparently knows exactly what is to be done in each individual case. The control also gives instructions to the patient to help the healing by placing his or her hands in line with one another. Patients frequently report feeling as if heat were going through their own bodies at such times. There is a question-and-answer period between the control and the patient, and apparently this period is used to calm the patient sufficiently for the healing to take place. While in her trance, Betty hears this voice directly in her right ear, and it sounds to her as if a definite and direct connection is set up between the control and herself, transmitting, as it were, all the sound into one location within her head; she hears nothing in her left ear. When coming out of the trance state she feels exhilarated and far from tired—though frequently she is dripping with perspiration—and extremely relaxed. Often she lies down and sleeps for a while after a session. She is told that the spirit control also takes care of her health while she is in trance. "I feel the movement of my own body but have no control over it," Betty explains. "Often the movement is awkward and the spirit control asks for assistance from the patient in placing the hands or in aiding me to stand. I cannot stand on my own, but when helped to my feet I can remain there until the treatments are over and then I am put back into the chair."

Returning to James DePass, we should note that on March 31, 1971, he signed a notarized affidavit stating: "This is to acknowledge and certify that on a Sunday night in December 1970, Betty Dye with her spiritual healing talent did absolutely beyond doubt heal me of a stomach ailment. I had suffered nausea and stomach pain for a week. I had definitely decided to see my medical doctor the next day. No one knew of my trouble except my wife Hazel. It was an absolutely effective spiritual healing case administered by Betty Dye for which I am very grateful."

Mrs. Floyd Cummings, also of Atlanta, came to Betty Dye a frightened woman, unable to look into her face. Her fears were due to what her medical doctors had told her. As Mrs. Cummings later related it, formally: "In December of 1970, my doctor, A. N. Ullea, of East Point, Georgia, found a growth in my throat. He made an appointment with a throat specialist, Dr. Robert P. Tuma, also of East Point, Georgia, to perform surgery and remove the growth. Before going to the specialist, however, I went to Mrs. Betty Dye and she gave me a treatment. During the treatment I experienced a wonderful feeling of healing, cleansing, and extreme heat coming from the hands of Mrs. Betty Dye while in trance. Several days later I went to the specialist. When he examined my throat, the growth was gone. It has not returned. That was four months ago. I have had no further trouble with my throat."

This was a case of instantaneous healing, requiring but a single session with the healer.

Betty Dye holds regular Friday night sessions for healing at which anyone in need of her help may attend. Some come from great distances. In 1971, for example, Sgt. Charles Piper drove in from Alabama to partake in the sessions, and he was so elated at the results of his healing sessions with Betty, both in the regular circle and privately, that he volunteered the following statement. "Since I was six years old I have had headaches. I started to wear eyeglasses and my mother always blamed eye strain. In 1960 I went on sick call for a severe headache and was told by the doctor that I had a chronic sinus condition. Since that time until September 18, 1970, I have had a recurring sinus problem. The attached sheet shows the many times I have been on sick call for sinus or related illnesses. The frequency of my headaches was about once every two weeks or more often."

Sergeant Piper then listed each instance in which he was on sick call, the information being taken directly from his military records. There were twenty-one single instances between August 15, 1960, and September 17, 1971. "On September 17, 1971," the sergeant continued his statement, "I attended a sitting at the home of Mrs. Betty Dye. During the sitting she went into a trance and a healing spirit entered her. I stepped forward when the control asked me to and asked to have my sinus problem cured. At the time I had a headache and swollen glands in my throat. The medium placed her hands into the sinus area and said they would be cured. Two hours later the swelling in my throat was gone and so was the headache. Since that time I have not had any sinus problems."

The number of those healed by Betty Dye, sometimes instantly, is large and impressive.

> I wish to state that I received spiritual healing from Mrs. Betty Dye for prostatitis. The back ache which often goes along with this condition was helped and the swelling in the prostate was reduced after treatment.—Dr. John P. Bohanan, Veterinarian, Canton, Georgia.

> This letter is to confirm that I have received spiritual healing through my dear friend Mrs. Betty Dye and the grace of God. I had a whiplash which was painful to me. After several treatments I received a lot of comfort and feel that with a few more treatments I shall be cured completely.—Thomas C. Bennett, Canton, Georgia.

> The treatment I received was for a back problem. Since I took several treatments, the problem completely disappeared.—Mary Elizabeth Bennett, Canton, Georgia.

> I have known Betty Dye for the past two years; she has helped in my church with healing. She has helped my grandson. He has not had any asthmatic attacks since she started to come, before Christmas 1970.—Reverend Irene Hornsby, East Point, Georgia.

> This letter is to express my appreciation for the wonderful and complete healing I received as a result of my visits to a few

sessions held with you earlier this year. For many years I suffered from nervous stomach as well as inflammation around the tonsils occasionally. Doctors could find nothing physically wrong. Now I seem to be completely relieved of those conditions. —Bill Maye, Atlanta, Georgia.

In the latter part of February 1972, a nine-year-old boy named Peter Love was brought to Betty Dye in the back of a station wagon. Peter Love was in a cast from the waist down and had a steel bar permanently applied between his feet to hold him in a certain position. Doctors had said the child suffered from a bone disease and that he must wear the cast and apparatus for at least three years; he had been in it about six weeks prior to his visit to Betty Dye.

Betty Dye administered spiritual healing immediately. On April 13, 1972, she received word from the boy's father in Alabama that an X-ray had been taken, and that to the doctor's surprise the boy was found to be 90 percent better. As a result of this finding, the boy was taken out of the cast and put on crutches. An affidavit signed by the boy's father, Donald P. Love, stated that the patient's condition prior to healing included "upper extremity of left femur badly deteriorated from perthes disease." In this case, for which Betty Dye received neither a fee nor even a free-will offering, the medium had placed her hands on the affected area.

The boy's father later was visited by a spirit entity and an unseen force moved his hands to Peter's left hip; thus the father's energies were also enlisted in the treatment. The father was not in trance. It felt to him as if millions of tiny needles flowed down his arm and out of his fingertips into the boy's hip. When he repeated the treatment the following night, the same thing happened, but this time there was no feeling of the needles and the force was much smaller.

For a while the father felt a spirit force within him; then the force moved to the side, and the father felt he was in somewhat of a trance state during the healing treatment.

During the first treatment the boy felt the needles also and winced from pain while the flow of needles continued. On the second night the boy felt much less pain. Donald Love concludes his notarized statement thus: "The condition is nearly gone. All the bone shows clearly in the X-ray, indicating good calcium growth. Just a short time is needed to grow the cartilage back. Originally this was to take from sixteen months to three years."

Was Betty Dye responsible? Or the father? Or both? It doesn't matter to Betty Dye whether she gets credit for what she does so long as the results are positive. But the case is an illustration of the diverse ways in which healing can occur.

Upon Betty Dye's request a registered nurse, Peggy Allison, attended a healing session on October 29, 1971, to take her pulse and blood pressure before, during, and after her trance. According to nurse Allison, Betty Dye's blood pressure, normally 126/80, increased to 170/130 during the trance and fell to 126/80 immediately upon the end of the trance state; likewise, her pulse rose from a pre-trance level. These readings would indicate the dissipation of energies during and because of the trance state, a situation common to the great healers. Betty Dye may be reached at P.O. Box 69, Union City, Georgia 30291. If you contact her, be sure and specify the exact details of your illness or problem and what you have done about it: she will not let you see her unless she is reasonably sure she can help you. Her fees are modest, especially as compared to those of medical specialists.

For over thirty years the name of John Myers has been respected in psychical research circles and somewhat controversially in scientifically oriented and lay circles. The respect was due John Myers, who passed away in May 1972, because of his unusual contributions to the field of psychic photography, psychic healing, and the organization of a psychic study society called Psychists, Inc. The controversial aspect of Myers' career stemmed from two events in the British dentist's life: his encounter with a journalist, Lord Donegal, who tried to trap him by substituting marked plates in one of the psychic photography experiments Myers had agreed to submit to for the press, and Myers' own inability to present an effective public image of his talents, because of a personality that was as contradictory as it was unusual.

Myers the man was not without vanity, interested in the good things of life, keenly aware of the advantages of being wealthy (which in his later years he indeed was although not because of his psychic work).

On the other side of the ledger, there was Myers the mystic, the medium, the psychic healer.

Following the traditional spiritualist line of thinking, Myers divided his activities in the field of psychical research between two main areas: to demonstrate his unusual mediumship as a photography medium and as a healer, preferably with resulting publicity in press, radio, or television; and to organize a society of healers and psychics in which he himself would be the dominant figure but which would encompass the work of others as well. I knew John Myers for twenty years. At times his naive approach to scientific controls and his incredible appetite for publicity—any kind of publicity—exasperated one, especially since this publicity mania led him to confuse his genuine psychic accomplishments with his mundane affairs. Indeed, it is no wonder that casual observers were easily misled into taking Myers for a charlatan. In fact, he was one of the great mediums—and great healers—of all times. The cases Myers cured number several hundred; they are on record. But perhaps the most outstanding of his cases was also his first really important one: Myers' meeting with the American business executive R. L. Parish, who was then suffering from a chronic sciatic condition as well as from defective vision. Within a few days after Myers' application of healing, the pain from the sciatic nerve had ceased and for the first time in many years Parish was able to see without glasses. In gratitude Parish invited Myers to join his company (and thus the second half of Myers' career began, with his move to New York City).

Many years later Myers was able to repay Parish for his friendship. On March 3, 1960, Mrs. Parish was injured in an automobile accident during a snowstorm. Rushed to a north Westchester hospital, she was examined by the family doctor, Donald Richie, M.D. The examination showed multiple bilateral rib fractures, hemorrhaging into the right side of the chest cavity, partial collapse of the right lung, and a fracture of the right shoulder. John Myers, who was then in Mexico, rushed back to New York to be at the bedside of his friend's wife. He requested fifteen minutes alone with the patient. The second day after the healer's visit, Mrs. Parish was out of bed. On the eleventh day she left the hospital. Donald Richie stated at the time that "no medical explanation for a recovery in six days from injuries that would have taken even a young, active person three to four weeks' time can be offered."

Interestingly, Myers was even able to heal himself, something very few psychic healers can do. In 1957, he suffered a serious hemorrhage and in the middle of the night was taken to Medical Arts Hospital in New York City. His personal physician, Dr. Karl Fischbach, examined him and discovered a growth over the right kidney. Several cancer experts examined Myers subsequently, and biopsies were taken in the operating room to determine whether or not the growth was malignant. The uninamous verdict was that an immediate operation was imperative, that any delay might prove to be fatal.

John Myers steadfastly refused. He informed his doctors that he had no intention of being operated upon but would do for himself what he had often done for others. Myers remained in the hospital for one week for observation. During that time he healed himself, calling upon the divine powers that had helped him so many times before in the case of others. The cancer disappeared at the end of the week, never to return.

A similar happening occurred in 1958, when John Myers suffered an acute inflammation of the appendix. The examining physician, Dr. Samuel Schwartz, insisted that he submit to an operation at once, saying that otherwise he could not be responsible for Myers' life. Myers, unconvinced of the need for the operation, checked into Knickerbocker Hospital in New York City, where the diagnosis was confirmed by a panel of doctors. Again, Myers politely refused to be operated upon. Two hours later all pain had ceased, and he spent a peaceful night. Examination the following day revealed that the inflammation had entirely disappeared. Myers had no further trouble with his appendix.

Among the diseases John Myers cured successfully were gall bladder trouble, cancer, heart disease, and many lesser ills, such as headaches, arthritis, and just plain muscular pains. He worked by passing his hands over the afflicted area or touching the patient just as he was directed by what he described as his spirit control, an American Indian who had passed on many years before.

Myers' own death did not come due to illness or any state of general weakness; he lived to a great age, though during the last few years, when he had retired from all active work, he complained of being somewhat tired.

The late Lotte von Strahl was most interested in following a career as a psychic healer. Although she saw people at her studio in Westwood, any healing work she did was always done in conjunction with a medical doctor. Mrs. von Strahl began her career as a psychic healer in South Africa during World War II when a leading South African surgeon asked her to try to help his mother, who was suffering from blindness in one eye and partial blindness in the other. Mrs. von Strahl placed her hands upon the old woman, who reported immediate relief. Altogether twelve sittings were necessary to accomplish what was asked of Mrs. von Strahl. After that, the mother could read and even do her knitting.

About the same time another patient came to her because the medical doctors had dismissed him as a hopeless case. After he had fallen from a ladder, a tumor had formed at the base of his spine. Mrs. von Strahl started to treat him by placing her hands upon the spot where she psychically saw the tumor. At the same time she prayed for help. She kept her hands on the spot until an inner voice or feeling told her that she had done enough. Soon after, the patient reported that he was completely cured, so much so that he took a physical job as a gardener.

Mrs. von Strahl was even able to heal long distance, by going out of her physical body and visiting a sick friend. While the von Strahls were living in London, a friend of hers, Ida Gravestein, wrote to her from South Africa to complain that she was suffering from a swollen foot and that medical doctors could not help her or relieve the pain. That night Lotte von Strahl visited her ailing friend astrally and put her own hand on the injured foot. As soon as she felt that she had done enough, she returned to her own body, back in London. Soon afterward she received a letter from her friend in South Africa to say that a miracle had happened. (She was of course not aware of Lotte's astral visit.) "In the middle of the night I could suddenly move my foot and I had no pain," she said.

Mrs. von Strahl worked fully conscious. She looked at a sick person and drew conclusions from the condition of the aura. For instance, when she saw a large black spot, she knew that there are weaknesses in the area corresponding to the black spot. If the discoloration was very severe, she would actually feel the pain of that person.

Originally, Leonard Parsons was a police officer in England for twenty-five years. In the middle 1930s Parsons became acquainted with Harry Edwards, the famed British healer. Edwards told him that he would someday be engaged in psychic work himself—an idea Parsons thought ridiculous. Later, at the beginning of World War II, Leonard Parsons and his wife adopted a little girl orphaned by the blitz, and he continued to serve as a policeman. However, when the child was four months old, she developed a cyst on the side of her head. Her parents took her to Jenny Lind Children's Hospital in Norwich, where she was X-rayed and the condition was diagnosed as a tumor. An operation would have to be performed in a matter of several months.

Parsons, not taking this advice very kindly, went back to see his old neighbor, Harry Edwards, for advice. To the constable's amazement, Harry Edwards informed him that the child would be healed and that he, Parsons, would be the instrument. Edwards told him simply to put his fingers around the tumor. Dumbfounded, Constable Parsons did as he had been directed, and in three weeks the tumor had completely disappeared. When the pediatrician reminded Parsons that it was time for the operation, Parsons informed him of what he had done. To his surprise, the physician was not shocked. Indeed, he suggested that the hospital be informed, and Dr. Bulman at Jenny Lind Children's Hospital, who had heard of Harry Edwards, far from scorning the police officer's healing efforts, asked that Parsons help them with other cases.

"Now I felt entirely differently," Leonard Parsons explained to me when we met in Houston, Texas, where he now makes his home. "I was keen to do more work. I never had any contact with spirits; I wasn't aware of them; and I frankly didn't know how to do it. All I knew was that when people were sick, and it didn't matter how sick they were, something seemed to come over me and I was being used to heal them."

When Parsons left the police force, in 1955, he became interested in spiritualism and visited a number of churches in England. About eight years later, while sitting in a spiritualist circle, he went into trance and somebody spoke through him. A spirit guide identifying himself as Hassan manifested and informed the other members of the circle that he would henceforth be guiding the destiny of Leonard Parsons. The spirit control spoke of his own life on earth near Jerusalem. He mentioned an abbey at Quamram and said that some scrolls would be discovered there in the near future. (This was prior to the discovery of the Dead Sea Scrolls.)

Another healer who lives in Houston is a retired electrical and mechanical engineer named Don C. Overstreet. Overstreet, who now teaches therapeutical hypnosis to classes of interested believers and works as a healer with his wife, became interested in the psychic world when he was still a small boy as a result of some visionary experiences, but his activities were severely curtailed by his German father. Thus it was not until the late 1960s that he renewed his interest in the field.

In recent years, however, partially as the result of taking a course in mind control with Joe De Silva of Laredo, Texas, the Overstreets have begun to help those coming to them because of illness by visualizing their bodies and by going down to the deepest levels, attempting to see whatever abnormalities are present and then to correct them.

Mrs. Overstreet, working with her husband, has visualized, and then dissolved, many blood clots, taking no more than half an hour to do so and working in an adjoining room. She described her state as that of a semi-trance; she uses the Lord's Prayer to begin with and then visualizes the person she wants to work on.

The Overstreets explained that they were getting advice concerning their patients from spirit counselors; it was not merely a matter of getting down to a deep level of consciousness. As Don Overstreet explained: "You're given the name and age of a person or the initials. Then you go to your level and ask the counselors to bring this person to you. They bring the astral or etheric body to you. Then you start analyzing it from the head on down, and any dark areas indicate malfunction. Then you go clear through it and find all the dark areas; then you go back and analyze them one at a time. Our teachings tell us that we are learning to use our minds to detect abnormalities in any kingdom, whether animal, vegetable, or human. We are learning to use our minds to bring back to normalcy any abnormalities found just by thought processes."

"It's not really good to do this in the presence of the person," Mrs. Overstreet added. "The healing proceeds more positively if the person is not in the same room with the healer," she explained.

Probably the world's most famous psychic healer was England's Harry Edwards. Edwards heard the call at a spiritualist seance when he was told by the medium that he should use his gifts for psychic healing. Soon afterward he developed trance mediumship and realized that he had been chosen as an instrument to manifest healing from the spirit world. He is convinced that his spirit guides are Drs. Louis Pasteur and Lord Lister, but he attributes the essence of his powers to God.

From time to time Edwards undertook mass healing services at London's Albert Hall or Royal Festival Hall, places large enough to hold several thousand people at one time. He welcomed the spotlight of press, radio, and television and had an impressive record of actual healings performed in the glare of precisely such spotlights. Crippled individuals stepped up and explained their affliction to the healer. He then made some passes over them or touched their bodies, at the same time praying for divine assistance. Not infrequently, the healing was instantaneous and the crippled person, unable to walk before, in many instances, walked off the platform briskly—cured. At other times, several consultations or healing sessions were necessary.

The majority of Harry Edwards' work was done at his healing

sanctuary at Shere, Surrey, England, where he used the early morning hours to meditate and tune in on the power he would use during the day. Only a small number of those seeking to be healed by him actually journied out to his sanctuary. Many thousands of others, unable to do so, were in correspondence with him for absent healing, and some absent healing does indeed work, although there is no question that the physical presence of the healer with the patient is much more likely to yield results than a mere exchange of correspondence.

Dr. Danny Abse, in his book *Medicine on Trial,* states that Harry Edwards told him that "the majority who write to me have been told that they are incurable; as a result of my meditations eighty percent record a measure of improvement, thirty percent of these have a complete recovery."

One of the first cases Edwards worked on involved a neighbor named Gladys Cudd, a teenager dying of consumption. Edwards placed his hands on her head and asked for healing. At that point he became conscious of a power flow through him. His body felt alive with energy, which flowed down through his arms and from there into the patient. Something within him made him tell the girl's mother that she would be up and well within three days; the physician had told the mother that her daughter was about to die.

That same afternoon, the high fever which she had long been suffering from was gone from the girl. The following day she vomited large quantities of a red substance and started to take food again as if she were not suffering from any deadly disease. Two days later she was up and about, cured. For a while Edwards kept in touch with his erstwhile patient through absent healing correspondence; then he lost track of her. Over the years she married and raised a family. In 1970 she paid the healer a surprise visit at his shrine in Shere to inform him that she was about to become a healer herself, opening a center for healing the sick in Devonshire, England.

Harry Edwards, who liked to work in his shirtsleeves, was a heavy-set, physical type oozing with robust health. Even in his eighties, he worked, assisted by four other healers, Ray and Joan Branch and George and Olive Burton, and each healer specialized in one

particular part of the human body. The mansion at Shere is a sprawl-
ing Tudor style manor house, surrounded by greenery and a large
garden, secluded from industrial and other pollution, an ideal spot.
Edwards maintained an efficient staff to respond to the large volume
of mail he received and to set up appointments for those seeking
in-person treatments. There was even a bus service from the nearest
railroad station to enable those coming for a healing to arrive just
before the scheduled appointment and to depart immediately afterward. Everything was done quietly and efficiently, just as if Edwards
were running a quiet country hospital. Payment for all treatments was
by voluntary donation.

I arranged for a visit at the sanctuary by my wife Catherine and
myself for July 16, 1970. When we arrived at Burrows Lea, the
sanctuary, we were ushered into a pleasant, good-sized study in
which the general healing sessions took place. Harry Edwards felt that
my witnessing the healing of various patients might give me a better
insight into his methods and approach.

A number of books contain detailed accounts of Harry Edwards'
amazing healing powers, especially his own *Thirty Years a Spiritual
Healer* and Paul Miller's *Born to Heal*, but what I witnessed was a quiet
consultation taking place between individual patients and their healer.
Evidently some of the people had come to Harry Edwards before.
There was quiet, subdued discussion as to the state of the condition;
then Edwards placed his hands upon the afflicted area or, in some
cases, asked one of his associate healers to take over.

In our case it was Olive Burton. I placed myself into a comfortable chair across from Mrs. Burton. She then extended her arms and
made a number of passes over my closed eyes and ears. My complaint
was, as ever, an incurable noise in my left ear; my wife's, general
irregularities involving hormones and other circulatory factors. During the treatment I had the impression of concentric circles surrounding my head, and I felt energy surging from the healer's hands into my
ear. I did not expect a single treatment to show dramatic results, and
it did not. But I felt better.

After the healing session was over, Harry Edwards sat down
with us for a few minutes to discuss psychic healing or, as he prefers to

call it, spiritual healing. He attributes the majority of diseases to frustrations on the spiritual level and feels that spirit healing is necessary to undo the damage of such frustrations before the physical body can be healed. I asked whether he was cooperating with medical doctors.

"Not with the medical profession as a whole, but some doctors as individuals come here and bring their patients or send them to us," he explained. "I don't think you can mix up the two therapies. Medical therapy is based on physical science, and this is spirit science. Both are complementary to each other."

"I noticed you always asked your patients whether or not conventional treatment had been administered before you treat them," I said.

The healer nodded. "Yes," he said, "because if conventional treatment has been used and it is the right kind then it obviously will help the person. I think the two approaches are compatible, if there is understanding and one works with the other. For example, let us take the dispersal of arthritis in a joint. If we can get the joint free by our methods, the patient will still need physiotherapy in order to carry on."

"Are you being troubled in any way by the authorities?"

"The British Medical Counsel threatened to strike off the register any doctor who cooperates with us. Nevertheless some doctors do. No one has yet been struck off for it. But there are one or two things we can't do, such as advertise a cure for cancer or epilepsy. And we are not permitted to prescribe for animals nor allowed to do dental treatment or venereal treatment."

Some medical doctors explain the amazing percentage of cures accomplished by Harry Edwards and his associates as being due either to spontaneous remission or to psychological therapy. In fact, this holds true only in a minute percentage of actual cases, since he treats physical ailments that cannot be "suggested away." In a majority of Edwards' healings, *physical* changes do take place in the body of the patient. Whether or not the action in the patient's body is triggered by suggestion, prayer, or Edwards' laying on of hands is really beside the point: if the patient is cured, the method worked.

On a much less spectacular scale, the sanctuary maintained by Philip and Kathleen Wyndham at 56 Narford Road, London, England, follows similar avenues of healing. The Wyndhams work through private appointments, prayer links for those tuning in at certain times following individual healing sessions, and public healing demonstrations, generally held at Caxton Hall in London. They also maintain absent healing correspondence along the lines of Harry Edwards' voluminous correspondences, requesting free-will donations only in return. What makes them especially interesting, however, is the fact that in addition to their spiritual healing, the Wyndhams suggest certain dietary approaches, based primarily on Dr. D. C. Jarvis' book, *Folk Medicine*.

England, in fact, can boast of many important healers—and healing partnerships. But none is so effective as the partnership of Willian Lang and George Chapman. Dr. William Lang, an eye surgeon and a respectable member of the British medical profession, has much in common with George Chapman. To begin with, both heal the sick in their own way, although Dr. Lang's ministrations are now done in a somewhat unusual manner. Both men live in the same house, a quiet, better-than-average private house—at 149 Wendover Road; it is known as St. Bride's—in a side street in the town of Aylesbury, Buckinghamshire, England. Both men love the house and rarely leave it. But here the similarity ends. George Chapman is the trance medium for the dead Dr. William Lang, who continues his practice in what used to be his old home through the entranced hands and talents of medium George Chapman.

Although a number of books and many articles have been written about this strange partnership, probably the most interesting work dealing with George Chapman and his work is Bernard Hutton's *Healing Hands*. Those who seek help from the healer include even medical doctors. According to *Psychic News*, November 27, 1971, "A young staff doctor at a famous London hospital where Lang used to work says the spirit surgeon has cured his pancreas deficiency." A woman doctor from Ireland who visited George Chapman's sanctuary explained that the medium, operating under trance instructions from the dead eye surgeon, "performed various operations in the area of her liver and lower abdomen and finally felt her fingers, confirming their rheumatoid arthritic condition." According to the newspaper, the doctor felt fine on her return to Northern Ireland and on the following day felt as if she actually had had an operation. There was severe pain and she had to lie down. Her husband, also a surgeon, was convinced that the healer and his spirit partner had actually done something to her body. Shortly afterward, she felt fine again.

What George Chapman does is called etheric surgery; he passes his hands over the affected area of the body of his patient and makes the movements of performing surgery—without, however, actually doing any cutting or entering the body whatsoever. In this respect he is quite different in his methods from the so-called wonder healers of the Philippines, who actually enter the body of the patient and extricate unwanted matter from the body. Similarly, the late Arago of Brazil also used actual tools, a penknife in many instances, to operate physically on his patients and in this manner would remove diseased tissue. With George Chapman there is no blood, no surgery tools, nothing physical whatsoever.

Among Chapman's patients was a lady from Puerto Rico on whom the healer performed etheric surgery. Looking at her stomach later, she found that there was a "new mark about four inches long, like a fine scar." The scar disappeared after a week.

According to George Chapman, he has signed a contract with a group of medical doctors, some of whom actually knew and worked with the late Dr. William Lang. The idea is to continue to utilize that late eye surgeon's great talents through the mediumship of Chapman and to make that knowledge available to conventional eye surgeons. Apparently the group of doctors who had known Lang in his lifetime were convinced by the trance performance George Chapman undertook in their presence. The doctors tested the medium by submitting case histories of their patients for Lang's opinion. Since George Chapman has had no medical training whatsoever, he would not have been able to diagnose or prescribe for these patients in his own right.

Nevertheless, the entranced Chapman was able to give the correct answers in each and every case, convincing the doctors that they were indeed dealing with the spirit of their late colleague, manifesting through the body of medium George Chapman.

On September 25, 1967, my wife and I entered Chapman's healing sanctuary. We had been sent an appointment card in advance, which I now surrendered to Mr. Chapman's secretary. The card instructed us to refrain from smoking and not to bring pets, tape recorders, or cameras into the healer's presence. We were given to understand that each patient could have only one in-person sitting with the healer. After that the healing would be continued by distant healing; we were instructed to link up with Chapman long distance every Monday night at 10:00 P.M. for fifteen minutes. There was no set fee for our appointment, and when I asked afterward what I should leave, I was told that a one-pound note a person—less than three dollars—would be quite enough.

Catherine had gone in first while I was waiting outside for my turn. "He was extremely friendly to me," Catherine explained later. "First he started to show me the room, explaining the various objects in it. Then he told me to sit down and to relax and began to examine me by putting his hands on my back and sliding them down. When he came to the area of my heart he said that everything was fine up to that point. Then he went over the stomach area, sliding perhaps half an inch above the body, and when he arrived in the area of the abdomen he explained that was there where my problem was. He also asked me not to be surprised if he snapped his fingers and mentioned the names of other people whom I could not see. He was only speaking to his late wife and to the dead surgeon helping him. He then asked me to get up and walk around the room while he explained some of the photographs on the walls to me. After a tour of the room, he told me to lie down again on the couch and this time he would operate on me."

"But he didn't actually operate, did he?" I asked.

Catherine shook her head. "Not exactly," she said, "when he wanted a certain instrument or an injection done he would snap his fingers and call out the name of the operation and then he would hold his hands over my stomach area. He pushed them over it and was moving them and doing all sorts of things which of course I could not see because my head was up and my eyes directed toward the ceiling."

"Did you actually feel anything?"

"Yes and no. I think I felt a slight sensation toward the end, especially on my right side. That was where I had the two injections. It was not painful. I felt it more after I was out of the room. But at the time when it was being done I didn't feel a thing."

"Do you feel anything right now?"

"I still feel the sensation in the area of the abdomen, sort of like mild cramps, but nothing uncomfortable."

My own experiences with George Chapman were similar. After I had taken the chair, I was told that I had a problem with my hair and that something should be done about it. With his eyes closed, the medium then diagnosed my problems as a matter of being over-weight, a problem itself stemming from a retention of water in the body. He described this condition in great detail, at the same time assuring me that my heart and lungs were very strong and in good condition. All this was entirely correct and known to me from previous orthodox examinations, but it is a little difficult to see how a stranger without medical training could so quickly diagnose these conditions without ever touching me and with his eyes closed. In fact, George Chapman does go into trance at the beginning of his day, and he does not leave that state until all patients have left at the end of the day. Most of the time his eyes are closed, and at times when they seem to be open he is not actually acting as himself but as the entranced instrument of the late Dr. William Lang. I looked into his eyes at such moments and am satisfied that he was fully in trance.

Since he had not brought up the primary question of my visit, I brought it up myself, saying only that I had some problem with my ear and what could he do about it. He informed me that the noises were due to a fissure in the middle ear bone, and he then "operated" on me in a manner similar to that applied to Catherine when she was in his "operating room." I felt absolutely nothing at the time, but my ear noises seemed to *increase* a little after I left Mr. Chapman's house. Later on they were back to what they were before. Chapman also remarked that he would have to operate on my eyes and remove some "tartar" so that the muscles could be extended and relaxed more easily. While I had never heard a reference to eye tartar, but was familiar with the term from dentistry, I must admit that my eyes seemed a great deal more refreshed after I left the office.

In summing up what Chapman did and did not do, I recall that he promised me nothing in relation to the ear noises but did say that my hair and eyes would improve. The fact is that while I have not grown any new hair since then, I have lost almost none; while I wear glasses occasionally, my eyes are in excellent condition. He also mentioned he was correcting a liver problem by giving me an injection into the liver. He did this by calling out for help from his unseen spirit associates and snapping his fingers whenever that help was needed, going through the motions just like a real flesh-and-blood doctor. He used many technical terms apparently quite correctly, and the entire operation took less than half an hour.

To be sure, Chapman's healing in our case was neither spectacular nor radical. But then our ailments were of the kind one could live with. Quite possibly, had we continued the distant healing technique demanded by George Chapman from his patients, and kept it up, additional improvements would have occurred. Two things are certain: he has cured others; during the spirit operation, there was definite change. Something happened. This was not suggestion, imagination, or wishful thinking. We both felt it.

Probably the most personable psychic healer I ever encountered was the late Gordon Turner, who frequently served as the president of the National Federation of Spiritual Healers of Great Britain. Gordon Turner, a writer for BBC radio, discovered his healing talents accidentally in the course of taking an interest in occult matters. Because of his position within the radio industry he was able to explain and frequently defend the position of psychic healing on the airwaves of Britain. In his early middle years, he was the picture of health, and perhaps more scientifically oriented than such people as Harry Edwards or Phil Wyndham, who stand more firmly on spiritualist ground.

Gordon Turner maintained a healing center at 796 Fulham

Road, London, and was especially interesting because he differed from most psychic healers in that he also healed animals. In 1971, for example, he saved the life of an Alsatian German shepherd dog that had been condemned to death. The dog suffered from a malignant growth as a result of having had her womb removed in surgery. The dog's owner refused to have her put away and instead brought her to Gordon Turner. Because the dog's wound was very painful, the healer could only hold his hands over the affected area. This treatment was continued through absent healing for some time. Gradually the growth started to disappear, and after five months of weekly treatments, supported by absent healing, the dog was well again.

My wife and I, who visited Turner in July 1967, were treated individually. Turner asked us to sit quietly in a comfortable chair for the treatment. In my case I very definitely felt a vibration going through my entire body when Turner stood behind me and placed his hands upon my shoulders. He then passed his hands about a quarter of an inch alongside of my entire body, stopping briefly in the area of the ears, since I had indicated to him that it was in that area that my problem was. For twenty-four hours after the treatment I felt strangely charged with energy. There was a hum in my left ear that had not been there prior to the treatment. Several days afterward, the ear noises resumed their normal level again. I am sure that continuous visits to the healer, perhaps once a week for several months, would have yielded more permanent results. As it was, my "sample treatment" was proof that something happened when Gordon Turner put his hands upon me or when he passed them along my body.

Another London healer is portly, jovial E. G. "Ted" Fricker, who as a child heard a voice that convinced him that he had a mission to fulfill. In 1955, when he himself was seeking help from another healer, he was told that he had the divine gift of healing himself and that he would someday practice it. At that time Fricker worked in an office, in a subordinate position, and the idea of becoming a psychic healer was far from his mind. Nevertheless, this is exactly what happened.

In his biography of Fricker, *Psychic News* editor Maurice Barbanell says, "Almost every ailment known to man has yielded to his ministrations. He specializes, however, in treatment of those two modern afflictions, ulcers and slipped discs, which, if there are no complications, are cured in a single treatment . . . innumerable patients have discarded their spinal belts and supports which they have been told were medically indispensable . . . former ulcer sufferers, as their testimony demonstrates, have left his sanctuary and consumed foods that have been forbidden as dangerous to them."

Fricker operates mainly by the laying on of hands, although he uses a peculiar form of rubbing them prior to administering his power. He ascribes his healing power to God and his sanctuary in North London bears testimony to his religious leanings. Fricker's healing work demonstrates the quandary a healer can be in at times, when his desire for worldly position comes into conflict with the essential humility required of a truly great healer. Fricker treats his gifts as if he were a Harley Street specialist. It is true that he may treat the poor without expecting to be paid; it is equally true that he charges those able to pay, at times handsome sums, far beyond the customary one guinea.

In this respect, Fricker parallels the approach by the late Austrian physician R. Zeileiss, a miracle healer in the 1920s and 1930s whose name went around the world at the time. Zeileiss touched his patients with a rod of crystal, claiming that mysterious radiation flowed through his staff. The conservative medical establishment had little use for him, but he did not seem to violate the law and thus was left alone. Thousands of people went to see him and came away cured. Whether by suggestion, spontaneous remission, or because of his treatments, the fact was that there were many cures.

Another famous healer, the late Achille D'Angelo of Naples, Italy, known as the "Magus of Naples," also obtained both a sizable reputation as an effective healer and considerable fees from those he healed, especially among the "well heeled." There is nothing inherently dishonest in such a worldly approach to healing, for the vows of poverty are an individual and personal choice, not something prescribed by either law or custom. To lash out at men like Fricker or D'Angelo merely because they charge some people substantial fees for their healing ministrations is unfair; so do doctors and specialists, without regard to their success.

Of course, healers are found internationally. For example, the Mannheim-born Arthur Orlop, who lives at 68 Mannheim Dammstrasse 4, West Germany, found a new profession as a clairvoyant when his acting abilities were no longer appreciated by the many small theaters in West Germany. In a climate that was far from friendly toward his new profession, Orlop managed to acquire a good reputation as a man who could foretell the future and on occasion also heal the sick. Eventually this brought him into conflict with the authorities, and on two occasions he was prosecuted for his work. In his defense he managed to submit many testimonials from those he had worked for, and in time the city of Mannheim, which had tried to put him out of business, let him be.

Most of Orlop's work consists in the evaluation of people's characteristics and potentials; he has many private clients who engage him to read for them, pretty much the way an American medium reads for her clients. In Germany this is done somewhat more precisely and with greater skepticism, perhaps because the climate of Europe is not a believer's world and clairvoyants are still considered fringe people whose ability has to be proven over and over again.

My wife and I met the *Hellseher*, as clairvoyants are called in German, at the Hotel Carlton in Nuremberg on September 7, 1967. His medical advice was precise and consisted mainly in pointing out the weaknesses in the physical condition of both my wife and myself. He prescribed certain homeopathic medicines and warned us to take care of certain conditions, which we did. By and large his appraisal of our physical condition coincided with the diagnosis given us before and after our visit to Nuremberg by our physician, a man who specializes in dietary medicine. It was neither startling nor overwhelming in any sense, but coming from an untutored clairvoyant who did not know us, it certainly was worthy of attention.

Much more significant, however, are the witnessed reports of his healings. From the voluminous material at my disposition, the following will suffice to establish Orlop as a psychic healer to be reckoned with.

According to the written report of Mrs. Therese Honnecker of Mannheim, Germany, dated November 15, 1950, "I suffered from a severe stomach ailment which had progressed to the point where I could not stand the pains without morphine injections. . . . In my despair I went to see Mr. Orlop. He prescribed a simple natural remedy. Eight days later I felt greatly relieved. Two weeks after that I went to see Mr. Orlop again to confirm that my stomach troubles had completely disappeared."

Evidently Orlop's gift is twofold: diagnosis by psychic means followed by advice on what remedies to take. The remedies prescribed by Orlop are primarily homeopathic or naturopathic remedies, generally available from drugstores without prescriptions. In this respect there seem to be some parallels between Orlop's methods and those of Edgar Cayce, who also prescribed certain rare or forgotten remedies for diseases where modern physicians would use other methods.

> "I want to thank you for recognizing my trouble on the basis of my handwriting and your clairvoyance. The remedy you prescribed, namely Luwo's healing of bladder treatment, has helped me a great deal during the first few days. So much so that I was cured several weeks later. To me this seems a miracle — Rudolf Kispert, Mannheim." So reads another report.

An insurance inspector named Helmut Jaeckel, also of Mannheim, certified in March 1956, that Orlop had given him proof of his clairvoyant abilities in areas having to do with his business. "On January 28, 1956, Orlop predicted to me that there would be a large fire, caused by explosion, in the area of Weinheim-Bergstrasse, around the middle of February of this year. There was no way in which he could foretell such an event, of course. As a matter of fact the event did occur as predicted, on February 18, and caused damage of several million marks at the quarters of the Freudenberg Company in Weinheim. Since I had heard that even medical doctors were consulting with Orlop in cases of difficult diagnoses, I consulted him myself in the matter of an annoying fungus infection in my feet. For years specialists had failed to remedy the situation. Orlop listened to my description and then recommended a certain harmless remedy which I was to take internally. This remedy was easily available in all pharmacies. I received this advice with great skepticism, but several days later there was an improvement and four weeks after our initial conversation, just as Orlop had predicted, the infection was completely gone."

Few U.S. specialists would have the courage to give written testimony to the ability of an unorthodox healer, especially when that healer had been recently in the courts for violation of an old paragraph dealing with fraudulent membership, something that certainly did not apply to Orlop. But Hanns Probst, M.D., a surgeon in Ludwigshafen, Germany, did just that in a statement dated July 15, 1951. The case involved a certain Mrs. Dollinger, who had been to Arthur Orlop on April 30, 1951. Orlop had given her a prognosis concerning her health. Following up on the clairvoyant's diagnosis, the surgeon examined the patient. In addition to the surgeon, Dr. Wittenbeck, Chief of the Gynecology Department at the City Hospital, Mannheim, also was consulted. Mrs. Dollinger then became a patient at the city hospital and was later operated upon. Here is the statement by Dr. Hanns Probst concerning the case.

> "On April 30, 1951, Mr. Orlop diagnosed an area of infection in the patient's uterus, the size of a fist. Dr. Wittenbeck confirmed the presence of a tumor the size of a fist. It was removed surgically. Mr. Orlop also stated with firm conviction that Mrs. Dollinger's pregnancy could not be saved. Dr. Wittenbeck was of the opinion that the pregnancy of the woman could be saved. However, he confirmed later in a letter dated June 12, 1951, that several days after the operation the fetus was lost spontaneously. In retrospect it can be stated that the diagnosis of Mr. Orlop concerning Mrs. Dollinger was almost 100 percent correct. —Dr. Hanns Probst."

But Orlop does not simply diagnose the illnesses of patients. Frequently he gets spontaneous impressions about people, sometimes even long distance. In a letter dated March 29, 1971, he congratulated my wife and me on her pregnancy. I had expressed my expectation that our second child would be a boy, to which Orlop replied: "Unfortunately it will be a girl. I am sure you understand. After the birth I suggest your wife take liver injections for some time." Five days later we had a little baby girl. Independently our physician put Catherine on a regular program of Vitamin B_{12} shortly after the birth. Orlop had also told us that the little girl would be extremely sensitive to temperature changes, especially when breathing through the nose. This has been our daughter Alexandra's main problem in the oft-changing New York climate.

Probably the most controversial aspect of unorthodox healing involves so-called psychic surgery. In this process untutored individuals physically work on patients with various disorders, extricate diseased tissue, sometimes using non-sterilized instruments in their work. Psychic surgery is controversial both for the claims made for it and for the methods employed, which horrify those trained along orthodox medical lines. In fact, a man such as the late Brazilian healer Arago operating on a patient with a penknife would be inviting all sorts of infections *under ordinary circumstances*. However, one of the aspects of this type of healing is its disregard for conventional dangers: the power that allows untutored individuals to perform seeming miracles, guiding them intelligently and precisely, also sees to it that infections do not occur. I know of no single case where disease resulted from the intervention of an unorthodox healer or psychic surgeon.

Prior to the discovery of aseptic methods in medicine, the medical profession lived by antiseptic standards—that is, infections were accepted as part of the picture but could be fought by counter-agents. Is it not possible that there is a third order of things, known perhaps only to those on the Other Side of life, whereby infections cannot only be fought or avoided but ignored because of superior powers inherent in the process? I know for a fact that psychic photography, when it is genuine and spontaneous, follows its own optical laws in total disregard of conventional rules of photography. In such instances overexposure does not result in the destruction of the light-sensitive elements in film but, to the contrary, produces psychic images. By the same token I think that something not yet fully understood comes into operation when a psychic surgeon operates, even by primitive means.

The psychic surgery discussed here is not the same as that previously mentioned in the case of English healer George Chapman. In Chapman's case, the motions are undertaken and invisible instruments are used, but the body of the patient itself is not entered. With such world-famous psychic surgeons as Arago and the much maligned but as yet not fully understood Tony Agpaoa, as well as the half a dozen lesser known healers of the type in the Philippines and in Brazil, the skin is actually broken by the healer's hands and tissue removed from the body. No anesthetic is used; the patient is fully conscious but still feels no pain.

In Harold Sherman's *Wonder Healers of the Philippines* and Tom Valentine's *Psychic Surgery* actual cases are quoted with pre-surgery and post-surgery statements by medical doctors. "Dr. Tony," as he is popularly called, in particular has been the subject of much persecution and attempts to expose him by journalists and medical authorities alike. Some disclosures indicate fraud, but others show that actual healings did occur due to his work. On balance I see no clear-cut proof that Agpaoa really practiced out-and-out fraud, and Dr. Andrija Puharich, a medical doctor and pioneer in the field of hearing, as well as an experienced parapsychologist, spent much time with Arago and was treated himself by the Brazilian healer. He is convinced of the genuineness of the treatments.

There is a certain commerciality and overzeal on the part of promoters as well as blind belief on the part of some patients who cannot accept the possibility that even so renowned a healer as Dr. Tony may fail in single instances, but too many serious and reliable witnesses have seen healers of this type open skin and put their fingers into the wounds thus created, with no or minimal flow of blood, to dismiss psychic surgery as fraud. Psychic surgery is an observable fact, and sufficient numbers of cases exist to warrant proper scientific investigation.

Not all psychic surgery need be as dramatic as that practiced in the Philippines, of course. For example, the Reverend William C.

Brown, known as "the miracle healer of Georgia," is a psychic surgeon who operates as a spiritualist minister and under the protection of the law applying to religion in Arizona. He may be reached at P.O. Box 2205, Sedona, Arizona 86336. During his etheric surgery Rev. Brown is entranced by the discarnate English physician Dr. John Geoffrey Spaulding. But the medium has a number of controlling entities, all of them medical doctors in their earthly lives. These medical helpers from the Other Side of life include a diagnostician, Dr. John Murphy; a neurologist, Dr. Sean O'Hara; a heart specialist, Dr. Edward Fredericks; an orthopedic surgeon, Dr. Charles Chandler; and many other specialists.

Using methods somewhat similar to those employed by George Chapman, Rev. Brown, in his operation on the etheric body, puts on invisible rubber gloves and gives the patient an equally invisible hypodermic injection. As he moves about the body of the patient, he is handed invisible instruments by invisible nurses. The operations do not take as long as conventional operations, and afterward the patient can walk to his bed in one of the cottages near the healer's residence. According to Rev. Brown, the time required for the body to adjust to the changes initiated in the etheric counterpart varies with the extent of the surgery performed.

William Brown is careful in his letters and in his printed material to emphasize that he does not make any claims to cure people. What happens, he says, is that people cure themselves; he and his spirit helpers merely *induce* the cure in the patient. Brown's etheric surgery is performed without set fee, and voluntary donations are the rule. To stay at the nearby cottages used to cost only seven dollars a day, hardly an extravagant figure.

On January 12, 1970, Rev. Brown wrote to me to explain how he worked. "Often I become aware of a person's problem when I see them and sometimes without having seen them at all," he wrote, adding, "As I write this my left eye has a dull ache as does the left ear; if this fits your problem then we are on the right track." I had not told him anything about my ear problem, and at the time of our correspondence I also had some difficulty with the lid of my left eye. Finally, people whose judgment I respect, such as medium Ethel

Johnson Meyers, have been to Reverend William C. Brown and come back in better health, or at least feeling better.

I myself met Rev. Brown and his charming wife Sylvia Maria in Los Angeles a few years ago. He was then treating some twenty patients at the apartment of a friend on Wilshire Boulevard. I agreed to be a guinea pig also, so to speak, as I have for years suffered from a minor but annoying ear noise that is medically incurable, as it originates in the inner ear. I was placed face down on a table, wearing only a hospital gown, and then Brown began to perform his so-called etheric surgery on my ear. I felt absolutely nothing, one way or the other. When the British healers Gordon Turner and George Chapman had worked on me, I did indeed feel a burst of energy of sorts. Here I felt nothing. How then do we explain the undoubtedly genuine cures of some of his many other patients?

In his youth, Rev. Brown had always dreamed of becoming a surgeon—was he acting out a suppressed dream? Or was he a conduit for psychic power that somehow caused changes in the subject's physical condition? Brown thinks of himself as a true healer and to many people he is precisely that. The mechanics of his work remain unspecified. Is etheric surgery, performed through spirit surgeons, assisting him invisibly? Or is it true psychic healing from his own hands? Or even a combination of psychological persuasion and self-healing? Or all of these?

I was introduced to Henry Rucker of Chicago in December 1972, by a mutual friend, Penny South, the president of her own psychical research society. He had spoken for her group and given her and others known to her remarkable samples of his healing powers. Henry Rucker is in his early fifties, a well-spoken and well-educated black man, with a soft voice and a quiet sense of dedication that struck me immediately as being very much in line with his work. A native of Chicago, he attended De Paul University and since 1969 has headed his own psychic research foundation. Although his specialty is palmistry, on which he lectures extensively, he prefers the healing side of his development and has been very active in an antidrug program of his own. He has taught a course on "Other Dimensions and Sensory

Parameters" at Columbia College in Chicago, and though he cannot be classified as a spiritualist in the technical sense of the word, it would appear that his teachings are similar in some respects to the philosophies held by that American religion.

"How did you discover your psychic gift originally?" I asked him during our meeting.

"When I was eight years old, I had a tonsillectomy. While I was still partially under the effects of the anesthesia, I found myself leaving my body. It was frightening; I thought I was dead. Every time I relaxed, I was on the other side of the room. I mentioned this to a nurse, who told me that if I was a nice boy I would have ice cream in the morning. But this did not satisfy me; I had to keep myself in certain positions, so that I would not get out of my body. From that time on many strange things have happened to me. I knew of things that were to happen. People would ask me about their life, and without thinking I would rattle off the things I saw; I began to hear voices, even conversations."

"Did you ever recognize any of the voices?"

"Always. I would hear conversations and even the thoughts of other people, people complaining about their children, people praying, people that I knew."

"You mean *living* people?"

"Living people. There were times when I would sit in a room and hear exactly what a person was thinking. A person would think, 'I'm getting sick of this, I'm going to get up and walk out of here,' and the next moment I would actually see this person get up and walk out."

"Did the thoughts materially differ from the spoken words? Did they sound differently?"

"No. The voices I would hear would be *in their voice*."

"Have you ever heard from the so-called dead?"

"Many times. Twenty years ago I began to see spirits and had communications."

"What work were you doing at the time? "

"I was a salesman, and at the same time I was working for the

Board of Education as a truant officer. I also worked as supervisor in the Post Office."

"When did you first get involved in healing?"

"When I was a child, my mother used to be sick quite often, and I'd touch her or work on her, because I had the feeling I could do something for her and people who were sick."

"How did you heal them?"

"At that time I would heal them just with my mind, in their presence. It used to give me a terrific headache, because there seemed to be tremendous energies coming out of me, especially out of my eyes, and my hands seemed to be burning. One of the ways to get relief from this headache was to heal people, because the energy was backed up."

"Do you have a healing center?"

"Yes, the Psychic Research Foundation at 192 North Clark Street, Chicago. I give no guarantees of success, and there is no charge, either. I stay within the law; it is not illegal to pray for someone, nor to send forth energies from your mind. But we may not make diagnosis or touch a person or prescribe."

"If you don't touch a person, how do you heal?"

"We do etheric surgery. I would do an operation on a person without touching by working on the etheric *counterpart*, which I can see. The etheric body emanates a color that people describe as an aura, but to me it is simply the color emanations from one aspect of your total presence. I would see certain discolorations in certain areas."

"Then what would you do?"

"I wouldn't touch the person; I would begin to work on that person by using my etheric hands, and my physical hands would be moving as they are now."

"How close would you be to the person?"

"It wouldn't matter; I could be across the room, or right next to the person; I could do absent healing. If there were someone you knew who was sick, I would get a picture in my mind, and I could see that person through astral projection and work on him."

"Can you give me some recent examples of successful healings?"

"A ten-year-old boy had a brain tumor that has been diagnosed by a medical doctor. The boy dragged one foot and lisped and drooled at the mouth. I did an etheric operation and took the tumor off. The boy felt *immediate* results; he didn't drag his foot, he didn't lisp, and he stopped drooling. A week later he went back to the doctor to have the tumor removed, but it could not be found. Therefore there was no operation. He has not had an operation to this day; there was no relapse or anything of that sort."

"Can you give me another case where there were definite results?"

"Norman Esserman is my legal counsel. A friend of his, Yalina, was despondent because she had been given a diagnosis of terminal cancer; she had also been told that she would immediately have to have all of her teeth removed. She was in her middle forties. I gave her a healing. When she went back to the doctor the next week to have her teeth removed, it was unnecessary. She went for a further examination of the malignancy and it was found to be diminishing."

"What happened to her?"

"They've been making checks on her for at least four years. She is still alive."

"What diseases yield best to your healing?"

"I've had some good results with tumors and heart trouble."

While we were talking I noticed that Henry Rucker had been looking at my hands. Remembering that he was primarily a palmist, I asked whether he received any spontaneous impressions about me. He took my hands into his, gently touching them, and started to talk about me at a rapid pace, as if he had known me for many years. It was a strictly personal reading, and it was highly accurate. He touched some aspects concerning healing. My professional frustrations, he explained, were causing me a nervous stomach, a heavy feeling in my chest when I was emotionally upset, and a tendency toward diarrhea or constipation under the same conditions. He also mentioned that I had headaches and pointed to the side of the head where in fact I have them frequently. He suggested that I had sinus trouble due to weather changes, especially damp weather. "You can wake up in the morning and for no reason at all have a headache that comes right around in here from that sinus problem which may also affect the ear," he explained, again hitting it on the nose. Then he added, "There is some pressure inside your head; I don't know if you had an accident, it seems as if something damaged your drum or down into the Eustachian tube. Is there scar tissue or something like it down there?"

I was amazed. This man, without knowing anything about it or examining me with complicated and sophisticated apparatus, had come to exactly the same conclusion as four ear specialists had come to over the years. The only difference was that with the ear specialists I had to undergo lengthy and complicated examinations. Also, the specialists had shaken their heads and suggested that I get used to the idea of the resulting ear noises because there was nothing in the medical world that could be done about it. Henry Rucker thought otherwise. Although he felt that Tony Agpaoa of the Philippines could do a better job with psychic surgery, he would take a crack at it anyway. He asked me to put both my feet flat on the floor and sit back in my chair. "This will make you feel a little buzz in your ear, what I'm doing now will give you a sort of itchy or tickling sensation because you cannot reach where I am working and you feel you want to scratch it but you can't get at it." I knew he was working on me, but I felt nothing more than a vague sensation of pleasant comfort. Rucker then snapped his fingers, explaining that that was the way in which he was building up psychic energy. He wondered whether I felt the energy pulsating through me and added, "If I could describe it to you, you might be able to recognize it; this is not like hypnosis but much more undulating. It goes and comes." I acknowledged that I felt sensation along those lines going through my head.

Encouraged by my statement, Henry Rucker then offered to do more for me. Seeing that I was a little tired that afternoon, he said, "I'm going to do something to you in terms of working on the etheric body. I'm going to change your etheric body, smooth it out, by lifting it off you and then putting it back on you after it has been exposed to what metaphysicians would call the cosmic fire. I am still working on that ear too. Put your hands in between my hands and see if you can feel this nervous energy I am taking away from you."

I did and I could indeed feel a flow of energy between his large, deeply structured palms. As the healer continued to work on me, he suddenly spoke something in a language I did not recognize. "What were those words you just spoke?" I asked.

"Those were chants in Egyptian," he explained casually. "Sometimes I use Mongolian chants. These are like prayers and they have power."

My ear was not cured, but I felt very much better all over. The tension of the day was gone, and if nothing else, Henry Rucker had refurbished me with new energy from his own, well-stocked powerhouse.

The number of gifted healers among us seems to be on the increase. They come from every imaginable background and from every walk of life. Consider, for example, healer John Scudder, a former aeronautical engineer turned Spiritualist minister, who discovered he had the gift of healing the sick. The list of his successful cases is impressive indeed. When last heard from, he lived in Homewood, Illinois.

Blanche Myerson is a friendly lady living quietly in New York City at 138 E. 35th Street. I have seen her work as a healer and witnessed the relief she had brought to people by the laying on of hands and the more conventional holding of her hands over the afflicted areas of the body.

One of the world's most important healers is a former musician named Dean Kraft, who discovered his gift years ago and has been successful curing many, sometimes in hospitals, as he works well with traditional physicians. He does "touch healing" with amazing results, and frequent cures. Dr. Brian G.M. Durie, professor of medicine at UCLA, a cancer specialist, calls Kraft's work "energy transfer". Rep. Julia Howard of the North Carolina General Assembly, the State Legislature, witnessed how her husband, suffering from medically incurable Sclerosis, was immeasurably helped and eventually cured. Dean Kraft can be reached at 310 459-7564 or 310 286-1431 in Los Angeles, or in Amsterdam, The Netherlands, where he spends part of his time, at 011-3120-627 7677.

The Healing Light Center founded by Rosalyn Bruyère in Glendale, California, a part of Los Angeles, has a resident staff of several healers, each specializing in a particular area of affliction. The fees are very modest and the results gratifying. Rosalyn herself, who is no longer as active as in years past, has had a number of respectable articles published about her work and gift. She can be reached at 204 E. Wilson Avenue, Glendale, CA. Telephone (818) 244-8607.

My latest healing discovery is Catherine Paretti of New York City, who is both a professional psychic reader and a remarkable healer. In a recent case, a friend with a likely malignant chest tumor was told by her that her problem was not a malignancy, and a healing session ensued. The lady in question had the operation her doctor had ordered, a minor one, and the tumor indeed turned out to be nonmalignant.

Catherine Paretti came by her gift the hard way, and in a most unusual fashion. At age 22, a fall at work caused her to be paralyzed on one side of her body and to spend the next eight years in a wheelchair, helpless and in constant pain. Her condition had at first been misdiagnosed and the delay added to the nerve damage caused by the fall.

Eight years later, still bound to her wheelchair, she turned to unorthodox help for relief—psychic healers such as Art and Irine Ruzinski, who tried to do what the doctors could not, restored her to health.

Suddenly, while being treated in this way, she had a near-death experience in which she saw herself in a world she knew was another dimension, a dimension into which we all must pass eventually. A blinding light forced her to close her eyes; when she opened them again she saw her own body lying on the bed, motionless and lifeless, and her grandfather, who had died many years before, was there to comfort her. She did not want to go back into her body, but the spirits she met gently told her she must . . . and so she did, reluctantly, because the world she was leaving seemed so much better to her than the one she knew.

When she opened her eyes, back in her own body, she felt strange: something had happened. She got off the bed and walked; she was cured.

For six years she was fine and led a productive, normal life. Her own remarkable experience turned her interest to the psychic world and she began spending her energies helping others in need of healing.

But in 1982 she was to be tested again: she contracted a viral disease called Guillain-Barré Syndrome, a debilitating disease that caused her to be paralyzed from the neck on down. She survived only with the help of a special device, operated by her breath in a tube, to turn on the light, answer the telephone or do anything at all.

But her earlier experience convinced her she could fight for her life, regardless of dire medical prognostication as to her chances of survival. She willed her body to become whole, to recreate damaged nerve tissue, to restore to herself the nerve loss that was part of the dreaded disease. Step-by-step, slowly, painstakingly, she managed, through visualizations and self-healing, to first sit up, then gradually return to full health.

Today, she walks, runs, and dances as if nothing had ever happened to her. Except for some minor spots of limited sensitivity in her fingers and ankles, which she expects to overcome eventually through special exercises, Catherine is whole again. She works now as a full time psychic counselor and healer of others. The gift has stayed with her, as by a miracle . . . which it was.

Catherine Paretti can be reached in New York City at (718) 728-6836.

Finally, for those who might require a truly gifted psychic healer, in England there is the celebrated Doris Collins, who at various times also headed up the British Healers Association. She may be reached at 948-3316 in London.

Undoubtedly there are many undiscovered great healers among us, unaware of their special gifts. It remains for the right time and place and opportunity for them to discover what is within them; I am convinced that psychic healers of various kinds are as much part of the human establishment as are the orthodox medical practitioners, perhaps even more so, since they draw upon a more direct power link with the universal source. But even the greatest natural healer needs to be trained and disciplined, his services channeled in such a way that they are available to those truly needing them. Until we have independent research centers in parapsychology where healers can be recognized, tested, and trained, and where patients can be taken care of not according to their ability to pay but according to the severity and urgency of their illnesses, we will be dealing with the marvelous world of psychic healing merely on a hit-and-miss basis.

And this is a pity, considering the amount of illness in the world.

While some of the people mentioned in the previous section still practice (as of this writing), some may be out of the field tomorrow. New practitioners appear often, however, thus allowing people interested in finding a healer to do so.

Many healers contact me with a request to test them so that I may evaluate their efficiency and results. I do not, however, in any way guarantee results, I merely investigate and draw cautious, reasonable conclusions and report on them.

A new healer practicing his gift at the Theosophical Center in Wheaton, Illinois, contacted me recently to report on his progress as a healer. His name is Bob Smith, and he can be contacted at 211 Caddy, Carpentersville, Illinois 60110; his telephone number is (312) 428-7042.

In New Mexico, a healer named Joanna Corti has shown remarkable success with cases involving sciatica, infertility, cysts, and other problems. Having developed her abilities under a Philippine psychic surgeon's guidance, but also being trained in acupuncture and Oriental medicine, Corti uses the trance state to heal her patients. Much of her work is done via the telephone. Her patients are also put into a trance-like state as she goes about dealing with the illnesses or problems they have asked her to help them with. Joanna Corti lives in Sante Fé, New Mexico, and can be reached at (505) 989-1460.

Recently, the *New York Times* of September 5, 1993 reported the work of a registered nurse turned healer, by the name of Judy Wicker, who lives in New York City. Wicker calls herself a metaphysician, but what she really does is healing, using meditation to induce it. Considering that meditation is really a form of self-induced altered state of consciousness, during which energies can be made available for healing purposes more easily, we seem to be dealing with the same energy source all healers use.

Maria Cooper Janis, the daughter of the late Gary Cooper, has for years studied healers and psychics, and is herself a healer with considerable success in "absent healing"—when meditation is used to "tune in" on a patient at a distance.

While the question of authenticity still plagues the Philippine psychic surgeons, and much has been written either praising them or denouncing them as total fakes, I do not for a moment think that *all* psychic surgery is counterfeit, though undoubtedly some may be. But the underlying principle of removing diseased body parts without physical surgery is not so far-fetched as it might appear at first. If there are strong energy fields around the hands of the practitioner, momentary intrusion into the physical body and quick withdrawal seem to me to be within the realm of the possible. At any rate, a renowned Swiss doctor and head of the Swiss Society for Parapsychology, Dr. Hans Negele-Osjord, went to the Philippines to see first-hand what was real and what was not. His report does support the reality of some of the "operations" performed by Philippine "etheric" or psychic surgeons. At the same time, however, he points to imitators who charge large sums of money in what they have perceived to be an easy scam.

I recently received a request from a Philippine healer named Tilak Femondo to meet him in New York. He is not a psychic surgeon, but a healer who passes his hands over afflicted areas. I did feel strong energies when he did this to me and have no reservations about his sincerity and work. Femondo can be reached at 278 South 23rd Street, Philadelphia, Pennsylvania 19103.

In Los Angeles, there is a Spiritualist Center which has been doing excellent healing work for years, with a number of volunteer healers in attendance on certain days. It is located at 6417 Lexington Avenue, Los Angeles, California 90038; (213) 656-8646.

In Europe, healers also do much good work, even though some countries make it difficult for them to practice. In England, healers have a strong professional association which is self-policing. In Germany, the pragmatic attitude toward anything unorthodox still hampers an unbiased scientific but open-minded approach to the art of psychic healing. Still, there are healers there as well.

A man named George Rieder is reported to have "x-ray eyes"

which allow him to diagnose a patient by looking at him or her. Rieder claims to have discovered his gift through a spirit guide; he heals the etheric body, not the physical counterpart, which then falls in line with it. Cancer, even AIDS, are illnesses he has dealt with and is willing to deal with. Rieder ran into trouble in Austria, where the local medical association accused him of quackery: but the healer had ample proof that he had indeed been successful in the treatment of cancer patients and the matter was dropped. Rieder can be reached through the publication *VTF* of the German Verein fuer Tonbandforschung (Society for Electronic Voice Phenomena) at Hoehscheider Strasse 2, D 40591, Duesseldorf, Germany.

Even in Russia, psychic healing is becoming more and more acceptable. Parapsychology always was of interest to the authorities even under Soviet rule, but now, with the Church being back in power and religion finding new life, healing also has become more popular. The woman who healed the late Communist Party head Leonid Brezhnev is Juna Davitashvili, a Georgian, who uses energy emanating from her hands to heal the sick. While she does this, she experiences the patient's illness herself, tuning in on what the problem might be.

In Italy, Carmelo Di Stefano has a fine track record of having healed the sick, again by passing his hands over them, and also by the "power of his eyes." Di Stefano spent many years in Germany, where as a young man he worked as a shoemaker before he discovered his special gift. His father was in the shoe business, strictly Roman Catholic, and very much against his young son's interest in paranormal healing. Eventually, however, Carmelo broke free of these restrictions and became a much sought after psychic healer. He can be reached at Corso Independenza 303, 97011 Acate (near Ragusa), Italy, and his telephone number is 0932-989091.

Sometimes the line separating psychic readings and counseling and healing is not so clear, as some professional psychics also have the gift of healing. For example, Miriam Garabrant, has successfully dealt with "problems of the heart"; she does this through a trance state and at a distance. From originally dealing with emotional problems and conflicts, she has moved on to dealing with physical problems as well, and deals with them in the same, and apparently successful, way. Garabrant can be reached at 217 Montclair Avenue, Montclair, New Jersey 07043.

The psychic healers mentioned here are all successful with some cases, at the very least, and perhaps it is fair to say that their percentage of successful treatments is no more and no less than that of all medical practitioners, physicians, specialists alike. Perhaps it is their limit of knowledge, or of available energies at a given moment—or with a given patient—that determines the outcome of a certain case. Or perhaps we need to better understand the workings of "bio-energy" to make fuller use of it.

When it comes to bio-energetic forces, I recently met a man from Israel who must be the greatest paranormal healer of this age. By comparison, all other healers I have personally investigated, and been treated by, are much less powerful, though probably no less well intentioned. Ze'ev Kolman was stationed in the Sinai desert as part of his military service, at a base called Uhom Hasiba. The year was 1969. At 4 A.M., restless, he decided to take a walk up a mountain near the base. There he had an encounter with a UFO, and unaccountably lost five hours of time during which he must have been on that mountain. When he returned to the base he was a different man. He discovered that the touch of his hand caused electrical discharges to the extent that people he touched experienced the equivalent of an electric shock. Soon Kolman discovered he could heal the sick, and gradually this quiet, ordinary businessman became Israel's most famous psychic healer. People from all walks of life have since consulted him, and many were cured of illnesses ordinary medical treatment had failed to cure. Some Hollywood celebrities, major politicians in Washington, and an increasing number of ordinary people have flocked to this man because he has indeed healed the sick in many cases, sometimes with a single treatment. Kolman himself is not a cultist or religious fanatic. He is a man dedicated to scientific exploration of his gift, which he refers to as "bio-energy" or life force. His power is derived not from some extraterrestrial force (though that may have unleashed it originally) nor from spirit intervention, but from his own, somehow "activated" physical body.

"I personally experienced his therapy and was truly impressed," states Barry D. Mink, M.D., an internist practicing in Aspen, Colorado.

"I experienced a great increase in physical energy, mental clarity . . ." writes singer John Denver after a session with Kolman.

Prince Alfred von Liechtenstein, president of the Vienna International Academy for the Study of the Future, asked Kolman to treat a close friend, a woman who had suffered serious eye damage from the wearing of experimental extended-wear gas permeable contact lenses and was in great pain. The woman received three treatments from Kolman within a span of two weeks, and at the end of the treatments she was completely cured.

"I am personally familiar with Mr. Kolman's ability as a healer . . ." states Senator Claiborne Pell.

Dr. Enrique J. Teuscher, diplomate in psychiatry and a practicing neurologist, writes of Kolman, "[he] is a bioenergist of extraordinary ability."

Among the many cases Kolman has successfully treated include cancerous tumors, a punctured lung, broken bones, lost hearing, and many other types of illnesses and medical problems for which people seek treatment. When Kolman gave me a treatment, he passed his hands approximately six inches above my body—never touching it—and yet I immediately felt an extraordinary strong series of waves, as if something very tangible passed between his fingers and my skin. There was heat, there were nerve impulses, and responses, and yet I could not *see* anything passing between his hands and my body.

Lastly, despite his increasing popularity, Kolman follows a very strict rule of how and whom he treats. He has given up his dry goods business to devote himself full-time to bioenergetic work and seminars (where he teaches the techniques to others). His fees depend on the patient's ability to pay, and unlike some hospitals, Kolman will not turn away a sufferer for lack of funds. Ze'ev Kolman lives in Israel, but travels world-wide. He sees people in America from time to time, where he works both in a clinic in Los Angeles and in New

York. He can be reached at 50 West 34th Street, Suite 7C6, New York, N.Y. 10001; telephone (212) 566-5006.

Undoubtedly, there are undiscovered healers living all over the world, people who have this natural gift, and are not yet aware of its potential. But as we learn more and more about man's bioenergetic force, which we all have to *some* extent but which psychic healers seem to possess in far greater concentration, and as this realization spreads, potential healers will no doubt come forward.

Only ignorance and prejudice on the part of those who fear the widening of our knowledge in the health field can retard this development. If more energy was put into seeking new approaches to medicine, new remedies not manufactured in profit-making factories, and new techniques discovered by learned and dedicated researchers, perhaps humanity would be in a healthier state than it is now.

How to Avoid Fakers and Quacks

Whenever I am asked by someone unfamiliar with psychic research: how does one know the difference between the real and the false? I give them the same stock answer: by the results. Thus it is with psychic and unorthodox healing as well. Only by the results can one adequately judge whether or not the person is effective.

The faker is never likely to heal anyone, while even the honest but inefficient healer can bring forth positive if limited results.

Some elements of the lay public seem to think that there are vast numbers of fakers walking around the world, bent on taking money from the unsuspecting, preying on the afflicted, and doing all sorts of harm. Nothing could be further from the truth. To begin with, the number of professional healers of one kind or another, outside orthodox medicine, is comparatively small—simply because unorthodox healing in most countries is still on the forbidden list, or, at the very most, tolerated within certain limits. Second, while the gift of psychic healing may be more common than most outsiders believe, the realization of that gift and the practical application of it is a matter of instruction and knowledge which not too many people possess. Third, the number of out-and-out fakers and quacks in the unorthodox healing field is very small because the physical healing field polices itself very well indeed; no one is more likely to discover manipulations or fraudulent practices than those closely involved, the afflicted themselves. The reputation of a successful healer depends heavily on word-of-mouth fame, which in turn is possible only if actual healings occur. A fraud operating on a major scale, seeing many patients and fleecing them of their money, would be brought to the attention of the general public by the howls of the deceived, long before any governmental agencies could get into the act. On the other hand, one must always remember that it is not uncommon for self-professed medical experts to declare an unorthodox healer or healing fraudulent without investigating all circumstances, or simply because the conditions under which the healing took place are different from orthodox medical conditions. The opinion of orthodox medical practitioners as to the value or lack of value of psychic healing is seldom unbiased; frequently it represents the defense mechanism of a threatened element.

Yet for all the internal and external safeguards against fakery, quacks are to be found. Hence, here follow some commonsense suggestions on how to avoid being taken by fakers or quacks in the unorthodox healing field. First, have the patient checked out fully by at least one recognized *orthodox* medical doctor, if possible by more than one, and by a specialist in the patient's particular area of illness. If, as so often happens, the disease will yield to conventional medical treatment, have the medical doctors state this in writing. Second, before consulting a healer, speak to others who have been treated by that particular healer and examine the results even if their diseases are radically different from the one of the patient at hand. This kind of information may be supplemented with the answers to queries placed with psychical research societies, with newspapers or magazines specializing in this field, or with individuals known for their integrity as investigators or researchers. Such people will always be glad to pass on any information they may possess on a particular healer, if they have met or investigated the healer themselves.

Third, before letting a patient undergo any kind of unorthodox treatment, ask the healer whether he thinks he can deal with the disease in question, how long he thinks it will take, and what his fee will be. Reputable psychic and unorthodox healers will not take on any patient unless they are reasonably sure they can help him. A quack will take on anyone, make very broad promises, and demand a substantial fee. No one expects healers, who devote their entire lives and all of their professional time to the work of healing, to do so without proper compensation. Where proper compensation ends and exorbitant fees begin, one can frequently discover the quack, though some eminently successful genuine healers have at times charged large sums of money to patients well able to afford it, while asking very little or nothing of those who could not. Then, too, some ineffective healers may charge very little for individual visits.

There are those healers who practice their art very much the way a Park Avenue specialist might. If they are good healers, and their reputation holds up over the years, one cannot take issue with them on either legal or moral grounds. If anything, one might charge them with lack of humility, but that is an entirely personal matter and, I think, secondary to the question as to whether or not they perform valid healings. What it really boils down to is that one pays both an orthodox physician and an unorthodox healer for his efforts, not for any guaranteed results. The only difference is that one has gone through medical school and received a great deal of orthodox train- ing, while the other relies primarily on a divine gift. But men of both schools of healing may be equally dedicated to their tasks, and putting their best foot forward is all they are expected to do.

Fourth, observe very carefully what happens during the healing session. If the patient feels that "something is going on" that had not been going on prior to the healer's entering the picture, or if the patient has an immediate reaction as soon as the healing has been completed, then something did indeed pass from the healer to the patient. It is not as difficult to differentiate between the suggestion of healing and actual healing energies passing between healer and patient

as one might suppose. Very few genuine healers make verbal suggestions to their patients prior to or during treatment. Whatever suggestions are involved are almost always made by the patient, who puts
forward a hopeful attitude, or on the part of the patient's loved ones,
who encourage him to have a cooperative frame of mind. Genuine
healers do not need the power of suggestion to accomplish their ends;
the patient does it for them. Conversely, if the patient is negative or
hostile, an authentic healer will nevertheless proceed and frequently
succeed in healing the patient, since the healing power does not
depend on suggestion. Positive thoughts are the icing on the cake:
because of them, the healing power is more readily absorbed, but the
power of suggestion alone does not heal, make no mistake about that.

Fifth, and most importantly, the proof of the pudding is in the
eating, and the proof of the healing is in the well-being of the patient.
Depending upon the nature of the ailment, if there is recovery and if
recovery continues to be felt for a considerable amount of time, again
depending upon the nature of the disease, then the healing must be
pronounced a success. The majority of all unorthodox healings are
instantaneous or the result of short treatments, though absent healing
frequently is continued in order to reinforce the initial "shock treatment."

Many conventional physicians will not prescribe new and un-
tried medicines even if the patient's life is at stake and there is no
other hope. Likewise, the fact that a number of people were materially helped by the drug Krebiozen was considered insufficient evidence to those insisting on its suppression. Yet, many terminal cancer
cases received benefit from Krebiozen, and had research continued on
its properties, perhaps enough would have been learned to convince
those unwilling to accept its partial usefulness. Some authorities, such
as government medical authorities, or the Food and Drug Administration, are quick to declare certain natural medicines as "useless"
because by current medical standards they do not fit into any existing
treatment methods, even though, if one uses different channels of
healing, these very same substances may indeed yield positive results.
On the other hand, these same authorities allow dangerous synthetic
substances, such as Thalidomide, to be dispensed, only to discover

much later the damage they have caused. The same authorities who worry about the effectiveness of Ginseng root capsules and try to suppress their sale because they do not think the capsules enhance virility (and perhaps they do not), permitted the wholesale use of DDT for many years until it was discovered that the substance was dangerous to insect and man alike; these same authorities permitted the use of tar products as sugar substitutes until they became convinced that these substances were cancer agents.

In short, for all their education, the constituted authorities are not *necessarily* correct in their judgments.

Perhaps the best example of the conflict that can be seen in unorthodox and orthodox attitudes to psychic healing can be seen in the way psychic surgery is regarded.

In another chapter I briefly touched on psychic surgery as performed in the Philippines, and the controversy surrounding these unorthodox practices still has not died down. Actually, Brazilian psychic surgeons preceded the Philippine clinics by several years. Brazil, which has a large spiritualist population, has always taken a more up-to-date approach to unorthodox healing. According to John Frances-Phipps, and the *Psychic News* of November 29, 1969, there are hundreds of psychic surgeons in Brazil. In a series of articles Frances-Phipps described in vivid language his personal experiences with the then still living healer Jose Arigo and with Lourival de Freitas.

The late Jose Arigo saw at least one thousand patients a day at his clinic in Congohas Do Compo. Arigo's guide was a spirit doctor by the name of Dr. Fritz, who spoke with a marked German accent or in German, which Arigo did not understand. Through the entranced medium, this doctor would prescribe various medicines and treatments for those seeking his help. In some ways the approach resembled that of the late Edgar Cayce. Dr. Andrija Puharich, who spent much time with the late Arigo, is fully convinced of the genuineness of the phenomenon, and he himself had a growth removed from his arm by the spirit healer.

Arigo was killed in an auto accident at a time when he finally was getting recognition and protection from a jealous medical establishment that had attempted to jail him several times, and when a special hospital of 160 beds was being built in his honor and for his use. But he, the Brazilian psychic surgeons and the Philippines' Tony Agpaoa and others, less well known, practicing along similar lines, are by no means isolated cases.

Thus, in 1967 a British medium and healer, Isa Northage, performed psychic surgery on a Scottish bus driver by the name of Tommy Hanlon, who suffered from a stomach ulcer. The surgery was witnessed by the man's aunt, a registered nurse named Margaret Sim. Miss Sim was in the fortunate position of observing the healer's work from close by. To begin with, the healer massaged the patient's abdomen. Then, before the witness's astonished eyes, the man's stomach wall was opened up—in her words, "opened like a rose"—and the ulcer was taken out in two pieces with forceps. The healer then closed the wound. There was no trace of a scar. According to a reporter for the *Psychic News*, the man was able to eat normally an hour after the operation.

Isa Northage, of Nottingham, England, works with a spirit doctor by the name of Dr. Reynolds. Photographs of malignancies were offered in evidence of another psychic surgery success by the same healer. These malignancies came from the jaw of Sylvia Hudstone, who signed a testimonial to the effect that she was cured completely by Northage. During the operation by the entranced psychic surgeon, the patient felt no pain whatever and the entire proceedings took place in front of a large audience in Northage's spiritualist church at Pinewoods, Nottingham.

On the other hand, B. S. Sharma, a spiritualist from Delhi, India, who went to Manila to watch the Philippine psychic surgeons at work, claimed that the material taken from the bodies of the patients was in fact "a waxy substance dexterously palmed and skillfully twisted to make it appear as if it is drawn out of the patient's body. Few operators are ready to part with such a substance for chemical examination." In fact, when a team of "investigators," more accurately described as would-be exposers, visited Tony Agpaoa, they obtained some of the tissue removed from patients' bodies, and had it examined in a laboratory. The tissue was then declared, on the opinion of one medical researcher, to be of animal origin, and, again on the testimony of one researcher, the entire field of psychic surgery called fraudulent and the "wonder healers of the Philippines" referred to as charlatans and frauds.

In a similar vein is the complaint registered with me by a forty-five-year-old man disabled with rheumatoid arthritis for the past thirteen years who had borrowed money in order to go to the Philippines in 1967. He admits to having been helped "slightly" and later met the healer again in the United States. According to this witness, Tony offered to teach him psychic surgery and, as a result, he was shown "all the tricks of the trade." My correspondent wanted me to warn researchers of the terrible fraud going on under their very noses. For my part, I would have been a little more impressed with this complaint had he not added, "I will give you all the details but the actual fact should be worth some money to reimburse the money I had to borrow for the trip."

In November 1972, New York State Attorney General Louis Lefkowitz obtained a court order to stop the practice of acupuncture in New York by ten "unlicensed Chinese" that had been carrying out the ancient Chinese needle therapy. These men were working under the supervision of three medical doctors, but to the Attorney General this was apparently not enough. How the practice of the ancient art of acupuncture, could, in the words of the Attorney General, constitute a "clear and present danger to the health and welfare of the people of the state of New York" remains a mystery. Quite possibly, the complainants against the thriving acupuncture clinic were losing business in their regular hospitals or private practices.

You cannot tell a faker or a quack by listening to official opinions, to the majority of medical doctors—or even by assessing the size of the fee he charges. If you have been helped, the healer was genuine; if you follow the five steps outlined above, you stand a good chance of avoiding quacks.

With all that, a word of warning is in order. Strange-looking contraptions, electrical apparatus, unless they offer clear-cut reasons for their existence and methods of application, may very well be instruments of fakery. This does not mean that legitimate inventions in the advancement of medical knowledge cannot work well and perform healing services. Earlier in this book I have spoken of Dr. Douglas Baker and his biomagnetism and the machines that Delawarr Laboratories in England are manufacturing for that purpose.

It would also be wise to treat with caution unusual suggestions by suspect healers, such as an order to obtain certain ingredients in the middle of the night, from specific areas, or to perform peculiar rituals in mixing the concoctions. Much of what passes for authentic witch-craft prescriptions, such as the famous "eye of newt or the head of a toad," are in reality nothing but fantasies.

Lastly, Gypsy recommendations concerning healing, according to which you must secrete certain sums of money in a way that the Gypsy will find it, are of course not to be taken seriously.

In essence, healing is a straight interaction between healer and patient; something must pass from one to the other and results must be obtained, whether temporary or permanent.

THIRTEEN

How to Heal
Yourself

"Physician, heal thyself" was the admonition the pupils of Hippocrates, called the father of medicine, would toss one to the other. Anyone wishing to help the sick should first of all be in full control of his own health, both physically and spiritually speaking. At least that was the way the ancient Greeks looked at it.

Modern doctors are no different from ordinary people when it comes to illness: when they get sick they go to other doctors, or to hospitals or to specialists who are better equipped to handle the particular illness from which they suffer. Very few medical men are able to deal with their own troubles. Somehow there persists the fantasy that physicians are less likely to be ill than ordinary people. Nothing could be further from the truth; even though medical doctors understand the symptoms of disease better than laymen, they are just as prone, perhaps more so, to become ill as are those unaware of what the symptoms mean.

Yet while perfection in mind and body is desirable for all, not

only doctors, being afflicted in one or another area does not necessarily prevent the individual from being a good doctor as well. Thus
Dr. Robert Laidlaw, who has for much of his life walked on crutches,
is nevertheless one of the most renowned and respected psychiatrists
in the world. Physicians have treated patients while they themselves
were in wheelchairs; cancer specialists have died of cancer. For all that
it is nonetheless true that the command to "heal thyself," addressed to
everyone, can often be obeyed by everyone, whether healer or
layman.

Since the number of reputable and successful healers is very
limited, and the number of the afflicted unfortunately very large, it
stands to reason that many of those in need of healing treatments will
never get to a healer. Then, too, there are a number of diseases and
conditions that yield frequently to personal treatment and do not
even require the ministrations of another person. Disease is not local;
it affects the entire organism, body, mind, and spirit, and must
therefore be attacked on that basis. In the words of Edgar Cayce, "The
body is not structural, but functional." Spirit manifests a physical
body; consequently spirit can heal a physical body.

In practical terms, all self-healing involves thought processes.
Thoughts can influence specific illnesses. Orthodox medicine holds
that illness is due to one of three major causes: invasion by foreign
bacteria or viruses; damage to the system through accident; degenerative processes through usage, aging, or other forms of weakening
of the system. Psychic healing, on the other hand, holds that disease is
the result of imbalance in the total system, body, mind, and spirit.
Disease exists only so long as this imbalance is not corrected. Once it
is corrected, disease must vanish.

In this view—the view not only of Edgar Cayce but also of
most leading metaphysicians and esoteric thinkers—the spirit-mind
combination has created the body and continues to influence it.
Thoughts, therefore, can cause disease; just as other thoughts can
undo disease. Physical symptoms, pain, and afflictions are merely the
outer manifestations of parallel situations existing in the etheric or
"inner" body. By correcting the situations on that inner body, the

outer, grosser body must fall in line automatically and mechanically; it has no choice.

The psychic healing system holds that disease results from three main causes, which, however, differ markedly from the three causes put forward by orthodox medicine as the reason for disease. The three esoteric causes of diseases are erroneous thought processes, improper living habits, and accidents. Only the third cause coincides with the causes orthodox medicine recognizes as being the origin of possible disease, and there the similarity stops; the treatment prescribed for accidents differs again markedly from the orthodox view.

False thinking—the inability to accept human conditions in the proper light, applying one's energies to alter these conditions unintelligently, without understanding the underlying causes of dissatisfaction and thus leading to a state of frustration—can cause disease. Frustration—a condition where one cannot do anything about one's cherished goals—allows energies to break out from the containment of inactivity. The manifestation of these energies causes damage to the human system, taking the shape of one or the other physical disease. Once the disease becomes physical and affects the organism, the underlying cause, even if recognized as the originator of the disease, cannot be forced to "take back" the disease, as it were. Fresh thought processes are necessary to reverse the trend and fight the disease at that stage.

Thus no matter what the nature of the disease, the approach to personal healing must be a twofold one. First, there is the long-range approach, expressed primarily in an optimistic attitude that one will overcome the effects of the disease and eventually conquer it. This end is accomplished most successfully by verbalizing in brief but salient sentences a command to oneself to overcome the effects of the specific disease one suffers from and to repeat this exact command at frequent intervals, especially on retiring and arising. While speaking aloud, one must also visualize oneself in perfect health, with particular emphasis on that part of the body that may be afflicted at that time. In seeing oneself either in one's inner eye or as a projected vision outside of oneself, in a perfect state of health, one actually makes this come true.

All this may sound farfetched to the materialist or logically thinking person, but it is an established fact that thought processes are tiny electric charges, emanating in the brain by direction from the mind. These charges go out from the brain into whichever direction they are aimed. In sending thoughts from one's own brain to one's own body, one is in a manner of speaking rearranging one's electrical molecules, purifying and programming them positively and returning them to that part of the body where they are needed. At the same time these positively programmed electrical particles will set the body's own defense mechanism into motion, thus causing physical action as well as suggestion: the physical action works against the diseased areas by mobilizing antitoxins, or the natural healing abilities of the cells. The mobilization of the suggestive apparatus in the psyche creates a more positive climate for healing to take place while at the same time dealing with anxiety states. Such anxiety states are not only unpleasant and at times dangerous but impede the natural processes of healing through depressed or even traumatic states that affect the circulatory rate and bodily functions in general—thus closing the vicious circle that delays recovery.

How to deal with pain through thought processes is a problem perhaps more urgent than that of long-range healing. Once one masters immediate agony, it is easier to approach the underlying causes in a calm frame of mind.

Now both orthodox and unorthodox medicine accept the view that pain comes through our consciousness only because it travels from the area of trouble in the human system to the control center in the brain, which tells our conscious mind that something is wrong somewhere in the body.

In order to deal with the existence of pain anywhere in our body, we have two avenues of counteracting it through thought processes. The easier one of the two is blocking the message of pain somewhere between the origination and the control center in the brain. We do this by visualizing the area of affliction connected with the control center in the brain by a highway-like strand of nerves along which the message of pain travels. Halfway in between we visualize a block, very much like a roadblock. We see the pain energies streaming out of the diseased area and coming to a halt at the roadblock. We then visualize the rest of the road, that is the nerve tissue, empty of pain messages, and therefore the control center cannot receive the impulse reflecting pain. This thought message is coupled with verbal suggestion, tightly expressed in as few words as possible, that pain will not go through. We acknowledge its existence, but at the same time we command it to stop at the artificially created roadblock along the way. The more strongly we visualize this division between a nerve road filled with pain impulses and a portion free of it and therefore calm, the more successfully we will be able to block the pain from coming to our conscious attention, and thus we will stop feeling it within a very short time.

A second method, somewhat more tricky, addresses itself directly to the area of disease or injury in the body. If we are completely cognizant of the nature of the illness or injury and what is the cause of it, we visualize the wound or injury in great detail in our mind's eye; having visualized it and verbalized the fact of its existence and the causes of it, we then proceed to build a protective wall around it, effectively shutting off all outgoing stimuli. We are aware of nerve fibers leading from the affected area toward the control center in the brain, but at the same time we visualize and accept the total protection of this invisible shield around the wound itself. Then we begin to visualize the rapid recovery of the wound or injured area, first holding the thought of it in its injured or diseased state, then gradually visualizing its changing to a healed or perfect state.

This process can be accomplished very rapidly, taking perhaps no more than five or ten seconds altogether. At the end of this period we hold the visualization of the area as completely cured. By attacking the area in which pain originates we are in effect killing pain, not merely blocking its transit from the origination point to the control center.

This method works whether the diseased area is due to infection, degenerative illness, or accidental injury.

It seems, at first, far-fetched that thought forces could deal effectively with living organisms, such as bacteria or viruses. But esoteric theory, and the conviction of psychic healers in general, holds that the presence of bacteria and viruses in the system is *natural*; only when there is an imbalance between good and bad bacteria and viruses does disease result.

Although orthodox medicine considers invasion by outside bacteria or viruses the cause of most diseases, it has never been proven beyond the shadow of a doubt that these invasions of foreign entities cause diseases. It may well be that they link up with the existing bacteria and viruses in the system to create an imbalance of specific entities, which in turn causes disease. Psychic and unorthodox healing helps the body's own defense forces overcome either imbalances or invasions by activating them to the fullest. Thought commands do create electric forces that go into action where needed in the body. We do not as yet know enough about the importance of polarity to health, but it appears that *the balance between positively and negatively charged electrical particles within a cell and thus within the entire system is at the very heart of the well-being of man.* When the polarity is upset, the entire system suffers, even if only one part of it manifests a physical disease or injury. I would even suggest that the polarity or balance between positively and negatively charged electrical particles in the human system is the life force or operating power through which man performs all of his functions, whether physical, mental, or spiritual.

The second approach in combating disease on a psychic healing base involves "proper living habits." By that I do not mean anything remotely connected with morality or the social order. Proper living habits simply means a way of life in which the pressure balance between positive and negative forces is not impaired. Minimally, this program demands a person to have the correct amount of rest and sleep, as indicated for each individual (and it may differ from person to person) and not go against his or her natural inclination in terms of being a day person or a night person. If one is a nocturnal person, one should adjust one's living rhythm accordingly; conversely, if one is diurnal, one must not strain the system by living a nighttime existence.

Proper living habits also include a certain amount of physical exercise, although not necessarily calisthenics or gymnastics. They include the use of a largely organic or at least balanced diet. The less one partakes of artificial stimuli, such as drugs, alcohol, and tobacco, the more the system will be in balance. This does not mean that a glass of good wine will make one sick; it does mean that alcohol per se is hostile to the harmonious way of life.

Proper amounts of oxygen in one's breathing air are also necessary to maintain the balance in the system; much illness derives from living in polluted areas or unhealthy climates. Proper elimination of poisons and waste stuffs and periodical purification of the system are extremely valuable to the avoidance of illness; toxic matters in the system cause much disease.

None of the foregoing alters my view that all disease is caused by improper thinking; the very presence of such toxic substances in the system is due to the fact that one is ignorant of the dangers and thus guilty of improper thinking. Accidental injury to parts of the body, especially as a result of someone else's carelessness, cannot validly be blamed on improper thinking, of course. But in dealing with such injuries the same principles apply as if the damage to the system had been caused by disease. Pain is blocked in much the same way as with a disease-caused wound; suggestion as to quick recovery of the affected area will not eliminate the healing period entirely but will speed up the recovery process immeasurably.

Much has been said about the healing power of "love." What exactly is love? Seen through the eyes of the para-psychologist committed to the concept of psychic healing, love is a particularly strong positive electric force, created in the emotional system of one person and directed toward one or more other individuals. This positive energy carries various messages with it; it may be a personal one involving a desire to share, unite physically and emotionally, or it may be a desire to bring various values to large segments of the population. Either way, the love force is probably the maximum potential an individual is capable of generating within his or her system.

Conversely, hatred can create a parallel negative force. I have already pointed out that frustration, or the inability to express oneself as desired, whether in one's professional, artistic, religious, or emotional life, can lead to external manifestations through various diseases. These diseases are not necessarily connected with the immediate area of frustration. For example, a frustrated lover does not develop heart disease or problems with his sexual organs, but the outgoing power, having no outlet outside the system, turns within itself and causes havoc wherever the system is weakest. In some people, this may be a foot or a hand; in others, it may be a joint. Or it may manifest itself in loss of hair. Everyone's system has certain weak points where an attack will yield the most severe results.

There is no foretelling which way this deflected energy will go in any particular case, and consequently diagnosis of illness is difficult. Starting with the symptoms of disease, it is not always easy to trace the way back to the frustration at the base of it. Of course, if we eliminate the particular frustration that has caused an illness by simply changing the circumstances, we would effect an instant healing. Most frustrations do not yield that easily, however, simply because the conditions cannot be so easily, if at all, changed. It is therefore much more important to change the patient's attitude toward his particular frustration, thereby allowing energies liberated by the frustration to flow into more constructive channels.

Next to frustrations, fears cause numbers of illnesses, not only mental but physical. Fear is simply the absence of information. To cure fear it is important to pinpoint the exact nature of the fear and then to proceed to obtain as much information on the subject as possible. By informing oneself on the subject, fear will dissolve. It is important to remember that fear is brought on by the one who experiences fear, not by some outside force. It is further important to realize that that which we bring on ourselves, we are also able to do away with ourselves. This is not a question of belief or something available only to a favorite few; it is a cardinal law of nature that the fears we create in our own minds we can also undo in our own minds.

If fear is merely the absence of information, then suppression of natural instincts is the absence of freedom of expression. Within the boundaries of our society, and short of causing damage to others, we should be free to express our natural instincts whether or not they coincide with our upbringing or environmental standards. Irresponsible pomiscuity is as wrong as is carefully channeled sexual selectivity. What is freely derived from our libido should be expressed equally freely, if it is indeed an honest expression of our innermost desires. Sex for its own reward is worthless and can lead to further frustration, but sex as an outward expression of inner emotional impulses is a valuable tool in the prevention of disease, since it offers a safety valve to the pent-up energies within the system that might eventually turn inside and against the system otherwise, and without a chance to control the direction.

Although thought processes can be used to heal *oneself* with good results, even including the use of suggestions from one nerve center to another part of the system, the same does not hold true when it comes to psychic and physical healing through the laying on of hands or making passes *for oneself*. In the latter case some kind of "short circuit" seems to result, and the healing does not take place as desired. With the laying on of hands or the making of passes the healer is contacting the aura, and when one part of the aura enters another part of the same aura, energy is simply drawn from one part of the system to another. Evidently this is insufficient to cause restoration of diseased areas of the aura. The practice requires someone else's auric force for success.

*　　*　　*

If humanity were truly cognizant of the spiritual element in life, the majority of people would not regard illness as some kind of attack upon them by a virus or some other, invisible external force, with the need to defend themselves against it by all available means. Once we realize and fully accept our very nature as being triune, we will also understand that all disease affects all three layers of our existence equally, and must be dealt with on that basis.

I realize that this requires a completely different view of life and existence than the conventional one. Where exactly did we go astray in our thinking? Why is it that only some of us understand this real nature of mankind?

As incomplete as humanity's understanding of self is, just as incomplete will be the steps taken by it to heal us when we are not well. Theoretically at least, complete realization of our true, spiritual nature should allow us to get rid of illness of every kind. Some people are indeed able to do that. Many more cannot, however, and for them the surrogate psychic healer, the bioenergist, or whatever term is used, will stand in with the powers he has.

Of course, we will never have enough paranormal healers to be able to save the world's population from trouble and illness. Would it therefore not be wise to launch a vast program of popular education to teach the millions about how their own triune nature functions? And, at the same time, continue to research and develop alternative approaches to healing? Indeed it would.

PROF. HANS HOLZER, PH.D., is the author of 115 books, including *America's Mysterious Places*, *America's Restless Ghosts*, *How to Cope with Problems*, and *How to Win at Life*. He taught parapsychology for eight years at the New York Institute of Technology, lectures widely, and is an active television and film writer/producer. Dr. Holzer studied at Vienna University, Columbia University, and received a Ph.D. from the London College of Applied Science. He heads the New York Committee for the Investigation of Paranormal Occurrences, founded in 1977. Dr. Holzer lives in New York City.